CAPABILITY-PROMOTING POLICIES
Enhancing individual and social development

Edited by Hans-Uwe Otto, Melanie Walker and Holger Ziegler

First published in Great Britain in 2018 by

Policy Press
University of Bristol
1-9 Old Park Hill
Bristol
BS2 8BB
UK
t: +44 (0)117 954 5940
pp-info@bristol.ac.uk
www.policypress.co.uk

North America office:
Policy Press
c/o The University of Chicago Press
1427 East 60th Street
Chicago, IL 60637, USA
t: +1 773 702 7700
f: +1 773-702-9756
sales@press.uchicago.edu
www.press.uchicago.edu

© Policy Press 2018

British Library Cataloguing in Publication Data
A catalogue record for this book is available from the British Library

Library of Congress Cataloging-in-Publication Data
A catalog record for this book has been requested

ISBN 978-1-4473-3431-6 hardcover
ISBN 978-1-4473-3433-0 ePub
ISBN 978-1-4473-3434-7 Mobi
ISBN 978-1-4473-3432-3 ePdf

The right of Hans-Uwe Otto, Melanie Walker and Holger Ziegler to be identified as editors
of this work has been asserted by them in accordance with the Copyright, Designs and
Patents Act 1988.

Cover design by Hayes Design
Front cover image: istock
Printed and bound in Great Britain by CPI Group (UK) Ltd,
Croydon, CR0 4YY
Policy Press uses environmentally responsible print partners

Contents

List of figures

List of tables

Notes on contributors

Giuseppe Acconcia is an award-winning journalist and researcher focusing on the Middle East. He is a Teaching Assistant at Bocconi and Cattolica University in Milan (Italy), is a PhD candidate at the University of London (Goldsmiths), and is involved in an international research project (EU-FP7) on youth movements (Pavia University). His research interests focus on youth and social movements, Iranian domestic politics, state and transformation in the Middle East. He graduated from the School of Oriental and African Studies (SOAS) in London writing a dissertation on the role of the military in politics in Egypt, Syria and Iraq. He is the author of *The Great Iran* (Exorma, 2016), *Liberi tutti* (Oedipus, 2015), *Egypt. Military Democracy* (Exorma, 2014) and *The Egyptian Spring* (Infinito, 2012).

Paola Ballon is Researcher in Development Economics at the Smith School of Enterprise and the Environment, University of Oxford, UK, and Lecturer of econometrics and statistics at ESAN Graduate School of Business in Lima, Peru. Her expertise is on the measurement and the econometric analysis of multidimensional poverty in Africa and South Asia. Her research interests comprise the operationalisation of the 'Amartya Sen Capability Approach' and the use of mixed-methods for the study of water-security, female empowerment, and shame-poverty. She is Associate Editor for Oxford Development Studies, and former member of the Editorial Board of the *Review of Income and Wealth*.

Sharon Bessell is Associate Professor at the Crawford School of Public Policy at the Australian National University (Australia). Her research interests revolve around issues of social justice and human rights, and focus on two broad areas. The first is social policy, social justice and the human rights of children. The second is the gendered and generational dimensions of poverty. She has a strong interest in research ethics and methodology, and has published widely on undertaking research with children.

Guillermo Adolfo Bornemann-Martínez, Dean of the Faculty of Economics and Business Administration (2007–2014) of the Central American University, Managua, Nicaragua. Consultant for different international development agencies and local organisations. Chair of the International Conference on Human Development and Capacities, HDCA 2013 (Managua, Nicaragua). Researcher and professor on issues related to poverty and human development, especially in the analysis of the impact of public policies and development.

Pedro Caldentey del Pozo is a specialist in Central American countries, human development, international cooperation and comparative regional integration. He is Director of the Department of Economics of the Universidad Loyola Andalucía where he teaches Applied Economics. He is Director of the Research Master in Inclusive and Sustainable Development. He was former Director of the ETEA Foundation, the Institute for Development at Universidad Loyola Andalucía. Caldentey worked as Senior Advisor of the Spain-SICA Fund at the General Secretariat of the Central American Integration System (2007–2011). He has years of experience in the design of development policies and instruments in regional integration with the Ministry of Foreign Affairs and Cooperation of Spain, the European Union, ECLAC, OECD, IICA and the regional institutions of the Central American Integration System. He is a member of the Board of Trustees of the Entreculturas Foundation, ETEA Foundation and Secretary of the Board of Directors of Fairtrade Iberia.

Enrica Chiappero-Martinetti is Full Professor of Economics at the Department of Political and Social Sciences at the University of Pavia (Italy). For the term 2014-2018 she is appointed as an Extraordinary Professor of Economics at the Faculty of Economic and Management Sciences at the University of Free State, South Africa. She acts as an Associate Editor of the *Journal of Human Development and Capabilities* and she has been Vice-President of the Human Development and Capability Association for the terms 2004-2008 and 2010-2011. Her main research interests are in the field of poverty and income inequality measurement; multidimensional approaches to poverty and well-being, capability and human development approach; fuzzy sets theory and fuzzy logic for well-being analysis; gender inequality, unpaid work and female empowerment.

Ina Conradie is the Coordinator of the SA-German Centre for Development Research at the University of the Western Cape in Cape Town (South Africa). She is also a Senior Lecturer in the Institute for Social Development at the same university. Her research interests are the role of aspirations in capability achievement, gender policies, and social policies that impact on poverty and inequality.

Séverine Deneulin is Associate Professor in International Development at the University of Bath (United Kingdom), where she teaches in the MSc in International Development and Professional Doctorate in Policy Research and Practice programmes. Her research is on social ethics and development policy in Latin America, and the role of religion in development.

Brid Featherstone is Professor of Social Work at the University of Huddersfield (United Kingdom). She has an international reputation in the areas of gender, fathers and child protection. A co-authored book (with Sue White and Kate Morris) *Re-imagining Child Protection: towards humane social work with families* has been highly influential in stimulating dialogue about the need to reform child protection in England and internationally.

Franziska Felder is currently a visiting researcher at the School of Humanities and Languages at the University of New South Wales (Australia). Her work is in the field of philosophy of education, mainly on the topic of inclusive education and justice. She is the co-editor of *Disability and the Good Human Life* (with Jerome E. Bickenbach and Barbara Schmitz), published in 2014 by Cambridge University Press.

Reiko Gotoh is Professor (Economic Philosophy) at the Hitotsubashi University in Tokyo (Japan). Main publications are *Against Injustice: The New Economics of Amartya Sen* (with Paul Dumouchel: CUP, 2009), *Social Bonds as Freedom*, (Berghahn Books, 2015), *The Capability Approach – Ethics and Economics* (with Paul Dumouchel: Iwanami Shoten, 2017, in Japanese), *Amartya Sen, Economics and Ethics* (with Kotaro Suzumura: Jikkyo Shuppan, 2001, in Japanese).

Paolo R. Graziano is Professor of Political Science at the University of Padua (Italy) and Associate Fellow at the European Social Observatory in Brussels. He has published and edited several volumes and special issues on topics such as Europeanization, welfare state politics, European social policy, political consumerism and European governance. He published three books, and edited eight special issues for various international journals. His most recent book is *Sustainable Community Movement Organisations* (Il Mulino, 2016, in Italian – written with F. Forno). His work has appeared in the following journals, among others: *Comparative European Politics, Mediterranean Politics, European Journal for Political Research, European Political Science, Regional and Federal Studies, Social Policy and Administration, Governance, Global Social Policy, Journal of*

European Social Policy, Journal of Social Policy, International Journal of Social Welfare, The Annals of the America Academy of Political and Social Science.

Anna Gupta is Professor of Social Work at the Royal Holloway University of London (United Kingdom). Her recent research explores the perspectives of families living in poverty who have experienced the child protection and family court systems in England. Together with Brid Featherstone, Sue White and Kate Morris, Anna is developing a social model for protecting children and supporting families that draws upon the Capability Approach.

Christian Christrup Kjeldsen is Associate Professor of Educational Sociology at the Aarhus University, DPU (Denmark). Furthermore, he has been the Vice Center Director for the National Center for School Research (NCS) in Denmark. Kjeldsen's research is focused on children and young people with special needs in a number of different educational programs. In addition, the transition from education to labor market has been a key research interest over his many years of research experience. He has published comprehensively on the Capability Approach related to education for disadvantaged youth and educational policies. He is both a qualitative and a quantitative researcher and has often conducted his research in a mixed-methods design. Since August 2017, Christian has been Head of Department of Educational Sociology at Aarhus University.

Elise Klein is Lecturer (Development Studies) at the School of Social and Political Sciences at the University of Melbourne (Australia).

Eduardo Lépore is Professor at the Department of Social Science at the Pontificia Universidad Católica Argentia (Argentina) and researcher at the Interdisciplinary Programme on Human Development and Social Inclusion. His research is on labour markets, urban segregation and social policy.

Indira Mahendravada is Professor of Economics at the Department of Studies in Economics and Cooperation, University of Mysore (India). Earlier she served as the Director of Centre for Women's Studies in the same University. She is the recipient of Best Teacher in Economics Award from Stars of Industry Group (USA) and Dainik Bhaskar Group (India) during 2013. She was a visiting fellow at the International Institute of Social Studies, The Hague during 2014. Her research covers diverse areas like agricultural marketing, policy analysis, gender studies and third sector. She coordinated national research projects in the areas of coffee marketing, women empowerment, nongovernmental organisations and co-operatives. Her publications include a book, *Gainers and Losers in Transition: The Case of Coffee Marketing in India* (Lambert Academic Publishing, 2014) and an edited volume, *Mainstreaming Cooperatives: Asian Perspectives* (International Cooperative Alliance, 2015).

Ann Mitchell is Professor at the Department of Economics at the Pontificia Universidad Católica Argentina (Argentina) and researcher in its Interdisciplinary Programme on Human Development and Social Inclusion. Her research is on impact assessment, poverty measurement, civil society and quality of life in informal settlements.

Emilio J. Morales-Fernández is Professor at the Department of Business Management at the Universidad Loyola Andalucía (Spain) where he teaches Human Resource Management, Management Skills, Organizational Behaviour and Strategic Management in graduate and postgraduate studies. He was former Director of Master in Research Methods in Economic and Business Sciences and he is professor of the Research Master and Doctoral Program in Inclusive and Sustainable Development. He is researcher of the ETEA Foundation, the Institute for Development at Universidad Loyola Andalucía. He has years of experience in university cooperation in Central America (Universidad Centroamericana de Managua, Universidad Centroamericana de El Salvador, Universidad Rafael Landívar de Guatemala, Universidad Nacional Autónoma de Honduras) and has participated in development projects in Ecuador, El Salvador, Honduras, and Nicaragua with the Ministry of Foreign Affairs and Cooperation of Spain, and the European Union.

Hans-Uwe Otto is a senior research professor for social services and educational science and director of the Bielefeld Centre for Education and Capability Research at Bielefeld University, Germany. He is an adjunct professor at the University of Pennsylvania, USA, and has been a guest professor at the universities of Chicago, Zürich, Bloemfontein and Shanghai. He has received honorary degrees from the State University St. Petersburg, University of Ioannina, University Halle-Wittenberg and Technical University Dortmund. His current research focuses on the critical analyses of the youth welfare system in Europe, reflexive professionalisation of social service and capabilities-friendly policy. He has been a coordinator of EU-funded international research projects concerning disadvantaged youth. He is editor of various publications including *Facing Trajectories from School to Work* (Springer Publications, 2015), ed., *Critical Social Policy and the Capability Approach* (Budrich Publications, 2014), ed., *New Approaches towards the Good Life* (Budrich Publications, 2014), ed.

Antoanneta Potsi is lecturer at Bielefeld University, Germany. She has studied early childhood education, worked as a research fellow at Wuppertal University, Germany, and has gathered didactic and practical experience in Germany and Greece. Her research interests include childhood studies, early childhood education, social policy, inequality studies and the capability approach as a justice approach.

Xavier Rambla is Associate Professor of Sociology at Universitat Autònoma de Barcelona (Spain). Currently, he is interested in the following research areas: education policy transfer between international organisations and governments, lifelong learning policies, and the implications of Europeanisation for education policies. Previously, he has also worked on early school leaving, Education for All and inequalities in Latin America, education policies targeted at vulnerable social groups (in Southern Europe and the Southern Cone) and critical coeducational action-research.

Susan C. Seifert is co-founder and director of the Social Impact of the Arts Project (SIAP), a research group at the University of Pennsylvania, School of Social Policy and Practice (USA). She is co-author (with Mark J. Stern) of publications based on SIAP research, which focuses on the relationship of culture and the arts to neighborhood revitalisation, community change and social wellbeing. Seifert has over 20 years' experience as an urban planner and policy analyst in Philadelphia and New York City. She holds a MSc. in Urban and Regional Planning from the University of Toronto, Canada and has done postgraduate studies in ecological planning at Penn School of Design.

Mark J. Stern is Professor of Social Policy and History at the University of Pennsylvania (USA). He is co-director of the Urban Studies programme at the University of Pennsylvania. He has authored or co-authored six books, including *One Nation Divisible: What America Was and What It Is Becoming* (with Michael B. Katz, Russell Sage Foundation Press, 2006) and *Engaging Social Welfare: An Introduction to Policy Analysis* (Pearson Educational, 2014). In 2017, Susan Seifert and he co-authored

The Social Wellbeing of New York City's Neighborhoods: The Contribution of Culture and the Arts (Social Impact of the Arts Project, 2017).

Ana Lourdes Suárez is Professor at the Department of Social Science at the Pontificia Universidad Católica Argentina (Argentina) and researcher with CONICET (the Argentine National Fund for Scientific Research) affiliated with UCA and its Interdisciplinary Programme on Human Development and Social Inclusion. Her research is on the sociology of religion, research methods and the religious presence in marginal neighbourhoods.

Melanie Walker is South African research chair in higher education and human development at the University of the Free State in South Africa. Her research interests include education, in/equalities and justice; higher education and the public good; and opportunities and agency through education. From 2014 to 2017 she was vice-president of the Human Development and Capabilities Association. She has published widely on higher education and social justice.

Holger Ziegler is Professor of Social Work at the Faculty for Educational Science, Bielefeld University, Germany. He has widespread experience in evaluating the effectiveness of youth welfare and social service interventions and in researching social work and active labour market policies, particularly with respect to hard-to-reach groups and within disadvantaged areas in Germany. He has published extensively on youth welfare, community work, social problems, research methods and methodologies, evidence-based practice, education, welfare and employment policy and social justice.

INTRODUCTION

ONE

Human development, capabilities and the ethics of policy

Hans-Uwe Otto, Melanie Walker and Holger Ziegler

How can we work to overcome unjust societies and achieve a better distribution of opportunities to flourish? How is human development best fostered? How can human development be revitalised in better-off countries where the role of social welfare is under scrutiny? These are some questions this volume aims to answer by analysing policies and conceptualising coherent and systematic strategies at the local, national and international level, and what seems possible in real-world contexts. We consider not just policy but also human development and capabilities expansion – 'picking out valuable ways of being and doing' – as the 'final ends' of responsible policy and policymaking and worth seeking for its own sake (Richardson, 2015, p 171). This approach is grounded in development ethics and an ethical approach to policymaking that seeks multidimensional measures of human progress of current and future persons. We identify and critically analyse policy interventions driven or influenced by the human development approach and examine how the approach has been operationalised and put into practice, as well as how far its implementation has been successful in contributing to human flourishing and increasing the opportunities available to individuals and groups to live the lives they have reason to value. The book therefore also discusses the discrepancies and obstacles that actual policies present to what a capability approach could mean in social policy practice. To this end, we hope to stimulate debate on overcoming obstacles in existing social policy scenarios of different kinds.

Our project serves as a response to calls to roll back or restrict social welfare and a call to dialogue, given the urgent need to come up with alternative social policies with a strong commitment to combat disadvantage, promoting individual and social development through human flourishing. The book makes a clear distinction between ordinary development programmes and those that seek to go further (even if imperfectly) by enhancing human security and augmenting individuals' and groups' positive freedoms and promoting democratic communities of mutual support and reciprocity. However, it also considers the nature of development interventions that follow human development principles and identifies shortcomings in existing programmes. Avoiding any stereotypical view of good social policy practices, the volume highlights challenging examples from diverse national and cultural contexts.

We consider human development policy intentions and interventions as a politically normative approach. In this approach, as Spence and Deneulin (2009, p 275) remind us, policy analysis is based on the notion that all areas of public policy should advance human freedoms and flourishing, and respect people's agency through an inclusive and democratic policy process. We examine how a human development approach has been conceptualised and operationalised into practice, and how far implementations of human development and capabilities expansion have been successful in contributing to human flourishing and enhancing people's individual and collective opportunities. We aim to promote policy dialogue by revealing processes of policy advancement, and thus have collected accounts of what human development and capability-oriented policies should look like, drawing on empirical evidence and experiences in diverse contexts, as well as examples of putting such policy into practice and of the enablements and constraints of operationalising human development policies. Both aspects are needed to inform current debates among those genuinely seeking to find solutions to the many pressing policy dilemmas that confront contemporary societies.

Human development and the capabilities approach introduced

Human development, Haq (2003, p 17) explains, requires that social arrangements are judged by the extent to which they advance human wellbeing so that the purpose of development is not wealth creation or economic growth for its own sake, but 'to enlarge people's choices'; such choices are dynamic and encompass the economic, social, cultural and political. Thus, the first page of the first Human Development Report published in 1990 famously reads:

> People are the real wealth of a nation. The basic objective of development is to create an enabling environment for people to live long, healthy and creative lives. This may appear to be a simple truth. But it is often forgotten in the

immediate concern with the accumulation of commodities and financial wealth. (UNDP, 1990, p 1)

Human development recognises that while economic growth is necessary and that income resources (personal resources as well as those acquired via social welfare) do matter, these are not on their own sufficient for multidimensional flourishing, nor as the single measure of good lives. As the first Human Development Report explains, human development is a process of enlarging people's choices, of which the most critical are to be able to lead a long and healthy life, to be educated and to enjoy a decent standard of living. Additional choices include political freedom, guaranteed human rights and self-respect, such as being able to mix with others without being ashamed to appear poorly dressed in public. The ends of development are not economic growth for its own sake but human wellbeing enabled by a variety of intersecting economic, political and social freedoms and supported by necessary resources of income, commodities, public policies and so on.

Alkire and Deneulin (2009) identify four interlocking human development concerns or principles that could underpin policymaking and analysis: equity, efficiency, participation and empowerment, and sustainability. These concerns could anchor development in a transformative direction that aims to change unjust structures rather than support an affirmative direction of surface reforms (Fraser, 2010). The value and principle of equity draws on justice, impartiality and fairness and incorporates a consideration for distributive justice between groups, drawing attention to those who have unequal opportunities. Efficiency refers to the best use of available resources so that an intervention offers the highest impact in terms of enhancing people's opportunities; however, it is not the same as neoliberal efficiency, which seeks the best return for the lowest investment. Participation and empowerment refers to processes in which people can act as agents – individually and as groups – and to their freedoms to make decisions in matters that affect their lives, to hold others accountable for their promises, and to influence development in their communities. Lastly, sustainability is often used to refer to the durability of development in the face of environmental limitations but is not confined to this dimension alone. It also refers to advancing secure human development and social cohesion such that human development endures over time.

These multidimensional human development principles and values are conceptually underpinned and operationalised as the expansion of people's 'capabilities' (Sen, 1999), that is, the opportunity freedoms each person has to choose the plural functionings (achievements) that make up a flourishing life that they have reason to value. Freedom both enables us to judge how good a deal each person has, but, Sen (1992) emphasises, freedom is also good for society: 'A good society … is also a society of freedom' (1992, p 41). Capabilities refers to different combinations of functioning that can be achieved, where functionings are 'the different things that a person can value doing or being' (Sen 1999, p 3). These beings and doings together constitute what makes for wellbeing and quality in a person's life. Capabilities and functionings thus constitute people's wellbeing freedoms and wellbeing achievements respectively, that is, the real possibilities and opportunities of leading a life a person has reason to value, thereby generating more human development in society. Alkire (2010, p 84) explains that 'in making interpersonal evaluations that can feed into analyses of poverty, inequality, justice or development, we should focus on what people are actually able to be and to do, that is, on their capabilities', and the capabilities each is able to generate based on the goods and services available to them, and of course where goods and services are missing or inadequate, policy needs to be active here too. Wellbeing is constituted by all the capabilities of a person and what he or she can then do and be (his/her functionings), including his or her agency, so that wellbeing is multidimensional with many valuable dimensions.

Because capabilities are positive freedoms – the freedom to do or be what one values – freedom thus plays a substantive role in development. Freedom is an end in itself, and not only a means for another type of utility. Thus, for a society to develop, the main sources of freedom deprivations must be reduced and eventually eliminated, including social policy that does not include a wide range of voices or does not advance human development in some way. While the approach focuses on the achievement of individuals, these individuals are located in society and are connected to others; the individualism proposed is ethical (each person is of moral worth) rather than ontological (the individual only for herself) or methodological (Robeyns, 2005). Importantly, the development of wellbeing depends on social and policy arrangements and relations with others so that wellbeing is always realised with and through others. Groups and their combined capabilities (or their group disadvantage) are then also important (Stewart, 2005).

Moreover, following Sen (2009), the capability approach (CA) seeks to advance democracy at the community, local and national level in ways that foster genuine possibilities for agency so that all can take an active part in shaping public policy. This means that people must be equipped with adequate resources (including endowments such as decent schooling, assets such as income, and so on), that is, they must have the ability to mount an effective defence of their political views and make them into a relevant part of public political discourse. The CA considers this participation a real freedom – intrinsically and instrumentally valuable – a chance to translate values into behaviour (beings and doings), to make reasoned and meaningful choices.

Policy into practice

The primary aim of the book is therefore to outline a new approach towards more socially balanced and innovative capability-promoting policy activities, models and programmes that reduce social and human suffering and have the potential to lead to more inclusive societies that make life worthwhile, and thus to their emancipatory transformation, even while acknowledging the substantial challenges involved in such a process. The central idea of the capabilities perspective is to merge substantial and procedural dimensions of a flourishing individual and social life. This perspective represents the essential fulcrum between the freedom and agency powers of individuals, the distribution of material conditions – that is, social and economic powers – to enable people to live flourishing lives, and the deep deliberative, democratic and solidaristic quality of societies, their modes of governance and their public, governmental and non-governmental institutions.

Sen (1999) reminds us that when drafting policy we need to make choices about the informational basis for making judgments; in choosing some information, we exclude other dimensions. For example, standard measures of unemployment may not show the constraints and unfreedoms that migrants face even when they have the same qualifications as citizens; individual migrants may then be blamed for lacking the 'right' cultural attitudes or ambition. If policy information focuses only on the amount of human capital each person has, it will overlook, for example, how men are advantaged in the labour market in patriarchal societies. We therefore need to ask whose voices are privileged in policymaking, and who participates in policymaking processes. Utilising the CA as the informational basis would ask that we assess policies for their impact in terms of functionings and capabilities (Sen, 1999). We would make the development of capabilities the objective of public policy, putting in place conditions for their development so that all persons have genuine choices in choosing the life each has reason to value. Thus policy and policy evaluation utilises some informational basis to make judgments about problem

X or problem Y, and will include and exclude certain information from the evaluation. In that regard, Alkire and Deneulin (2009, p 5) give examples of how normative selections can affect policy decisions and outcomes:

> They shape the data that we collect; they influence our analysis; they give certain topics greater or less political salience; they feed or hinder social movements; they may motivate professionals for moral or ethical reasons and they can be more or less philosophically credible.

Sen therefore calls for an enriched 'informational basis of judgment in justice'. He argues that the 'bite' of a theory of justice 'can be 'understood from its informational base: what information is – or is not –taken to be directly relevant' (1999, p 57). We need also to keep in mind that the processes and outcomes of both policymaking and policy interpretation and implementation are interwoven, the latter processes shaped by local actors and local dynamics under conditions of intersecting contextual conversion factors, including contexts of inequalities. New policy is not written onto a blank slate but will be affected by other policies already in place. As Ball (1993, p 11) points out, 'the policy, its context, its interpreters and implementers all have histories'. In the chapters in this book, we have examples of policies that look good on paper but on closer inspection display patchy and uneven implementation, or policies whose claims to effect human development turn out to be hollow in practice. Policy texts can also simply be ignored. This also means that policy is not a value-free technical process, but takes place in complicated human settings suffused by power (overt or invisible) and politics; these political forces, as we see in the chapters in this book, act as a key conversion factor in shaping what is possible, but human agency also plays its role in advocating for policies that foster wellbeing so that voice is redistributed and power and authority reconfigured in some way through human agency and collective advocacy.

At the same time, we recognise that we live in an imperfect world and changing the informational basis for policy design and implementation may not be so straightforward, for example shifting education policy from a dominant human capital perspective to a more expansive capabilities approach. Sen's (2009) emphasis on comparative assessments of justice in real-world situations is important – the question then is which policy is more just or which policy is less just in its effect for people's wellbeing and agency. Furthermore, Carpenter (2009) warns that only appealing to reason and normative principles is not sufficient where the actual conditions for agency are poor. He argues that political struggles are needed to design and translate policy into human development and capabilities-forming practices. The importance of a political analysis of the forces that shape public policy is also highlighted by Spence and Deneulin (2009), who point out that a detailed analysis of power relations is essential. According to this, the success of policies should be assessed according to whether they promote not only people's freedoms but also their agency. Moreover, one of the main contributions of human development thinking has indeed been to construct new narratives in the field of development policy (Deneulin, 2014), showing that a potential for change does exist even if, at the present time, human development policies could be considered as contra-hegemonic compared with mainstream approaches. Ibrahim (2014, p 20) captures the challenge well when she says that:

> the operationalization of the capability approach is difficult but not impossible. There are some tough choices that need to be made to render the capability approach more 'policy-friendly,' but the real challenge lies in doing so without foregoing its conceptual richness.

Finally, Spence and Deneulin (2009) also remind us that policymaking happens across many moments, in a web of many decisions from the street to government, and as a process shaped by power, so that a political analysis is also required to understand which forces are influencing policy. Taking all this into account, we think that a human development and capabilities approach offers a rich alternative to mere critique of current policymaking by asking what we can and what we should do in the interests of justice. Still, despite extensive academic discussions regarding the capabilities approach, the key question of how to put it into practice is less easily resolved: how to design and operationalise public policies that fully encapsulate its central idea that policy actions should aim at enhancing the 'capabilities that people have reason to choose and value'. Despite the obstacles alluded to, progress has nonetheless been made in recent years in the direction of developing more capability-promoting poverty and policy evaluations measures, but how to bring these insights to bear on the making of social policy – one of the key instruments for making the human development ideal a reality – remains relatively unchartered territory. There is also a gap regarding how the collective responsibility and solidarity for bringing about such change would happen, moving from a focus on the real lives of individual agents to people acting as agents together. There is a gap between the legitimating egalitarian and democratic ideals and the reality of social policies across the world, whether in advanced capitalist societies or societies where agricultural and informal economies prevail. Within a capabilities perspective, the final aim of development is not simply to produce goods and services (crucial as these are as means), but to create opportunities that contribute positively to people's wellbeing and agency, both in the economic realm and beyond. Therefore, from the perspective of this book, public policy actions and social intervention should focus on the enhancement of opportunities for people fully to achieve their potential and on supporting a sense of collective responsibility and agency to achieve that aim.

While social policy can lay the groundwork for enhancing capabilities, its contribution to human flourishing may be limited by the social context. Putting human development into practice is a rather challenging exercise as any effort to do so may be accompanied by detrimental effects (for example, producing another sort of social inequality such as harm of the natural environment). The challenge lies in making a clearer distinction between ordinary development programmes and those that go further by enhancing human security and augmenting individuals' and groups' positive freedoms and fostering democratic communities of mutual support and reciprocity.

In our view, the CA is currently among the most appealing and convincing of the theoretical approaches with respect to issues of integrating social justice and human flourishing and development. Nonetheless, despite significant progress in political and academic discourse, policymakers are not required to wait until academia finds the way towards a perfectly just society. It is challenging but essential to identify policy and action initiatives that take into account the insights of human development and the capabilities approach in their design and implementation. However, capability-promoting policies are not only to be judged in terms of their outcomes; they also have a procedural dimension. They point to issues of democratic and deliberative processes. Thus to put the capabilities approach into practice is not a straightforward exercise. Capability-promoting politics should not be considered as managerialist or technocratic programmes with somehow more benign performance indicators.

Towards capability-promoting policies and policy analysis

To address the challenges of developing a different kind of social policy to achieve more just communities and countries, the book has been divided into five sections, including the introduction and the conclusion; together all the sections provide a kind of an intellectual and empirical map, not only of the overlapping subject matter of capability-promoting policies but also of the significance of, and the major themes in, contemporary social policy. We have set things out in this way because it is the conjunction of the five dimensions – the introductory case for the approach; conceptual challenges; modalities of structure and civil society; children, youth and education; and the conclusion pulling these threads together – that has in large part brought about the current fruitful condition of our subject. The range of ideological and normative perspectives the contributions entail is indeed the main strength of this collection. The chapters single out different areas of capability-friendly or capability-promoting policy for discussion and highlight examples from diverse settings as well as the successes and difficulties faced. Furthermore, the book brings together a team of distinguished contemporary contributors to the subject from the Global North to the Global South and demonstrates the flexibility of the CA approach as well as its relevance to diverse development contexts. The authors offer a wide range of examples of CA policy operationalisation in countries as diverse as Australia, South Africa, India, the UK, Germany, Central America, Switzerland, Argentina, Mali and the US. Throughout the book, the authors foreground the way in which capability-promoting policy influences a wider world of ideas and practice.

Following on from the Introduction, Part 1, on conceptual challenges, comprises four chapters that examine substantial conceptual challenges of how the CA can be operationalised and transferred as an instrument for innovative policy programmes within the discussion of political liberalism and the role of the welfare state in fostering reflective examples of agency, care work and women's employment. In Chapter Two, Reiko Gotoh contemplates what has been left behind by political liberalism and the welfare state by connecting Rawls' theory of justice with Sen's capability approach. She describes how, after the Second World War, Japan adopted a pacifist constitution and developed a respectable system to secure basic wellbeing for all underpinned by individual rights – a system that has produced rich arguments concerning the relation between rights and public welfare, freedom and democracy. However, Gotoh makes the point that discussions focusing on individual rights may, paradoxically, have caused concerns about individual wellbeing to recede into the background. When there is an implicit assumption that anyone can exercise his or her own rights, individuals who have not done so are regarded as having chosen not to do so. There is danger in justifying this, which may even result in threatening people's rights to wellbeing (above a minimum standard of wholesome and cultured living). In other words, the violation of rights could be justified as a consequence of respecting people's will and subjective evaluation. Gotoh argues that the Japanese welfare state has established a universal social security system that covers common risks but has lost sight of individuals who are struck by bad luck and have no other help than from their close family members. Gotoh asks if we can recover these exceptions and residuals or what has been forgotten by the welfare state of post-war Japan. By connecting Rawls with Sens' capability theory, we can re-examine the foundation of modern theories of justice in terms of individual wellbeing (hardship and suffering).

In Chapter Three, Elise Klein and Paola Ballon discuss agency and the capabilities approach. While at a normative level, placing people at the centre of development is an achievement, some scholars have pointed to the simplistic notion of agency and personhood expressed in the CA; this thin picture of personhood can provide an inadequate basis for conceptualising wellbeing and human development more generally. Drawing on research carried out in Mali in Africa, the chapter examines agency in the capabilities approach, proposing the psychological domain of agency as a way to expand the concept.

Chapter Four, by Indira Mahendravada, looks at a shift in public policy from welfare to the empowerment of women, drawing on experiences from Karnataka in India. Mahendravada notes that historically glaring inequalities between men and women have been observed in all development indicators in India, although these inequalities have been reduced in recent years. Although women's development has been a long-standing priority, there is now a paradigm shift from welfare to empowerment, with gender considered as a cross-cutting theme and each sector assessed through a gender lens, highlighting the need for ending gender-based inequities, discrimination and violence faced by girls and women by ensuring optimal learning outcomes in primary education, interventions for reducing poor nutrition, and maternity support. While some of these policies and programmes are centrally sponsored, state governments such as Karnataka also develop their own policies and programmes. Working with non-governmental organisations, the promotion of self-help groups is the empowerment strategy that has been adopted on the premise that access to financial resources empowers women. However, the impact of this approach on capabilities is little explored. An attempt is therefore made in the chapter to understand the impact of these efforts in the empowerment of women measured using the CA.

In the final chapter in this section, Guillermo A. Bornemann-Martínez, Pedro Caldentey del Pozo and Emilio J. Morales-Fernández explore the contribution to human development of social policies in the Central American Integration System (SICA). SICA, they explain, is the oldest such system in Latin America and is a very prominent area for the design and implementation of development public policies. Its progress has been interesting but not especially relevant compared with other dimensions of integration like the economic or political. However, SICA has recently approved a new strategic approach to the social dimensions of integration in the context of the post-2015 Sustainable Development Goals. The chapter presents the hypothesis that the conceptual foundations of the social dimension in SICA are not adequately defined and raises suggestions for the social dimensions to be redefined on the paradigm of human development and the CA.

Part 2, on modalities of structure and civil society, discusses key normative concepts, theoretical issues and how the dialectical relationship between personal development and structural preconditions is analysed for the policy productivity of the capabilities approach. The central issue posed here is what capabilities-promoting policy does or may look like, how it can be justified and implemented in different political, institutional, cultural and socioeconomic contexts, frames and traditions, and how civil society can be a space for collective demands for participation, equality and justice. Chapter Six, by Severine Deneulin, Ann Mitchell, Eduardo Lépore and Ana Lourdes Suárez, considers urban policy, describing how the capabilities approach is being integrated into the policies and priorities of the local government of the federal city of Buenos Aires, which is deeply fragmented between the formal and informal city. Informal settlements are characterised by unsuitable accommodation, little public infrastructure, weak rule of law, and high levels of unemployment. The first part of the chapter discusses the insights that the CA offers to concrete actions to reduce urban fragmentation, promote a better distribution of wellbeing opportunities within the same urban territory, and integrate physically, socially and symbolically its marginal areas with the rest of the city. The second part discusses how these insights are being translated by the local government in its decisions. The chapter focuses on three specific insights of the capabilities approach that are particularly relevant for urban integration policies: multidimensional and multisectoral perspective on policy; an institutionally integrated vision of wellbeing: and agency focus.

Chapter Seven, by Mark J. Stern and Susan C. Seifert, begins by noting that economic inequality has been rising in the United States for 40 years without influencing political discourse. However, in the wake of the recession following the 2008 global economic crisis and the subsequent recovery, politicians and policymakers have finally begun to pay greater attention to the gap between the most and least advantaged residents. The chapter specifically explicates the construction of a multidimensional index of social wellbeing for New York City's neighbourhoods based on the CA. In some neighbourhoods, dimensions of disadvantage reinforce one another, while in other neighbourhoods disadvantage can be counterbalanced by dimensions of strength. One of the most common sources of strength in low-wealth neighbourhoods, Stern and Seifert propose, is affiliation – being able to live with and toward others – and one aspect of social affiliation is the community's level of cultural engagement. This chapter therefore uses a measure of cultural engagement based on the presence of institutions (non-profit and for-profit cultural resources), artists and cultural participants in a neighbourhood. It concludes by viewing capability-promoting cultural policy as a means of addressing long-term social inequality in two ways: public sector commitment for achieving cultural equity by improving residents' access and opportunities for cultural engagement; and, in low-wealth neighbourhoods with existing cultural resources, philanthropic investment in these assets to improve other dimensions of social wellbeing.

Next, in Chapter Eight, Giuseppe Acconcia, Enrica Chiappero-Martinetti and Paolo R. Graziano write about third sector associations and the development of capability-oriented policies in Italy. By adopting the CA as a basic framework to analyse social phenomena, they disentangle the role of third sector associations at the local level in increasing socially innovative processes to enable the integration of groups formerly excluded from the labour market (such as disadvantaged youths). This chapter asks to what extent third sector stakeholders trigger greater policy integration and social innovation and explores this question with reference to fieldwork research involving the *Libera* network (*Libera. Associations, names and numbers against mafias*), a grassroots association supporting community empowerment projects engaged in managing confiscated lands owned by mafias in two disadvantaged urban areas in Italy (Milan and Naples). The driving forces for the differential impact of a CA approach to social innovation are identified through the analysis of two in-depth case studies. The chapter argues that social innovation can be produced by a capabilities-promoting approach that enables intermediate actors to bring about enhanced capacity on the part of disadvantaged persons to define their aspirations or to be able to aspire. The case studies show how limited the third sector actors' participation has been both at the meso and micro levels with respect to policies aimed at contrasting youth unemployment. The final section of the chapter asks what the consequences of the findings are for more general questions of human development; more specifically, they discuss to what extent, especially at the local level, the effectiveness of third sector associations in activating social innovative processes is particularly relevant.

Ina Conradie concludes the section with an account of social insurance for informal workers in South Africa. She outlines a social policy proposal to introduce a savings plan based on the Mbao scheme in Kenya that might address poverty, given that – in spite of good policies – South African development indicators have not shown as much positive impact as had been hoped. Low-wage workers, unemployed and underemployed people, and who have given up on finding a way to earn an income, are unprotected and vulnerable in a reasonably affluent, middle-income country. In providing social insurance for informal workers in South Africa, a tool is therefore needed that would make inroads into the cycle of over-indebtedness among the poor and the emerging lower middle class. It should contribute to activating economic engagement by the poor, and attract informal workers into different sectors of the economy – into trading, small-scale manufacture, small-scale service industries, information technology, and many more areas. A tool is also needed to help the poor and the emerging lower middle class to save, in order to have protection against economic risks. Such a project could play a role in giving informal workers in South Africa a bigger choice in how they would like to live and finance their lives. It might contribute to a (small) shift in the structure of income in South Africa, and to increased quality of life for the large sector of economically excluded South Africans. With more policy options available to them, they might come to feel that the economy serves them, rather than the other way round.

Part 3, on children, youth and education, deals with and provides informed insights on capabilities-promoting policy aspects that relate to children, youth and education. Education is a central arena in which to apply the CA as an evaluative framework that assures human rights and strives for the respect of human dignity. It opens with a chapter by Anna Gupta and Brid Featherstone on what the CA offers child protection policy and practice in England as an alternative conceptual framework for social work that challenges the dominance of neoliberal ideology in ways consistent with the promotion of human rights and social justice. However, the authors note that contemporary child protection policy and practice in England adopts a narrow approach to child and family welfare and the role of social work. Practice is taking place amid increasing poverty and inequality, severe cuts to local authority budgets and a highly risk-averse context, reducing the 'means' available to families, while cuts to local authority and community-based support services are diminishing conversion factors that could enhance capabilities in adverse circumstances. The chapter then considers what the CA can offer the development of a more humane and socially just system that promotes children's and their parents' human rights, capabilities and functionings. Finally, the authors examine how support services and practitioners can incorporate CA ideas into practice and work with families to promote strengths and capabilities.

In Chapter Eleven, Sharon Bessell considers the CA as a way to make real the Australian ideal of the 'fair go'. She points out that capabilities approaches have had relatively little influence on policy debates in Australia despite ideals represented as fundamental to Australian identity having strong resonance with the CA. Ideals of egalitarianism and what is colloquially referred to as a 'fair go' for all to achieve their life goals are essential to the Australian national self-image and are used by politicians to frame and promote a broad range of policy initiatives. While studies have questioned the depth of commitment to the ideals of egalitarianism in practice, and particularly in relation to marginalised groups, those ideals remain fundamental to the Australian national psyche and to political and public debate around key policy issues. This chapter first explores the value a CA brings to the Australian ideal of the 'fair go'. The second section of the chapter examines the dominant narratives that have shaped social policy in Australia over the past decade. Specifically, this section examines the increasing dominance of workforce participation as the objective driving social policy using the CA as a critical lens. The final section returns to the relationships between Australian ideals of egalitarianism and the CA, suggesting ways in which social policy can be transformed to move beyond the narrow agenda of workforce participation to an agenda of social inclusion, social justice and opportunity.

Next, Franziska Felder examines the role of schools in inclusion and capabilities formation; inclusion is indisputably one of the most discussed moral values in the field of education today and the chapter sheds light on the normative implications. More precisely, it inquires into the contribution of inclusion to the building of human capabilities

– and vice versa – and adapts this picture to education in schools. The chapter suggests the concept of 'capabilities to be included' and how schools as institutions are able to foster these. Lastly, it discusses some examples of corresponding best practice in the field of education, drawn from international empirical research and practice. Felder proposes that the CA fills two gaps: on the one hand, it offers a normative framework that is able to enlighten important theoretical questions on the quest for inclusion, especially with regard to the freedom aspect. On the other hand, it is able to inform and inspire public policy concerning inclusion, especially in education.

Chapter Thirteen, by Antonneta Potsi, considers early childhood educational curricula. This chapter explores the potential of the CA as a framework of normative aims for early childhood education curricula. More specifically, the author considers Martha Nussbaum's list of basic human capabilities, developed as a relatively definite standard of minimal justice and as the minimum entitlements a person should have, as an adequate frame for capability-promoting policy in early childhood education (ECE) and especially in curriculum development. Nussbaum's basic human capabilities are deep-rooted in the normative principles that govern early childhood education and care and contrast with the reductionist and instrumental view of the ECE curriculum that prevails within contemporary policy frameworks.

Next, Christian Christrup Kjeldsen examines youth education for all in Denmark, asking questions as to whether freedoms exist only on paper or are achievable in context. His chapter focuses on the actualities and change for young people with special needs in terms of capabilities, formal rights and disadvantage in relation to policy and relates these to macro-level changes in public discourse and development for young people. The author notes that if we only focus on the intention of the policy it may be interpreted as succeeding in its capability-promoting aspects, but investigation into how intentions and formal entitlements becomes actualised in practice presents a more blurred picture. It becomes evident that the public discourse on 'work first' and the latest changes arising from active labour market policies have pushed forward a second wave of modernisation of the welfare state for the most disadvantaged youth within society, where the mantra now is 'making work pay'– giving a return on investment in terms of reducing the expense of social benefits. Thus even what appears to be a highly effective capability-promoting policy on paper may in practice become less so. In order to develop and operationalise fully capability-promoting policies, they would need to have an evaluative dimension, where a part of the policy is to empirically evaluate its actual results.

In the final chapter in this section, Xavier Rambla asks if public policies impinge on the values of education looking specifically at Latin American countries. He notes that a number of writers claim that basic human capabilities are fostered not only through the positional values of education but also – and most importantly – through its intrinsic and instrumental values. The chapter argues for the potential of this theoretical framework to evaluate education policies. In recent decades, the governments of Argentina, Brazil and Chile have attempted to overcome 'middle-income trap(s)' that hinder human development by either targeting the poor through pedagogic and organisational innovation or by coordinating various levels of government to plan educational development. Rambla's analysis discusses the formulation of these policies, their implementation by means of various sectors and levels of government, and ultimately, their impact in terms of enrolment, performance and inequality. The case studies pose relevant questions about how to promote intrinsic values and reveal that education and social policies are instrumental to one another, while the author's conclusions highlight that the final impact on social positions is extremely complex.

The book concludes with a chapter by Hans-Uwe Otto, Melanie Walker and Holger Ziegler drawing everything together to sum up the arguments for new principles and aspirations towards capabilities-promoting policy.

To summarise, the book sets out a 'final ends' (Richardson, 2015) approach to policymaking, implementation and analysis, attending to capabilities expansion as the means of achieving the ends of human development and more just societies. We advocate a richer informational basis to make judgments about the context and conversion (structural) conditions under which policies are operationalised, about whether interventions are more or less just, and about whether they inflect more or less in the direction of human development in an imperfect world. We intend the book to be an invitation to and stimulus to wider public reasoning about the ends of policy, how we get there and how we are doing.

References

Alkire, S. (2010) *Human development: Definitions, critiques and related concepts*, Human Development Research Paper 2010/01, New York, NY: UNDP.

Alkire, S. and Deneulin, S. (2009) 'A normative framework for development', in S. Deneulin and L. Shahani (eds) *An introduction to the human development and capability approach: Freedom and agency*, London and Sterling, VA: Earthscan, pp 3-13

Ball, S. (1993) 'What is policy? Texts, trajectories and toolboxes', *Discourse*, vol 13, no 2, pp 1-17.

Carpenter, M. (2009) 'The capabilities approach and critical social policy: lessons from the majority world?' *Critical Social Policy*, vol 29, no 3, pp 351-373.

Deneulin, S. (2014) 'Constructing new policy narratives:the capability approach as normative language', in G.A. Cornia and F. Stewart (eds) *Towards human development*, Oxford: Oxford University Press.

Fraser, N. (2010) *Scales of justice: Reimagining political space in a globalizing world* (reprint edition), New York, NY: Columbia University Press.

Haq, ul M. (2003) 'The human development paradigm', in S. Fukuda-Parr and A.V. Kumar (eds) *Readings in human development*, Oxford: Oxford University Press, pp 17-34.

Ibrahim, S. (2014) 'Introduction. The capability approach: from theory to practice – rationale, review and reflections', in S. Ibrahim and M. Tiwari (eds) *The capability approach: From theory to practice*, Basingstoke: Palgrave MacMillan, pp 1-28.

Richardson. H. (2015) 'Using final ends for the sake of better policy-making', *Journal of Human Development and Capabilities*, vol 16, no 2, pp 161-72.

Robeyns, I. (2005) 'The capability approach: a theoretical survey', *Journal of Human Development*, vol 6, no 1, pp 93-117.

Sen, A. (1992) *Inequality re-examined*, Oxford: Oxford University Press.

Sen, A. (1999) *Development as freedom*, Oxford: Oxford University Press.

Sen, A. (2009) *The idea of justice*, London: Allen Lane.

Spence, R. and Deneulin, S. (2009) 'Human development policy analysis', in S. Deneulin and L. Shahani (eds) *An introduction to the human development and capability approach*, London: Earthscan, pp 275-94.

Stewart, F. (2005) 'Groups and capabilities', *Journal of Human Development*, vol 6, no 2, pp 185-204.

UNDP (United Nations Development Programme) (1990) *Human Development Report 1990: Concept and measurement of human development*, New York, NY: Oxford University Press.

PART 1:

Conceptual challenges

What political liberalism and the welfare state left behind: chance and gratitude

Reiko Gotoh

Introduction: the visit of a wounded bird

Four men stand in four different corners of a room, each holding a gun. They all set their sights on each other and none of them can turn down his gun. They are at a deadlock in a four-way standoff.

Then, suddenly, a wounded little bird flies down and falls right in the middle of the four men. Strangely, its faint breath travels across their guns and is perceived clearly on their hands.

At this moment, the four men all lower their guns, deeply appreciating the fact that they have escaped the worst situation at the last minute.

Can we call what was perceived by the four men beauty, truth, goodness, or love? What does it mean to be 'perceived on their hands?'

We are not going to discuss whether it is a bodily sense, empathetic feeling, intellectual interpretation, or rational reasoning. Nor do we have to specify what is symbolised by the wounded little bird. After all, it does not matter what went through the minds of the four men; this could have been different for each one. What matters is the fact that the four men put down their guns, the fact that something other than bullets struck the four men, who then lost whatever reasons they had to continue holding their guns, and the fact that the unexpected presence of the small bird suddenly changed the critical situation faced by these individuals and in turn totally changed their behaviour.

Let us continue with the tale. The four men abandon their guns and take up hoes instead. They cooperate in cultivating the soil, resulting in a rich harvest in autumn. Now many lively birds visit the field and their songs can be heard. Wealth and peace are finally achieved, and they live happily ever after.

However, here is one question we have forgotten to ask: What then happened to the wounded little bird?

The wounded little bird was left behind and ascended quietly to heaven. No one noticed it. When autumn came the leaves covered it, and snow covered it in winter. There was no sign at all of the injured bird by early summer when the four men began fighting with each other again, this time with hoes: "To whom do these crops belong?"

This fight continued, again, until another wounded little bird fell down from heaven. The unexpected appearance of the injured bird brought the four men to their senses, and they put down their hoes.

How many times on earth must people repeat the same mistake, which can be summarised as follows?

... Crisis of conflict → unexpected visitor → sudden change of situation → change in behaviour → achievement of cooperation → neglect and oblivion → collapse of cooperation → recurrence of crisis → ...

Cooperation among 'ourselves' is not only unjust but also unstable if we forget and neglect the visitor, the other who triggered our cooperation, and if we delude ourselves that cooperation was achieved by 'ourselves' only, pushing the visitor's existence into a category essentially similar to our own, based on (as explained later) a scientific cognition of continuity.

However, how can we understand the tiny bird that is entirely different in nature from 'ourselves' without losing equality as a norm? Is there any risk that the asymmetric being is going to be treated as a means for symmetric beings to achieve their cooperation? Before talking about this, let us briefly reflect on the reach and limit of the welfare state, looking at the constitutionally guaranteed welfare system of post-war Japan as an example in order to elaborate on our theme.

The modern welfare state and democratic equality

After the Second World War, Japan adopted a pacifist constitution and developed a respectable system to secure basic wellbeing for all. To use Rawls's words, the constitutional idea of Japan's social security and welfare system can be summarised not only as embodying the concept of 'liberal equality', but also as stepping in the realm of 'democratic equality' (Rawls, 1971a, p 65 onwards).[1] Let me begin by explaining these concepts.

According to Rawls, 'liberal equality' means equal treatment of equal beings, that is, all individuals should formally be treated equally as legal subjects. It is represented, for example, by the equal guarantee of 'rights to civic liberty', which says that no one should have his/her body, mind, or conscience violated without a legitimate reason.

The idea also means securing rights to political liberty, that is, equal access to various social decision procedures, especially to those crucial to oneself. In contrast, what Rawls calls 'democratic equality' refers to the effective or 'real' equal treatment of unequal or substantially different beings. For example, it is represented by securing 'rights to wellbeing', which demand compensation of income or wealth for individuals below a certain threshold level of wellbeing.

Japanese constitution declares that realisation of individual rights may be restricted, apart from general conditions of circumstances, only by similar rights of other individuals or similar effects of other kinds of rights, not by values of the state or society beyond its constituent individuals. It is also declared that anyone is entitled to pursue his/her own interest, express his/her own will, and change various social decision procedures by exercising various rights he/she holds, as long as one follows a due procedure (equal rights to civic liberty and political liberty). In addition, everyone should have an equal access to education, work and public services; moreover, anyone in a difficult situation is entitled to receive public assistance in order to maintain a minimum standard of wholesome and cultured living (equal rights to wellbeing freedom).

The concept of rights is indeed a 'trump' political value (see Dworkin, 1977). According to Rawls, '[T]he only reason for circumscribing the rights defining liberty' is that 'these equal rights as institutionally defined would interfere with one another' (Rawls, 1971a, p 64). It reminds us of the intrinsic value of persons that stands against the logic of number, holistic values and power.[2] Such a micro as well as universal perspective of a right certainly describes the political ideal of *equality* in its highly abstract form. However, discussions focused on the endowment of rights may have caused, paradoxically, concerns about individual wellbeing to recede into the background. Why? We can find some of the reasons for this by looking at theoretical premises and the common-sense thinking supporting individual rights.

The statement 'anyone is entitled to some rights' has a passive connotation. It does not mean that these rights are actually exercised or that goals of the individuals exercising them are actually achieved. In order to exercise their rights, individuals have to visit a particular place, follow a particular procedure, fill out an application form, and so on. Furthermore, after exercising their rights in this way, they have to prove by themselves that they satisfy the first condition. Many factors exist that can prevent or interfere with one fulfilling this process.

Suppose, for example, a woman is reduced to poverty. There can be innumerable conditions that have to be met before she learns of the existence of public assistance that would allow her to achieve basic wellbeing, decides to receive it, and finally completes the necessary application. Once completed, this application may turn out to lack some of the required conditions, or the woman may face certain obstacles in meeting its demand.[3]

Even if this process discourages her from securing her rights to wellbeing and only ends up making her even more tired and hungry, her individual rights are not regarded as violated or threatened, unless and until events or acts that prevent the exercising of her rights are clearly recognised. When there is an implicit assumption that anyone can exercise his or her own rights, individuals who have not done so are regarded as having chosen not to do so. In other words, the non-exercising of their rights could (if anything) be justified as a consequence of respecting their will and a subjective evaluation of their own interests.

In this context, we must recall that Rawls clearly distinguishes between guaranteeing liberty and securing the worth of liberty. He explains that the latter could be a social goal only in political liberty (for example, voting) and a kind of social and economic liberty that is stipulated by the 'difference principle' under the 'fair equality of opportunities'.[4] When it comes to liberties of speech or the pursuit of happiness, Rawls (1971a, p 204) noted that 'the worth of liberty to persons and groups is proportional to their capacity to advance their ends within the framework the system defines'.[5]

Concerning the worth of social and economic liberty, Rawls admits that social intervention should be carefully checked when it may discourage people's will and efforts, and the purpose and scope of compensation policies are to be restricted to the effects of factors that cannot be chosen or controlled by individuals.[6] This implies that when someone wants to realise his or her rights and ask for compensation because of the shortage of basic wellbeing, he or she has to prove that the result was not due to his or her choice but to bad luck or an unfavourable environment.

Who, though, could clearly prove this to someone else in words? And can he/her do so while maintaining his/her will and continuing to act to realise his/her rights against overwhelmingly depressive prospects? Usually, as Sen has pointed out, it is difficult for an individual to choose his/her possible actions, unless he/she can take part in the process of setting possible actions with the help of an informed adviser, since individuals' choices are strongly framed by the set of alternatives available to them, or by the decision-making procedure itself (Sen, 2002, chapters 3 and 4).

In addition, we can observe the following problem. When someone claims that individual choices can affect the result, even in an extremely unlucky situation, this claim is praised as evidence of the triumph of human beings' free will. On the other hand, when someone else states that luck can change the outcome of even the wisest choices, this statement emphasizes the fundamental boundaries of reason and rationality as well as of legal fictions. Either proposition tends to invite negative views on designing policies for compensating the worth of liberty.[7]

Finally, as clearly explained in the following sentence, which was critically introduced in Sen's (1997 [1980], pp 365–6, including note 28) criticism, Rawls' theory of justice was first developed for symmetric relations among rational and reasonable individuals, leaving aside 'hard cases'.

> I also suppose that everyone has physical needs and psychological capacities within the normal range, so that the problems of special health care and of how to treat the mentally defective do not arise ... prematurely introducing difficult questions that may take us beyond the theory of justice, the consideration of these *hard cases* can distract our moral perception by leading us to think of people distant from us. (Rawls, 1999 [1975], p 259, emphasis added)

Consequently, it turned out that very serious problems were left to individuals to solve in the welfare system. Family became a social fortress containing individuals in situations of destitution, hardship, or rebellion. Changes in family structures and household types meant that only stem family members shared a destiny with individuals in need (husbands, children, grandchildren, sisters and brothers), in isolation from other distant relatives, based on the natural (but, in reality, socially and historically constructed) sense of responsibility. As the welfare state gradually established a universal social security system (pensions, and health and nursing care) covering common risks, it lost sight of individuals who had met with bad luck and received no help other than from close family members.

These 'incidents' are usually considered 'exceptions' or 'residuals', carefully separated from and sidelined by the main legal system. They may deeply disturb people's ordinary life for a short while through images on the TV screen but they are soon overwritten by another new 'exception' or 'residual' and easily forgotten.[8]

Can we recover these exceptions and residuals or what has been forgotten by the welfare state? In the following sections, we consider this problem by examining academic studies of the theories of justice and, more broadly, political liberalism in general. Institutions and policies occasionally change the normative consciousness held by people drastically, while institutionalised academic studies influence institutions and policies to some extent.

Theorising conceptions of political liberalism: tolerance and non-discrimination

To begin with, we sketch an outline of political liberalism by drawing on works by Rawls. A conception of political liberalism is characterised by the fact that its content is prescribed by the reciprocal acceptance of 'real' people who are situated in some ideally *fair* conditions. Here reciprocal acceptance means an acceptance that is presumed and expected by anyone situated in a similar condition.[9]

It has been postulated that people seeking freedom and independence avoid committing themselves to any comprehensive doctrine on the conception of the good including libertarianism, which attaches the supremum value to freedom. The most important virtue for political liberalism is to take an equal distance from any particular religion, moral doctrine, or belief, as well as to be equally tolerant of them.

It is natural for political liberalism to renounce any unequal or discriminatory treatment, based on particular factors such as origin of birth, profession, gender, disability and ill health, or income and wealth. These factors are called by Rawls 'social or natural contingencies', or 'morally arbitrary' matter.[10] When we apply the device of a 'veil of ignorance' to our daily life, shutting out all kinds of individualised information not only about ourselves but also about other people, it becomes effectively impossible to discriminate against anybody based on these particular factors.[11]

The analytical framework of the welfare economics on distributive justice has contributed not a little to supporting the idea of non-discrimination in political liberalism. Take the Lorenz curve as an example, which captures the extent of income inequalities by referring to the straight, 45-degree line that represents perfect income equality and gives a strong visual impression of continuity among individuals (Lorenz, 1905). Qualitative distinctions in all other aspects disappear into the background and only quantitative and continuous differences represented by income remain. This implies that categorical distinctions such as poor and non-poor vanish and only relative positions such as lower or higher remain.

A similar logic leads us to neglect categorical distinctions between those with and without disabilities, if we can order individuals with physical or mental disabilities from slightest to severest in a real number scale, for example. If we imagine the sequence of points converging to zero with a large number of people, only quantitative and continuous differences would remain, while the rationale of discrimination for those with disabilities disappear.

What happens if we adopt the framework of multidimensional indices as a composite (vector) of different dimensions showing different continuous quantities? It would then be difficult to regard someone as being more or less disadvantaged, even if he/she is at the lowest level in almost all dimensions but one. This is because, first, considering the limitations of human cognitive ability, we cannot deny any possibility of the crossover of rankings in a yet-to-be recognised dimension that may overwhelmingly dominate the other dimensions in its importance. More generally, it is because we have no objective criterion to weigh and substitute different dimensions for one another across different individuals.[12]

As Kenneth Arrow points out by drawing on Leibniz's principle of the identity of indiscernible, 'value judgments may equate empirically distinguishable phenomena, but they cannot differentiate empirically indistinguishable states' (Arrow, 1963[1951], p 112), the welfare economics has denied the logical possibility of discrimination. This is apparently the academic contribution to non-discrimination in political liberalism.[13]

We must note, however, that the logic that denies differences across individuals as a fact has led to a cautious approach to the acceptance of any principle of redistribution that accommodates essentially asymmetric relationships among individuals. When individual characteristics are quantitatively continuous, it becomes arbitrary to identify those who should receive resource transfers.[14]

This is indeed why people are too cautious about Rawls' difference principle. As is well known, it has attracted a wide variety of people concerned about the distribution of income and wealth, partly because its expression is modest and restrictive in claiming that social and economic inequalities are permitted only when they contribute to maximising expectations of the worst-off people (Rawls, 1971a) instead of claiming to eradicate social and economic inequalities completely. It suits to the intuition that there must be a limit to reducing inequalities even though equality is important.

The welfare economics confirms this intuition by pointing out its effects on individuals' work incentives. In other words, productive people must lose their willingness to work as the income tax rate progressively increases. This has led to an argument about the extent to which redistribution will maximise the share of the worst-off people, when taking into account labour supply responses to such redistribution system.[15]

It suggests that, for example, giving greater weight to the transfer for maximising the incomes of the least advantaged might result in a miserable income for them or for society as a whole because it may invite the reduction of capable individuals' work incentives. This possibility gives policymakers a good reason for adopting a lower weight of transfer, either for avoiding negative effects on the least advantaged or for promoting gross national income in a whole society.

The argument is developed not only for individuals' rational behavior in choosing the optimal combination of income and leisure but also for the following feelings of unfairness brought about by the difference principle.[16] Why should we privilege a specific position by calling for the 'maximisation' of the 'worst-off' position despite the fact that, if individual differences are only quantitatively continuous, the non-worst-off positions are also interchangeable by resource transfer?[17]

In summary, the analytical framework of welfare economics, which does not provide an argument for going beyond agnosticism about qualitative differences among individuals, cannot provide a sufficient reason to support inter-personal transfer.[18] The problem of distributive justice, therefore, tends to be reduced to intra-personal distribution under uncertainty or inter-temporal distribution across different life-stages of an individual.[19] We need to find a new theory now.

Expanded social cooperation or 'patronal treatment' scheme?

Let us go back to the tale we discussed before. What was symbolised by the wounded little bird?

Among essentially unsettled symmetric beings,
Unexpectedly appears an asymmetric being,
Who can shake the relation among them,
Hence, can provide a chance for cooperation.

Symmetric beings owe their cooperation to an asymmetric being. Supposing this is true, we can infer a reasonable axiom of reciprocity that says we should respect and thank the asymmetric being who brings about cooperation. This could be substantiated as a resource transfer scheme from symmetric to asymmetric beings, when 'asymmetric beings' are people whose positions are not interchangeable with others' positions merely by transferring resources, or people whose hardships or sufferings cannot be adequately compensated for with resources in the first place.

This is an attempt to reformulate Rawls' theory of justice by incorporating those hard cases (such as severe physical or mental disability) excluded by Rawls himself. It is at the same time an attempt to restructure the scope of his conception of the 'system of social cooperation' by accommodating people who are not yet recognised and included in 'social cooperation' (see Figure 2.1).

Figure 2.1: Social cooperation including symmetric and asymmetric relations

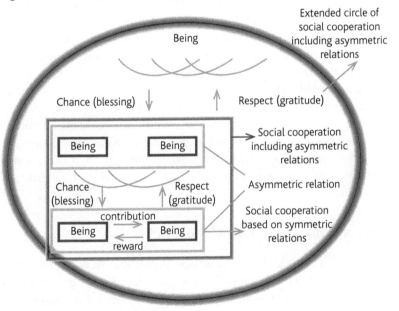

However, we must bear in mind the following serious problem when expanding the system this way. Is there any risk that asymmetric beings are going to be treated as a *means* for symmetric beings to achieve cooperation? Is the expanded system of social cooperation any different from an imperialist state that expands by swallowing its peripheries into its territory?[20]

It is true that welfare governance can sometimes go hand in hand with power. The benevolence (by means of benefits) and protection for specific minorities provided by power is often loudly advertised and quietly accepted by people, as it could make up for the oppression or violence forced on other minorities by the same power. An attempt to develop the system to include those outside the system has the possibility of overturning the trend from treatment to contract, a possible setback from a contract between free and equal agencies to a patronal treatment by the governor for the governed. Or, it might produce a gigantic governance power like hydra with 'contract relationships' at its centre and 'benevolence and protection' at its periphery, leaving asymmetric beings rarely treated as an end itself.

How can we possibly follow Kant's (1785) moral principle to 'treat any individual as an end, not merely as a means'?

Let me briefly state my conclusion in advance. Key to answering this serious question is to seek a normative conception that prescribes a resource transfer scheme from symmetric to asymmetric beings, going beyond the concept of 'fairness', which prescribes conditions of contracts among symmetrical relations based on equality as a fact. For example, equal treatment for equal cases, the same wage for the same work, or the same reward (benefit) for the same contribution (cost).

The wounded little bird cannot do the same work nor bear the same cost as symmetric beings. However, this very fact can provide a chance to bring and maintain cooperation among symmetric beings. In order to remember the chance (benefit) brought to symmetric beings by the asymmetric being and to keep the respect (and gratitude) given in return, we have to move to a less conditional normative concept than fairness.

The core thought of Rawls' theory of justice

Let us revisit Rawls' theory of justice. Rawls indeed recognised that the maximised expectation of the least advantaged actually varies with individuals' choices of work times, or, in general, with their behaviours related to labour incentives in society. Rawls himself, however, rejected the so-called 'maximum criterion', which reduces the problem to a kind of rational choice under uncertainty (Rawls, 1999 [1974], p 247).

Moreover, Rawls acknowledged the gravity of the effects of various natural or social contingencies. Consider, for example, Rawls's words in explaining that the philosophical background of the difference principle contains deep insight into the effects of social or natural contingencies.

> [N]o one should benefit from certain undeserved contingencies with deep and long-lasting effects, such as class origin and natural abilities, except in ways that also help others. (Rawls, 1999 [1974], p 246)

Here, Rawls questions the legitimacy of the 'principle of distribution according to merits'. What is usually taken for granted and attributed to individual merits can in fact be based on collective merits'. Alternatively, an individual owes his/her 'merit' at least partially to the fact that he/she can escape some natural or social contingencies that strike his/her neighbour, but not him/her. In this case, it is not obvious to what extent those merits can be attributed to 'the person himself/herself'.

In addition, the following notes made by Rawls in the context of how to identify the least advantaged in society suggest a possibility that goes beyond the concept of fairness that is essentially based on symmetrical relations.

> If, for example, there are unequal basic rights founded on fixed natural characteristics, these inequalities will single out relevant positions. Since these characteristics cannot be changed, the positions they define count as starting places in the basic structure. Distributions based on sex are of this type, and so are those depending upon race and culture. (Rawls, 1971a, p 99)

In order to achieve substantively equal basic rights, some asymmetrical treatments according to fixed characteristics are needed. The philosophical background of Rawls' theory of justice provides a perspective that makes it possible to interpret 'social cooperation' as accommodating not only those who can work but also those who cannot work and are in need of resource transfers. If society recognises that there remain some individuals who suffer severe disadvantages in the exercising of basic rights, they are to be treated with a necessary concern in implementing Rawls' difference principle.

However, unfortunately, Rawls did not fully develop this core thought of his theory. Rather, as clearly explained in his reply to Sen's criticism, Rawls left aside 'hard cases' (those of disability, hardship, or destitution) after all, hoping these would be dealt with at the legal stage in a real society (see Sen, 1997 [1980], Rawls, 1982). Below, I outline two ways in which to restructure Rawls' theory of justice to include this core thought.[21]

Two ways to restructure Rawls' theory of justice

First, in conceptualising the relationship between asymmetric and symmetric beings, sketched earlier by the metaphorical tale of the wounded bird, let us examine the concept of reciprocity that Rawls focused on, namely, 'justice as reciprocity', along with 'justice as fairness'.[22] It is similar to retributive justice but also different from it in the following way – that is, typically, in a way that can be illustrated by the following quotation.

> [T]hey are ready to propose principles and standards as fair terms of cooperation and to abide by them willingly, given the assurance that others will likewise do so. (Rawls, 1993, p 49)

This quotation expresses the idea of political reciprocity,[23] which recognises equivalent retaliations as just, observed in practices of explanation to others and of acceptance from others based on a bilateral relationship. The phrase 'given the assurance that others will likewise do so' is interpreted as indicating something that alleviates 'the strains of commitment to justice'[24] (see Figure 2.2).

Figure 2.2: Justice as reciprocity

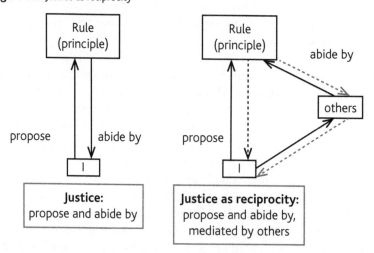

Gotoh (2009) developed an idea of public reciprocity based on Rawls' idea of 'justice as reciprocity'. Public reciprocity is similar to but different from the concept of mutual advantage that motivates private contracts or cooperative games, in that public reciprocity does not require symmetry or proportionality in its contributions and rewards relationship; moreover, it does not rule out cases where only one side will gain without a corresponding burden.[25] It is similar to but different from the concept of 'gift', which is realised in the context of direct or personal relationships followed by a counter–gift at some time in the remote future, in that public reciprocity does not presume that relationship. Instead, it is realised through certain rules, which are adopted through political reciprocity, and which in themselves represent bilateral correspondences in society as a whole.[26]

The following rule is taken as an example: if you can work and afford to provide, do so; if you are in need, receive help and be well. With this rule, we can rely on the fact that a neighbour with similar abilities to us would also work and provide, and that a neighbour with similar difficulties to us would also receive, though the amount provided or received may be quite different for the neighbour than for us. Moreover, we can rely on the fact that someone who provides nothing and only receives would also provide if he/she had the ability to work, as long as he/she could accept the same rule we follow. This kind of reasoning invites the idea of public reciprocity (see Figure 2.3).

Figure 2.3: Social cooperation with public (rule-based) reciprocity

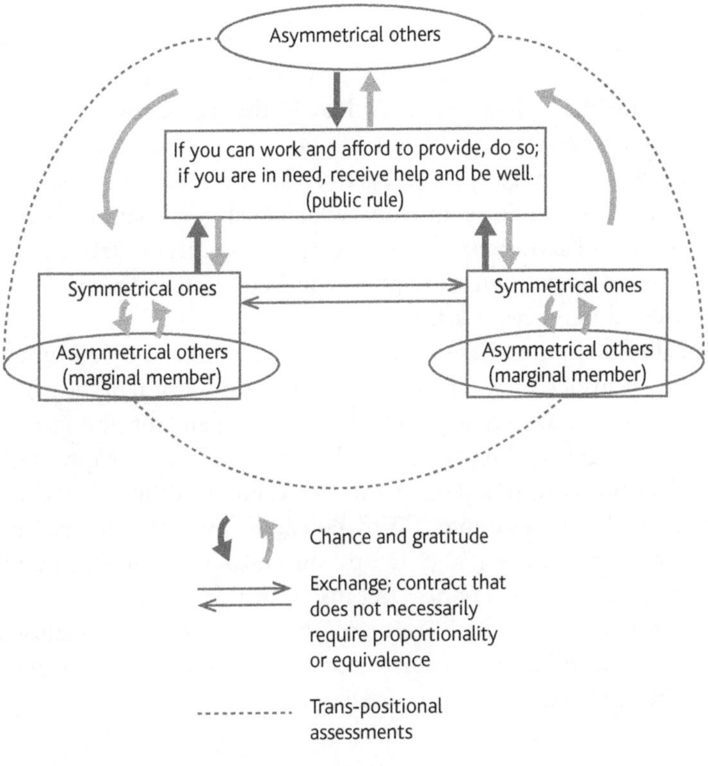

Second, we should try to describe and understand the situation of the wounded little bird as accurately as possible in order to provide better social assistance, without leaving the bird as an exception or a residual. Whether or not we can conceive of such a situation as something that could possibly be experienced by ourselves, we can admit the fact that it has happened to someone somewhere, and can then find a way to help the person in this situation as a social responsibility, respecting him/her as an equal being in society.

The capability approach proposed by Sen can be quite effective in describing and understanding individuals' concrete situations in detail (for example Sen, 1985, 1999). This approach makes a partially interpersonal comparison in multidimensional indices, by evaluating various contributions, burdens, meanings and benefits in specific historical, cultural and social contexts from the viewpoint, or 'position', of those individuals. To capture a person's capability is essentially to understand his/her predicament from his/her own position. Sen suggests further that multiple positions actually occupied by an agency himself/herself should provide a basis for 'trans–positional assessments' and for 'open impartiality' in his/her cognition as well as in the construction of public judgments (see Gotoh, 2014, pp 150-1).[27]

Conclusion

Connecting the core thought of Rawls' theory of justice with the capability approach of Sen's makes it possible to expand the concept of fairness conceived almost exclusively for symmetric beings to the concept of public reciprocity, which includes relations between symmetric and asymmetric beings. Underlying this process should be 'equality as a norm', which requires equal concern and respect for all, accepting 'differences as a fact'.

Equality as a norm here cannot be accommodated by a criteria of distributive justice such as formally uniform distribution or distribution aimed at universally equal results. It is an independent political value in its own right, and does not need to be based on or supported by any other political, moral, or economic value. In other words, when someone asks, for example, "Why equality?", we can answer simply and finally "Because equality is a paramount social value", instead of excusing ourselves by saying "Because it leads to social stability and, hence, our own benefits in the end." Note that having equality as a norm is compatible with having Rawls' veil of ignorance, as well as public reciprocity.

Confirming these points, let us go back to the original question. How should we understand the little bird, which is completely different from 'ourselves'?

Adam Smith would suggest putting ourselves in the position of the little bird through an 'imaginary exchange of positions'.[28] Immanuel Kant could tell us just to be kind to the little bird, and we do not have to understand it.[29] Rawls might recommend that we share the products of our cooperation with the little bird regardless of whether he/she can work or not. What would Sen suggest?

Sen would propose that we find out what the little bird has reason to value through public discussion in which the little bird takes part as an agency, say, expert of the position he/she actually occupies. Once that is clear, we can start producing goods and services that we all value. I may add here that perhaps Martha Nussbaum would suggest that we play with the little bird after waiting for its recovery and rest (see Nussbaum, 2000, p 78 onwards, 2006).

Notes

[1] For details of the relationship between Rawls's political liberalism and Japan's welfare state system, see Gotoh (2015b).

[2] Here 'trump' means 'priority', that is, not to be outweighed without any justification. The essential characteristic of a right is that it is ultimately attributed to an individual (to his/her will or interest). To use Dworkin's words, an individual can claim 'equal concern and respect' from society. See Dworkin (1977).

[3] Two sisters in their forties starved to death in January 2012. The elder sister had visited a welfare office three times prior to this, but she did not apply for public assistance after all.

[4] The 'fair equality of opportunities' and 'the difference principle' is contained in the second part of 'the difference principles of justice' proposed by Rawls (1971a).

[5] In contrast, the capability approach proposed by Sen focuses on the worth of liberties. See Gotoh (2015a).

[6] Note that as will be mentioned later, Rawls is more interested in securing basic wellbeing for all rather than making a clear selection of factors, since he recognised that a real problem is that we cannot clearly distinguish between responsible factors and non-responsible factors.

[7] This is because the former claim leads to an argument for respecting the free will of human beings, and the latter statement leads to the psychological justification of neglecting sufferers because of bounded rationality.

[8] This is the main criticism of Rawls' theory of justice by Sen; see Sen (2009).

[9] Rawls drew on Kant's moral theory and looked at the conclusions reached by reasoning using a political constructive procedure. For example, imagine that different individuals, under the 'veil of ignorance', are going to reason from a free and independent standpoint, while the 'veil of ignorance' covers up one's birth, attributes, social states, personal preferences and characteristics. And suppose they base their reasoning on the fact that there must be 'the least disadvantaged' depending on the distribution of 'social primary goods' in any society. Then what

kind of principles can they derive concerning the distribution of 'social primary goods'? See Rawls (1971a, 1993).

[10] It is not permissible to prevent someone from exercising his/her rights, damage his/her self-respect and dignity, or restrict his/her access to education, work, or public services, based on differences in these factors.

[11] The 'veil of ignorance' is a device for detaching oneself from his/her individualised information in choosing principles of justice in *A theory of justice* (Rawls, 1971a), whereas in *Political liberalism* (Rawls, 1993) it is developed to represent the core idea of political liberalism, which requires detaching oneself from all individualised information.

[12] For example, the internal organs of someone with a severe mental disability are not themselves necessarily severely damaged.

[13] In reality, people discriminate against certain individuals based on common sense and their gut feelings. This occurs by picking one disadvantage in just one dimension as something that dominates the other dimensions, and attributing it to a particular individual. On the contrary, the 'science' of political liberalism denies as fact the very existence of differences as a decisive disadvantage dominating other dimensions, considering the limitations of human cognitive ability.

[14] People can perform at the highest level even if their income is at the lowest quantile. Even today in Japan, there are many cases where an individual's poverty is retrospectively recognised only after he/she 'starves' to death.

[15] It provided an inspiration for the development of important research fields in economics such as the optimal taxation theory or incentive theory (endogenous theory of optimal redistribution).

[16] In neoclassical economics, this is explained by a decrease in the price of leisure (real wage). See Varian (1980) on optimal tax rates under uncertainty about the ability to work. See Gotoh (2014) for criticisms against the work incentive argument based merely on neoclassical economic models.

[17] Rawls recognised these arguments but he realised that a real problem is the fact that we cannot make a clear distinction between responsible factors and non-responsible factors. People can perform at the highest level even if their income is at the lowest quantile.

[18] Refer to, for example, Sen's criticism of the new welfare economics, condensed into 'welfarism'. See, for example, Sen (1997 [1977]). See also Gotoh (2001).

[19] For example, insurance systems equalise the expectations of persons who suffered dangers and those of persons who escaped dangers by transferring money from the latter to the former.

[20] According to Gunther Teubner, this is exactly the kind of *aporia* faced by Luhmann's system theory based on the concept of 'autopoiesis' as well as Derrida's 'justiciance' (Teubner, 2008).

[21] In Gotoh (2014), I have indicated that the framework of Rawls' 'justice as fairness' is inevitably restructured if the concept of 'capability' is introduced into his theory of justice, although Rawls himself considered that the concept of 'capability' could be smoothly introduced in the legislative stage without changing its basic framework.

[22] '[T]hey [the concepts of justice and fairness] share a fundamental element in common, which I shall call the concept of reciprocity.... It is this aspect of justice for which utilitarianism ... is unable to account; but this aspect is expressed, and allowed for, even if in a misleading way, by the idea of the social contract' (Rawls, 1971b, pp 190-2).

[23] For a detailed view of this conception of reciprocity in the context of Rawls, see Gutmann and Thompson (1996) and Gotoh (2009).

[24] The 'strains of commitment to justice' is explained by saying that 'the parties must weigh with care whether they will be able to stick by their commitment in all circumstances' (Rawls, 1971a, p 176).

[25] On this point, Lawrence Becker, the author of *Reciprocity*, seems to take a similar position, since his concept of 'proportionality' goes beyond the literal meaning of the term: '... when we seem unable to do anything that equals either the benefits we have received or the sum total of the sacrifices that have gone into producing those benefits. Here it is important to remember that such benefits typically come to us by way of people's participation in on-going social institutions.... What is fitting is reciprocal participation in those institutions' (Becker, 1986, pp 113-14).

[26] This definition of gift is different from the classical one, and closer to what Marcel Henaff calls a 'ceremonial gift', which is a form of reciprocity and not a unilateral transfer. See Henaff (2009). See also Gotoh (2009, 2013).

[27] Related to this point, an interesting issue is argued in Frazer (2014).

[28] Smith (1969 [1759]). The 'imaginary exchange of positions' is a refined method, if we do not end up jumping on the stereotype of 'suffering' in general, or unconsciously imposing 'my' own aesthetic idea or moral codes, or making judgments based on 'our' own customs and common sense, and if we can obtain the viewpoint of an 'impartial spectator'.

[29] Even if one is not moved by the suffering of others, he/she can perform 'an act of kindness' for others as his/her moral duty from his/her own good will, which Kant considered sufficient.

References

Arrow, K.J. (1963[1951]) *Social choice and individual values*, (2nd ed) New York, NY: Wiley.

Becker, L.C. (1986) *Reciprocity*, London: Routledge & Kegan Paul.

Dworkin, R. (1977) *Taking rights seriously*, Cambridge, MA: Harvard University Press.

Frazer, L.M. (2014) 'Including the unaffected', *The Journal of Political Philosophy*, vol 22, no 4, pp 377-95.

Gotoh, R. (2001) 'The capability theory and welfare reform', *Pacific Economic Review*, vol 6, no 2, pp 211-22.

Gotoh, R. (2009) 'Justice and public reciprocity', in R. Gotoh and P. Dumouchel (eds) *Against injustice? The new economics of Amartya Sen*, Cambridge: Cambridge University Press, pp 140-60.

Gotoh, R. (2013) 'Justice as reciprocity reexamined in the context of catastrophe', *Study on Languages and Cultures*, vol 24, no 4, pp 33-42.

Gotoh, R. (2014) 'The equality of differences: Sen's critique of Rawls's theory of justice and its implication for welfare economics', *History of Economic Ideas*, vol XXII, no 1, pp 133-55.

Gotoh, R. (2015a) 'Arrow, Rawls and Sen? The transformation of political economics and the idea of liberalism', in P. Dumouchel and R. Gotoh (eds) *Social bonds as freedom*, New York, NY: Berghahn Books.

Gotoh, R. (2015b) 'What Japan has left behind in the course of establishing a welfare state', *Proto Sociology*, vol 32, pp 106-22.

Gutmann, A. and Thompson, D. (1996) *Democracy and disagreement*, Cambridge, MA: Belknap Press of Harvard University Press.

Henaff, M. (2009) 'Gift, market and social justice', in R. Gotoh and P. Dumouchel (eds) *Against injustice? The new economics of Amartya Sen*, Cambridge: Cambridge University Press.

Kant, I. (1785) 'Transition from popular moral philosophy to the metaphysics of morals', *Groundwork of the metaphysic of morals: Immanuel Kant*, edited and translated by J.B. Schneewind, M. Baron, S. Kagan and A.W. Wood, New Haven and London: Yale University.

Lorenz, M.O. (1905) 'Methods of measuring the concentration of wealth', *Publications of the American Statistical Association*, vol 9, no 70, pp 209-19.

Nussbaum, M.C. (2000) *Women and human development: The capabilities approach*, Cambridge: Cambridge University Press.

Nussbaum, M.C. (2006) *Frontiers of justice: Disability, nationality, species membership*, Cambridge, MA: Belknap Press of Harvard University Press.

Rawls, J. (1971a) *A theory of justice*, Cambridge, MA: Harvard University Press.

Rawls, J. (1971b) 'Justice as reciprocity', in Samuel Gorowitz (ed) *John Stuart Mill: Utilitarianism, with critical essays*, Indianapolis, IN: Bobbs-Merrill, pp 190-224.

Rawls, J. (1982) 'Social unity and primary goods', in A. Sen and B. Williams (eds) *Utilitarianism and beyond*, Cambridge: Cambridge Unviersity Press, pp 159-85.

Rawls, J. (1993) *Political liberalism*, New York, NY: Columbia University Press.

Rawls, J. (1999 [1974]) 'Reply to Alexander and Musgrave', *Quarterly Journal of Economics*, vol 88, pp 633-55.

Rawls, J. (1999 [1975]) 'Kantian conception of equality', in S. Freeman (ed) *Collected papers*, Cambridge, MA: Harvard University Press, pp 232-253.

Sen, A.K. (1985) *Commodities and capabilities*, Amsterdam: North-Holland.

Sen, A.K. (1997 [1977]) 'On weights and measures: informational constraints in social welfare analysis', *Choice, welfare and measurement*, Oxford: Blackwell, pp 226-63.

Sen, A.K. (1997 [1980]) 'Equality of what?', *Choice, welfare and measurement*, Oxford: Blackwell, pp 353-69.

Sen, A.K. (1999) *Development as freedom*, New York, NY: Alfred A. Knopf.

Sen, A.K. (2002) *Rationality and freedom*, Cambridge, MA: Harvard University Press.

Sen, A.K. (2009) *The idea of justice*, Toronto: Allen Lane.

Smith, A. (1969 [1759]) *The theory of moral sentiments*, Delaware: Arlington House.

Teubner, G. (ed) (2008) *Nach Jacques Derrida und Niklas Luhmann: Zur (Un-) Möglichkeit einer Gesellschaftstheorie der Gerechtigkeit*, Stuttgart: Lucius and Lucius.

Varian, H.R. (1980) 'Redistributive taxation as social insurance', *Journal of Public Economics*, vol 14, pp 49-68.

THREE

The capability approach, agency and sustainable development

Elise Klein and Paola Ballon

Introduction

For the past 15 years, there has been a coordinated effort by the international community to track countries' progress for addressing extreme poverty, disease, lack of adequate shelter, and exclusion while promoting gender equality, education and environmental sustainability, in a quantifiable manner or 'target' as framed by the Millennium Development Goals – MDGs. However millions of people have been left behind by such 'progress'. Many live in entrenched poverty, rising inequality and face discrimination. This is exacerbated when looking at marginalised groups: the old, people with disabilities, ethnic and religious minorities, and in particular women and girls, and sexual minorities (Stuart et al, 2015).

In September 2015, the High-level Political Forum on Sustainable Development adopted the 2030 Agenda for Sustainable Development, which includes a set of 17 Sustainable Development Goals (SDGs) to end poverty, fight inequality and injustice and tackle climate change by 2030. Thus the SDGs, under the umbrella tenet 'leave no-one behind', put social justice and equity at the heart of the wider agenda for eradicating extreme poverty (UNDP, 2016). To achieve this, there is a need to assess the progress in the circumstances of disadvantaged groups, but most importantly to ensure that disadvantaged groups are not passive actors of 'change'.

In development policy and practice, community development programmes have arguably caught on to the importance of 'participatory' approaches to varying degrees (see Chambers, 1977). Nevertheless, while the SDGs allude to the empowerment of girls and women, they do not explicitly refer to purposive agency, democratic practices and authentic self-determination more generally. This was a critique of the MDGs, and some commentators have argued that the lack of attention given to agency has limited their success. The seriousness of the omission of agency from the MDGs is illustrated by the observation that the goals could be achieved even if the entire world's poor were put in gaol, which challenges the dramatic neglect of the poor's freedom (Alkire and Deneulin, 2006).

From a capability perspective, agency is important and should be central to all processes of development (Sen 1999; Alkire 2002; Nussbaum 2011). Agency is central to the capability approach, where 'the people have to be seen ... as being actively involved – given the opportunity – in shaping their own destiny, and not just as passive recipients of the fruits of cunning development programs' (Sen, 1999, p 53). Within the capability approach, social arrangements are viewed with respect to their ability to expand human freedoms on two levels, freedoms of opportunity and freedoms of process and agency (Sen, 2002).

Agency in the capability approach refers to both individual and collective processes. At an individual level, agency is the ability to act on values, or as Sen puts it, 'what a person is free to do and achieve in pursuit of whatever goals or values he or she regards as important' (Sen 1985, cited in Ibrahim and Alkire, 2007, p 384) At the collective level, Sen considers empowerment, agency and systemic process freedoms such as democratic practices, civil and political liberties to be central to creating social change. Furthermore, to Sen, agency is not just instrumental but also intrinsic (Alkire, 2008). Sen considers empowerment, agency and democratic practices also to be valuable independent of the outcome, where the process of achieving such freedoms has intrinsic importance at both individual and collective levels.

Furthermore, in the capability approach, both collective and individual agency are purposive. While Sen does not explicitly use the word 'aspiration' in his definition of agency, his idea of agency is aspirational, as it suggests an action or a response to what he calls 'constructive impatience' (Sen, 1999, p 11). Ibrahim (2011) has proposed an explicit discussion of aspirations within the capability approach, because it is what people reach for, and what they imagine, strive and hope for, even against all odds, that affects their actions as agents.

Notwithstanding, agency is contested within the capability approach. While at a normative level, placing people at the centre of development is an achievement, some scholars have pointed out the simplistic notion of agency and personhood expressed in the capability approach (Gasper, 2002; Giovanola, 2005). This narrow or 'thin' picture of personhood can provide an inadequate basis for conceptualising wellbeing and human development more generally.

Furthermore, there is not a deep understanding of habitual agency within the capability approach. While Sen and other capability scholars are not ignorant of the complexity between structures, culture and agency, hegemony and power are under-theorised in capability literature. Yet relations of power and social structures can be reproduced through subjectivities, agency and collective process freedoms such as democracy. For example, power underpins subjectivity and agency as seen in the work of post-structuralist theories where power is not just about oppression but also the emancipatory potential of power – indeed the element that constitutes subjectivity and agency. To Michel Foucault (1982), power is present in all human relations, social structures and the creation of subjectivity. Power, not only shapes the environment in which the agent acts, but constitutes the subjectivity that contests this very environment. Subjectivity is not just about being dominated or oppressed; it also constitutes agency. This is what Foucault describes as a paradox of subjectivity (Foucault, 1977; Butler, 1997). What this means is that while power constitutes and maintains the institutions that people act within, structural conditions are never fixed and are in constant motion within the dialectic of agency. Therefore, while subjectivity and agency are constituted within hegemony and oppressive structures, it is her agency and linking in with the agency of others that may shift and shape this process.

Further, the capability approach does not have a full account and theorisation of societal structures, hegemony and power in the shaping institutions of society (Otto and Ziegler, 2006; Zheng and Stahl, 2011). To put it differently, the racialised, liberal and economic constitution of society tends to structure agents' options and hegemony acts to exclude other options (Gramsci, 1971; Laclau and Mouffe, 2001). Sen refers to the market and human rights almost neutrally, which causes some difficulty in thinking about collective process freedoms such as democracy and public deliberation, which may further exclude or marginalise voices, reproducing asymmetrical power relations.

To be fair, the capability approach was not created as a theory to explain social phenomena per se, instead being designed to evaluate and conceptualise social phenomena, complementing other disciplinary perspectives (Robeyns, 2006). Yet overlooking such variation and difference when thinking about 'agency' could affect the goal of 'leaving no-one behind'. Drawing on research carried out in Mali, this chapter addresses the importance of including psychological and collective domains in the measurement of agency and proposes the use of 'local' metrics of agency: *dusu* and *ka da I yèrè la*. The chapter is structured as follows. The next section describes the Mali case study and the concept of psychological and collective agency emerging from it. We then explore the policy implications of the 'leave no-one behind agenda' for agency and multidimensional poverty by means of profiles and metrics. The chapter ends with a consideration of areas for policy integration and some concluding remarks.

The Mali case study

The Mali case study presented in this chapter draws from a study by Klein (2014). This study aimed to understand the elements of agency in a neighbourhood on the social fringe of Bamako by exploring mechanisms that were central to the purposeful agency of both men and women. Specifically, the study site is a neighbourhood of 423 households on the urban fringe of Bamako, Mali's capital. The neighbourhood can be characterised as a site of major urbanisation. The economic and social ties of the neighbourhood are very much mixed with those of the capital, which is only 15 km away; 70.9% of the people living in the neighbourhood were not born there, and had migrated from rural villages searching for work. The mix of the population makes the neighbourhood a site of complex social relations, specifically regarding gender and age. The educational level of people living in the neighbourhood is also diverse; according to the area household survey, the average number of residents' years at formal school was 5.9, and 53.1% of survey participants had five years' or less formal schooling. Further still, most people living in the neighbourhood struggle with deprivation and poverty where analysis of household deprivation shows that 73.3% of households were income poor,[1] and 71.7% of households were multidimensional poor.[2]

Methods

The study used an exploratory sequential mixed-methods design, which included inductive qualitative methods followed by quantitative methods to support qualitative findings. Specifically, the research was conducted over a total of six-and-a-half months, split over three trips. The first trip was a scoping and relationship-building mission lasting one month (December 2009); the second trip involved data collection for five months (November 2010 to March 2011); and the third trip reviewed initial results over the course of one month (November 2011) as a 'double-checking exercise'. The qualitative methods used included several months of observations while living in the neighbourhood, followed by data collection in the form of 26 life histories, four focus groups (one each with men, women, male youth and female youth) and another 25 key informant interviews. A household questionnaire was then used to collect data from every household in the neighbourhood to triangulate the qualitative findings about the psychological domain of agency and quantify levels of household deprivation and socioeconomic characteristics in the neighbourhood. There were 307 surveys completed out of a possible 423 households. A retest of the household questionnaire was then conducted with 12.2% of the population to test the stability of the questionnaire tool. Another 30 interviews were conducted to double-check the results a year later.

Agency on the urban fringe of Bamako

In the neighbourhood, purposeful agency – and specifically initiatives undertaken by both women and men to improve their livelihoods – was central to people's daily lives and to improving personal and collective wellbeing. We can think of this agency as purposeful and intentional in that it was directed towards what men and women in the neighbourhood called *hèrè*,[3] which in Bambara loosely translates as 'wellbeing' or the 'good life'. *Hèrè* describes not just wellbeing in the personal or immediate domain, but also the community domain, where the two are interlinked (respondents felt it was hard for the individual to have *hèrè* if others did not).

The psychological domain of agency

After spending time in the field engaging with this question of purposeful action, two important concepts emerged as being central to both men and women's intentional action: *dusu* (internal motivation) and *ka da I yèrè la* (self-belief). These concepts emerged time and time again when participants were asked about what was necessary for people to overcome hardship in their lives. Both *dusu* and *ka da I yèrè la* are psychological, in the sense that they are related to the person's self- understanding or *nakali* (the Bambara word to describe the mentality or self). *Dusu* (loosely translated as internal motivation) and *ka da yèrè la* (loosely translated as self-belief)[4] have a dyadic value to people in the neighbourhood. These concepts have an instrumental value to people, whereby they are inherent in the dominant narrative of change that implies that if you have *dusu* and *ka da I yèrè la* you can achieve aspirations even with limited means (financial and material).

Dusu and *ka da I yèrè la* also have an intrinsic value to informants, whereby it was argued that pursuing aspirations one cared about was an end and valuable to the agent or group in itself. The psychological constructs had an intrinsic and instrumental value to respondents with differing socioeconomic characteristics (years at school, household deprivation), which contributed to social change in the neighbourhood (Klein, 2014).

For example, one woman interviewed in the neighbourhood and living in a poor compound spoke of the problems faced by people each day because of their poverty. She said the only things to help were *dusu* and *ka da I yèrè la*. Specifically, she commented on their instrumental significance: "To get *dusu* and *ka da I yèrè la* is the start of everything. If you do not have this kind of thinking everything you undertake will collapse – it will not have success."[5] This woman then went on to say that *dusu* and *ka da I yèrè la* were the building blocks of working well in associations, as they motivated and energised the group to work towards the aim. Another woman living in the neighbourhood explained the intrinsic importance of *dusu* and *ka da I yèrè la* and 'loving' the initiative one undertakes: "If you love what you do, then you can do it and implement these things."[6] The psychological concepts were important to the purposeful agency of the informants.

Moreover, *dusu* and *ka da I yèrè la* were also important for collective agency. For example, when asked how someone can overcome hardship in their lives, a representative of the neighbourhood women's focus group, comprising seven women from poor households, said: "We encourage them to stand up with their *dusu* and do something. We invite them to join this association or another association as there are many associations to do something."[7]

'Leaving no-one behind': agency and multidimensional poverty across gender groups

In this section, we analyse the relationship between agency and multidimensional poverty to show how agency is an important policy consideration in leaving no-one behind. Specifically, we first examine agency in relation to power and gender in the study site, and then explore *dusu* and *ka da I yèrè la* in relation to multidimensional poverty measure and gender. This analysis will show the role of agency in leaving no-one behind.

Gender, power and agency

The qualitative research in Mali showed that life for women in the neighbourhood could be especially difficult; not only did they suffer household deprivation but also sometimes limited decision-making ability in key domains in their lives. *Dusu* and *ka da I yèrè* were seen as a basis for women's agency, to contest hardship and to undertake initiatives individually or collectively to enhance wellbeing. While *dusu* and *ka da I yèrè la* may imply elements of adaptive preference and the internalisation of social norms, they should not be dismissed as mere subjugation Mahmood (2005) has navigated such tricky analytical terrain, showing that even when agency is a 'product of the historically contingent discursive traditions in which they are located' (p 32), as was the case in her study with female participants in the mosque revival movement in Cairo, we cannot write off their agency as just submissive and oppressed. Instead, Mahmood (2005) follows Butler and Foucault in seeing the agent constituted by power, and while there is no freewill outside power, it is more interesting to examine how agents deploy their agency. Specifically, 'we should keep the meaning of agency open and allow it to emerge from within semantic and institution networks that define and make possible particular ways of relating to people, things and oneself' (Mahmood, 2005, p 34). For example, both men and women in the study site reported the use of relational processes that affected their *dusu* and *ka da I yèrè la*. Specifically, both men and women respondents reported that *dusu* and *ka da I yèrè la* were constituted by the relational processes of positive envy (*dusu*) and watching other people succeed (*ka da I yèrè la*). Positive envy was explained as a positive jealousy in seeing someone have what another wanted. It was positive because it then drove that person to undertake initiatives to achieve a similar outcome. Watching other people succeed was about people seeing people in similar socioeconomic situations achieve desired outcomes, which provided not only a road map of how one could go about trying to achieve such goals, but a solidary that gave a person confidence to act. Therefore, we can see *dusu* and *ka da I yèrè la* within structures of power and gendered institutions, but neither can be reduced to mere mechanisms of adaption, as they are inherent in women's agency to contend social change more broadly.

Profiles of agency and multidimensional poverty by gender

The concepts of *dusu* and *ka da I yèrè la* that are important to people living in the neighbourhood on the urban fringe of Bamako have clear implications for the 'leave no-one behind' sustainable development agenda of the country. Under the SDG framework, policies aimed at eradicating extreme poverty in Mali must take all population groups, and in particular the marginalised ones, into account. In the case of gender equality, SDG 5, the elimination of all forms of discrimination against women and girls, and a successful eradication of the many dimensions of poverty, requires an acknowledgement of the psychological aspects of agency such as *dusu* and *ka da I yèrè la* within structures of power and gendered institutions.

To illustrate this, we analysed the gender profiles of multidimensional poverty and psychological agency of the 307 adults surveyed in the urban fringe of Bamako. Figure 3.1 shows the percentage of females and males surveyed. While 42% of respondents identified themselves as females, and 51% as males, 7% did not identify as either female or male. This highlights the importance of including forgotten or marginalised groups in development policies, as stated in the leave no-one behind agenda.

Figure 3.1: Distribution of respondents by gender

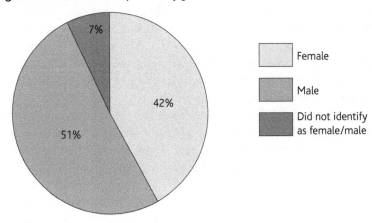

Measurement of agency

To measure agency, respondents were asked to rate their level of both *dusu* and *ka da I yèrè la* at an individual level and collective level on a ladder, or scale, from 1 to 10 (a picture of a ladder with rungs was used as a visual aide). Specifically, the question was: 'Today, if you are on a 10-step ladder, where 10 is a lot of *ka da I yèrè la/dusu* and 1 is no *ka da I yèrè la/dusu*, how much *ka da I yèrè la/dusu* do you have to undertake the initiatives for your family, and for your community?'

The household questionnaire also included questions measuring relative autonomy (compare Ryan and Deci, 2000, 2006). Klein and Ballon (2015) have shown that there was a very weak association between relative measures of autonomy and local measures of autonomy of *dusu* and *ka da I yèrè la*, and that the latter were more appropriate as metrics of psychological agency in Mali.

Measurement of multidimensional poverty

To study the multidimensional poverty situation of respondents in Mali, we applied the Alkire and Foster (2011) counting method of poverty measurement, referred to as the AF method. The AF method uses the joint distribution of deprivations to identify the people (or households) that live in multidimensional poverty. To obtain the joint distribution of deprivations of a person (or household), the method begins by comparing the wellbeing of the person in each indicator with the corresponding normative cut-off. The deprivation cut-off for an indicator shows the minimum achievement level or category required to be considered non-deprived in that indicator. If the wellbeing of the person in an indicator is below the cut-off, that person is considered to be deprived in that particular indicator.

Given that the importance of each indicator in a society may not be homogenous, each deprivation is 'weighted' according to its ethical importance in the society. The weight or deprivation value affixed to each indicator reflects the value that a deprivation in that indicator has for poverty, relative to deprivations in the other indicators. The joint distribution of deprivations is then obtained by counting the number of weighted deprivations that the person or household experiences.

Then, to identify the people who are multidimensionally poor, the AF counting approach proposes the use of a cross-dimensional cut-off. This second form of cut-off shows what combined share of weighted deprivations is sufficient to identify a person as poor. Thus, a person whose weighted deprivations are equal to or above the cross-dimensional cut-off is identified as living in multidimensional poverty.

The construction of an AF-type poverty measure thus entails several choices, among which we find the choice of indicators, dimensions, weights, deprivation cut-offs and poverty cut-off. The measure is thus sensitive to these choices and requires robustness analysis to assess the sensitivity of the results to the choices made (compare Alkire et al, 2015).

After identifying the people who live in multidimensional poverty, the AF method aggregates their status into an overall index (or indices).

The aggregation employs the Foster, Greer and Thorbecke or FGT (Foster et al, 1984) measures appropriately adjusted to account for multidimensionality. This leads to a family of indices among which the adjusted headcount ratio (M0) is the one reported internationally (compare UNDP, 2010–2015). The adjusted headcount ratio is equal to the product of two sub-indices: the multidimensional headcount ratio or the percentage of people identified as poor using the dual cut-off approach (*H*), and the average deprivation share among the poor (*A*). Thus M0 provides an assessment of the composition of multidimensional poverty in terms of incidence (*H*) and breadth or intensity (*A*). As with the FGT unidimensional measures, M0 can be decomposed by population subgroups, and can also be broken down by indicator. These properties are keen for policy decisions, as they allow understanding the characteristics of multidimensional poverty for each group, as well as, those indicators that contribute the most to poverty for any given subgroup.

To assess the multidimensional poverty profiles of respondents of the urban fringe of Mali, we followed the global multidimensional poverty index (Global-MPI) developed by the Oxford Poverty and Human Development Initiative (OPHI) with the United Nations Development Programme (UNDP) for inclusion in UNDP's flagship Human Development Report in 2010 and published in subsequent reports ever since. The Global-MPI is an AF-type counting approach poverty measure that assesses acute poverty in the Global South. It comprises three dimensions – education, health and living standards – and 10 indicators, all (dimensions and indicators) equally weighted. To identify the poor, the Global-MPI uses a poverty cut-off of 33%. This means that people who suffer deprivation in at least one third of the weighted indicators are identified as living in multidimensional poverty (UNDP, 2010–2015; Alkire and Santos, 2014). Table 3.1 describes the normative criteria of the MPI constructed for the urban fringe of Bamako.

Table 3.1: Normative criteria

Dimension	Indicator/ variable	Poverty cut-off	Weight according to Alkire and Foster (2011)	Measure used in the current study?	Weight used in authors' analysis
1 Standard of living	TV, radio, telephone, fridge, motorcycle, car, truck	Poor: can own one of TV/radio/ telephone/fridge/motorcycle but not more. If owns car/truck is not poor.	1/6	Yes	1/6
	Floor	Poor: dirt/natural floor.	1/6	Yes	1/6
	Electricity	Poor: no electricity.	1/6	Yes	1/6
	Cooking fuel	Poor: wood, dung, charcoal.	1/6	Yes	1/6
	Toilet	Poor: no improved private toilet*	1/6	Yes	1/6
	Water	Poor: no drinking water**	1/6	Yes	1/6
2 Education	Years of schooling	Poor: no person in the household has finished primary school.	1/2	Yes	1
	School enrolment	Poor: any school-aged child up to 14 is not enrolled in school.	1/2	No***	–
3 Health	Under five child mortality	Poor: if a child born of a woman living in the house has died under the age of five..	1/2	Yes	1/2
	Nutrition	Poor: if any adult or child in the household is malnourished.	1/2	Yes	1/2

Notes: * If the toilet is flush or is a pit latrine with a slab, it is considered 'improved'. Otherwise it is not.
** If the water is piped into the house/compound, or comes from a protected well, the household is considered non-poor. Otherwise it is not. *** It was hard to collect exact data for this question as a lot of the informants did not know how many children lived in the house. We therefore decided to exclude this question and only have one indicator for the education domain.

Source: Adapted from OPHI, 2008.

Profiles

To profile agency and poverty across gender groups, we began by looking at deprivation by dimension, as an informative analysis. However, we should point out that an assessment of unidimensional deprivation remains silent about poverty, which reflects a condition of multiple deprivations. Following the deprivation profiles, therefore, we present the poverty statistics computed on the basis of the AF method and the Global-MPI empirical application previously explained. Using these poverty measures, we profile agency by gender.

Table 3.2 shows the headcount ratios or deprivation ratios by indicator per dimension or domain. The highest deprivation rates are found in the education and living standards domains, where 70% of respondents are deprived in years of education, and 95% live in households with very poor-quality cooking fuel materials. In the case of health, although the deprivation rates are lower than those for education and living standards, they are not negligible, as 40% of respondents live in households where at least one child has died.

By gender, we observe a pattern disfavouring females and the 'unidentified' group of respondents. Females exhibit higher deprivation rates than males across all living standard indicators, including nutrition. However, the trend is reversed for years of education and child mortality, where males show considerable higher deprivation rates than females. Deprivation in health exacerbates for the 'unidentified' group, where the rates of deprivation in child mortality and nutrition are the highest among all gender groups.

Table 3.2: Deprivation rates, by gender (%)

Gender	Education	Health		Living standards						
	Years of education	Child mortality	Nutrition	Improved sanitation	Electricity	Cooking fuel	Flooring	Safe drinking water	Assets
Female	64	31	14	29	20	96	52	28	7
Male	75	46	11	22	15	94	45	22	3
Do not know	67	52	19	29	14	100	43	38	0
All	70	40	13	25	17	95	48	26	4

Moving on to multidimensional poverty, in Table 3.3 we report the adjusted headcount ratio (M0) and its partial subindices of incidence (H) and breadth (A) of multidimensional poverty. Overall, we observe that 71.7% of respondents live in multidimensional poverty and experience average deprivation of 56%. In other words, 220 out of the 307 interviewees live in households that experience deprivations in at least a third of the weighted indicators considered in the analysis. The breadth of their poverty indicates that their average deprivation is equivalent to five out of nine indicators. When we disaggregate by gender, we observe that females are better off than males or the unidentified group. Females exhibit lower incidence rates (66%) than males, but the same intensity rate (56%). The unidentified exhibit the same incidence rate as females, but a higher intensity rate (60%) than that of females or males (56%). This leads to a larger M0 index for males (0.43) followed by the unidentified group (0.40) and females (0.37). Despite these group differences, the composition of poverty across all three groups tends to be quite homogenous. Figure 3.2 depicts the percentage contribution of each indicator to overall poverty, and shows that years of education is the indicator that contributes most to multidimensional poverty across all three groups, followed by child mortality and cooking fuel.

Table 3.3: Local measures of agency and multidimensional poverty, by gender

	Poverty index			Local agency measure: average dusu/ka I yèrè			
Group	H	A	M0	Dusu family wellbeing	Dusu community wellbeing	K I yere la family wellbeing	K I yere la community wellbeing
Female	66.2%	56%	0.37	8.8	8.7	**9.0**	9.1
Male	76.9%	56%	0.43	8.5	8.2	**7.9**	8.7
Do not know	66.7%	60%	0.40	9.1	7.9	8.6	8.8
All	71.7%	56%	0.40	8.7	8.4	8.4	8.9

Notes: Values in bold denote statistically significant differences at 5% level between females and males.

Figure 3.2: Composition of multidimensional poverty (%)

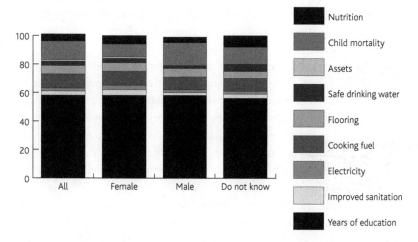

When looking at the agency profile among the poor, once again we observe that females exhibit slightly larger scores of *dusu* and *ka da I yèrè* than males and the unidentified group in both family and community initiatives, but only in the case of *ka da I yèrè la* do we find a statistically significant difference between the scores of females and males (9.0 females, 7.9 males). The unidentified group turns out to be the one with lower scores than males in all cases except for *dusu*

family initiatives. Thus we find that, in terms of multidimensional poverty and agency, respondents belonging to the unidentified group tend to be worse off than females or males. This clearly indicates that an inclusive development process leading up to 2030 should address policies where all groups – male, female and unidentified – are explicitly included and their agency is equally considered.

Conclusion

Agency has been promoted in development scholarship and policy (Jackson and Karp, 1990; Drèze and Sen, 1995; Kabeer, 1999; Sen, 1999, 2009; Nussbaum, 2001; Mahmood, 2005; Batiwala, 2007; Alkire, 2008; Narayan et al, 2009). Such approaches show that a failure to consider both agency and the dialectic between agency and structure disregards the discursive nature of individual agents negotiating their lives at psychological, collective and institutional levels (Long, 2001). Furthermore, the trend towards participatory development techniques in development policy and interventions has affected this shift towards promoting agency in development scholarship and policy (Chambers, 1997). However, policymakers must be careful in their treatment of agency, and specifically individual agency, because of the increasing individualisation of economic relations brought about through neoliberal ideologies.

On one level, the inclusion of agency in development studies can be helpful in conceptualising people as fuller beings, as we seek to move beyond the binary categories of deprivation level, gender, ethnicity, income group and so on. Yet, as contemporary development intervention is firmly rooted within wider structures of power and domination, there is a serious risk that political and economic actors could explicitly or implicitly target the psychological domain for instrumental purposes.

For example, in 2015 the World Bank released its annual World Development Report, entitled *Mind, society, and behavior*. In a press release just before the report was published, the Bank explicitly articulated its aim to 'look more deeply inside the economic actor, at the individual's mental processes'. The report demonstrates the instrumentality of targeting the psychological domain, specifically where 'new policy ideas based on a richer view of decision-making can yield high economic returns' (World Bank Group, 2015, p 1). Therefore it is imperative that any analysis of agency situates agency within broader structures of power, and that an inclusive development process in the run-up to 2030 addresses policies that cover all population groups.

Some possible ways for policy to engage in this important area include the following:

- **Development as human flourishing, not economic growth and integration.** The capability approach has the ability to challenge outdated and restrictive definitions of development. The capability approach maintains that expanding valued capabilities is the purpose of development, and that institutions (including the state and economy) should only exist to support capabilities that people value or have reason to value. The capability approach could support the creation of post-development or hybrid economies that would recognise the diverse meanings of development, where people subjected to development actively take part in defining their own trajectories of development.
- **Integrating the capability approach with critical social theory.** Combined with critical social theory, the capability approach could provide a suitable normative framework to guide policy to support meaningful engagement to ensure no-one is left behind. Critical social theory scholars focus on how social structures and power dynamics enable or restrict emancipation, that is, the discursive character of social structures that limit personal and collective freedoms (Zheng and Stahl, 2011). Without such critical social theory, the pluralism and flexibility built into the capability approach 'creates scope for more casual and indeed opportunistic appropriations and interpretations' (Sayer, 2012, p 582).
- **Creating context-specific policy formations where agency is central.** The capability approach provides a way to work through any top-down managerial approach, which often plays out at the expense of individual and collective process freedoms. Because it requires deliberation and democratic freedoms, the capability approach can help avoid individualisation, wherein actors use their privileged position to prevail over all others. Instead, the capability approach requires public deliberation in the formation and execution of policies with actors that are directly affected by the policy.
- **Making the means as important as the ends.** Another area where the capability approach could contribute to the leave no-one behind agenda is in rebalancing the relationship between the means and ends of policy. Currently, policy is outcome-focused (ends) and the process of getting to such outcomes is overlooked and undervalued. Within the capability approach, the policymaking process has intrinsic and instrumental significance in terms of people's ability to have more control over their lives.

Nonetheless, this short chapter shows the importance of agency for people living in the neighbourhood on the urban fringe of Bamako, and highlights the challenge faced by policymakers in including agency in the leaving no-one behind agenda.

Notes

[1] Income deprivation was calculated from the yearly household income based on the poverty line level of below US$1.25 per day.

[2] See the section on measurement of multidimensional poverty.

[3] *Hèrè* is Bambara for 'good things', things focused not so much on material goods, but on happiness and a general sense of wellness in life. When asking about wellbeing, it was the word *hèrè* that was used. Both the interviewees and the focus group participants understood this concept, and no examples of what it could look like were used as a probe. The question was posed using '*nièta*' when talking about the improvement of wellbeing. '*Niè*' means forward and '*ta*' means go.

[4] Writing about *ka da I yèrè la* and *dusu* is fraught. Nuance can be lost in translation where we have tried to articulate the inductive definitions of terms that have emerged in the research (by suggesting *ka da I yèrè la* and *dusu* may be understood as similar to self-belief and internal motivation). Therefore, we are not claiming any absolute definition of *ka da I yèrè la* and *dusu*.

[5] Female interview, the neighbourhood, 22 December 2010.

[6] Female interview, the neighbourhood, 5 January 2011.

[7] Women's focus group, the neighbourhood, 24 January 2011.

References

Alkire, S. (2002) *Valuing freedoms: Sen's capability approach and poverty reduction*, Oxford: Oxford University Press.

Alkire, S. (2008) 'Concepts and measures of agency', in K. Basu and R. Kanbur (eds) *Arguments for a better world: Essays in honour of Amartya Sen. Volume 1: Ethics, welfare and measurement*, Oxford: Oxford University Press.

Alkire, S. and Deneulin, S. (2006) 'The human development and capability approach', in S. Deneulin and L. Shahani (eds) *An introduction to the human development and capability approach: Freedom and agency*, London: Earthscan, pp 22-48.

Alkire, S. and Foster, J. (2011) 'Counting and multidimensional poverty measurement', *Journal of Public Economics*, vol 95, no 7, p 11.

Alkire, S. and Santos, M.E. (2014) 'Measuring acute poverty in the developing world: robustness and scope of the multidimensional poverty index', *World Development*, vol 59, pp 251-74.

Alkire, S., Foster, J., Seth, S., Santos, M.E., Roche, J.M. and Ballon, P. (2015) *Multidimensional poverty measurement and analysis*, Oxford: Oxford University Press.

Batiwala, S. (2007) 'Taking the power out of empowerment – an experiential account', *Development in Practice*, vol 17, no 4, pp 557-65.

Butler, J. (1997) *The psychic life of power: Theories in subjection*, Redwood City, CA: Stanford University Press.

Chambers, R. (1997) *Whose reality counts? Putting the first last*, Bradford: ITDG Publishing.

Drèze, J. and Sen, A. (1995) *India: Economic development and social opportunity*, Oxford: Oxford University Press.

Foster, J., Greer, J. and Thorbecke, E. (1984) 'A class of decomposable poverty measures', *Econometrica: Journal of the Econometric Society*, vol 52, no 3, pp 761-66.

Foucault, M. (1977) *Discipline and punish: The birth of the prison*, London: Allen Lane.

Foucault, M. (1982) 'The subject and power', *Critical Inquiry*, vol 8, no 4, p 18.

Gasper, D. (2002) 'Is Sen's capability approach an adequate basis for considering human development?', *Review of Political Economy*, vol 14, no 4, pp 435-61, doi: 10.1080/0953825022000009898.

Giovanola, B. (2005) 'Personhood and human richness: good and well-Being in the capability approach and beyond', *Review of Social Economy*, vol 63, no 2, pp 249-67, doi: 10.2307/29770307.

Gramsci, A. (1971) *Selections from the prison notebooks*, New York, NY: International Publishers.

Ibrahim, S. (2011) *Poverty, aspirations and wellbeing: Afraid to aspire and unable to reach a better life – voices from Egypt*, Brooks World Poverty Institute Working Paper 141, Manchester: BWPI.

Ibrahim, S. and Alkire, S. (2007) 'Empowerment and agency: a proposal for internationally-comparable indicators', *Oxford Development Studies*, vol 35, no 4, pp 379-403.

Jackson, M. and Karp, I. (1990) 'Introduction', in M. Jackson and I. Karp (eds) *Personhood and agency: The experience of self and other in African cultures*, Uppsala: Acta Universitatis Upsaliensis, pp 1-33.

Kabeer, N. (1999) 'Resources, agency, achievements: reflections on the measurement of women's empowerment', *Development and Change*, vol 30, no 3, pp 435-64.

Klein, E. (2014) 'Psychological agency: evidence from the urban fringe of Bamako', *World Development*, 64 (C), pp 642-53.

Klein, E. and Ballon, P. (2015) 'Rethinking measures of psychological agency: a study on the urban fringe of Bamako', Paper presented at the 2015 HDCA conference, Washington, DC.

Laclau, E. and Mouffe, C. (2001) *Hegemony and socialist strategy: Towards a radical democratic politics* (2nd end), London: Verso Books.

Long, N. (2001) *Development sociology: Actor perspectives*, London: Routledge.

Mahmood, S. (2005) *Politics of piety*, Princeton, NJ: Princeton University Press.

Narayan, D., Pritchett, L. and Kapoor, S. (2009) *Moving out of poverty. Volume 2: Success from the bottom up*, Washington, DC: Palgrave Macmillan and the World Bank.

Nussbaum, M. (2001) *Women and human development: The capabilities approach*, Cambridge: Cambridge University Press.

Nussbaum, M. (2011) *Creating capabilities: The human development approach*, Cambridge, MA: The Belknap Press of Harvard University Press.

Otto, H.-U. and Ziegler, H. (2006) 'Capabilities and education', *Social Work and Society*, vol 4, no 3, pp 269-87.

Robeyns, I. (2006) 'The capability approach in practice', *The Journal of Political Philosophy*, vol 14, no 3, pp 351-76.

Ryan, R. and Deci, E. (2000) 'Self-determination theory and the facilitation of intrinsic motivation, social development and well-being', *American Psychologist* vol 55, no 1, pp 68-78.

Ryan, R. and Deci, E. (2006) 'Self-regulation and the problem of human autonomy: does psychology need choice, self-determination, and will?', *Journal of Personality*, vol 74, no 6, pp 1557-86.

Sayer, A. (2012) 'Capabilities, contributive injustice and unequal divisions of labour', *Journal of Human Development and Capabilities*, vol 13, no 4, pp 580-96.

Sen, A. (1999) *Development as freedom*, Oxford: Oxford University Press.

Sen, A. (2002) *Rationality and freedom*, Cambridge, MA: Belknap Press of Harvard University Press.

Sen, A. (2009) *The idea of justice*, London: Penguin Books.

Stuart, E., Samman, E., Avis, W. and Berliner, T. (2015) *The data revolution: Finding the missing millions*, London: Overseas Development Institute.

UNDP (United Nations Development Programme) (2010–2015) *United Nations Development Programme*, Human Development Report Office, http://hdr.undp.org/en/global-reports

UNDP (United Nations Development Programme) (2016) Sustainable Development Goals, available at www.undp.org/content/undp/en/home/sdgoverview/post-2015-development-agenda.html.

World Bank Group (2015) *World Development Report 2015: Mind, society, and behavior*, Washington, DC: World Bank.

Zheng, Y. and Stahl, B. (2011) 'Technology, capabilities and critical perspectives: what can critical theory contribute to Sen's capability approach?', *Ethics and Information Technology*, vol 13, no 2, pp 69–80.

FOUR

Public policy: from welfare to empowerment of women in India

Indira Mahendravada

Introduction

Public policy addressing gender issues in India started with a constitutional declaration in 1950: Article 15(1) of the Fundamental Rights of Indian Constitution prohibits discrimination on grounds of religion, race, caste, sex or place of birth. Furthermore, Article 15(3) empowers the state to take affirmative actions in favour of women. These measures, however, did not ensure gender equality, as strong socio-cultural factors and patriarchy resulted in a greater gender gap in access to opportunities. This gap could be observed in all capability-enhancing inputs across the country. According to the 2011 census, the gap in the literacy rate of male and female was 16.7%. This gap was greater in rural areas (19.2%) than urban areas (9.65%). Affirmative action was identified as an important tool to include those who were hitherto excluded and make men and women equal partners in the development process. Various policy measures and programmes were introduced in different five-year plans. The promotion of girl child education has resulted in a considerable increase in gender parity in school enrolment, and more and more women have entered the paid labour market. However, this has generated a host of other issues, given the patriarchal norms in Indian society. For example, there has been a considerable increase in the number of cases of violence against women, divorce and so on. The pending ascent of the Women Reservation Bill[1] for the past two decades is a testimony to the influence of patriarchy. The Bill has not achieved the requisite majority despite being presented several times. Currently, India is in the paradoxical situation whereby reasonable gender parity in capability-promoting measures and enhanced gender-based violence coexist.

The objective of this chapter is to review the policy initiatives by the Government of India during the planning era and analyse empirically the impact of the policy interventions on the empowerment of women in Karnataka at the micro level by using the capability approach. The study tests the hypothesis that the policy of involving non-governmental organisations (NGOs) in the empowerment of rural women has a positive impact on the autonomy of women measured in terms of capabilities.

The analysis is based on primary data collected through sample surveys from two districts in Karnataka, India. Sample districts represent developed and underdeveloped districts based on the Human Development Report of Karnataka. Data was collected from 50 women randomly selected from each of eight sample villages. Of the eight villages, there is NGO presence in four villages; the remaining four are non-NGO villages (NNGO) constituting the control group.

This chapter is divided into three sections: the first discusses the capability approach; the second traces the shift in public policy from welfare to empowerment; and the third presents an analysis of field data and the findings from the study in Karnataka.

Capability approach

This section comprises a brief discussion about the capability approach, its application to women empowerment and agency, and indicators to measure autonomy.

The important concepts of the capability approach are 'functionings' and 'capabilities'. According to Sen the life of a person is seen as a sequence of things the person does, or states of being he or she achieves, and these constitute a collection of 'functionings'. On the other hand capability is 'the various combinations of functionings, reflecting the person's freedom to lead one type of life or another' (Sen, 1992, p 40). The capability approach focuses on what people are effectively able to do and to be, that is, their capabilities. Beings and doings, which Sen calls functionings, constitute what makes a life valuable. Functionings include working, being literate, being able to rest, being healthy, being respected, being part of the community and so on. There is a distinction between achieved functionings and capabilities. While achieved functionings are those that are already realised, capabilities are effectively possible functionings. What is important is whether people have the freedoms or valuable opportunities (capabilities) to lead the kind of life they want to lead, to do what they want to do and be the person they want to be. Nussbaum distinguishes three different types of capabilities; basic capabilities, internal capabilities and combined capabilities. The basic capabilities are 'the innate equipment of individuals that is the necessary basis for developing the more advanced capabilities and a ground of moral concern' (Nussbaum, 2000, pp 84-5). The internal capabilities are developed states of the person and these states are mature conditions of readiness. According to Nussbaum, internal capabilities develop only with support from the surrounding environment. The third category of combined capabilities is internal capabilities combined with suitable external conditions for the exercise of the function. According to the capability approach, the ultimate goal of all policies should be people's wellbeing in all dimensions, that is, their enhanced capabilities. The external interventions of these programmes are capability inputs. Monetary inputs like income, and non-monetary inputs like care, public goods and services, community culture and so on, are identified as capability inputs (Robeyns, 2005). In the capability approach framework, given the same level of inputs, the outcomes may be different due to different conversion factors like social norms, religion, skills, disability, living in a dangerous area or isolated area, and so on.

Empowerment and capabilities

Empowerment is defined as an increase in certain capabilities that are deemed particularly instrumental to the situation at hand (Ibrahim and Alkire, 2007). An increase in empowerment would therefore be reflected in increased agency. Empowerment enhances the assets and capabilities of the poor. However, agency influences people's individual and collective assets and capabilities. Collective assets that influence capabilities are voice, organisation, representation and identity, while individual assets and capabilities are material, human, social and psychological in nature (Narayan, 2002). Agency can be constrained by the 'opportunity structure', that is, the institutional climate and prevailing social and political structures (Alsop et al, 2006). In discussing the influence of circumstances within which women attempt to flourish, Nussbaum (2000, p 31) says that these circumstances 'affect the inner lives of people, not just their external options: what they hope for, what they love, what they fear as well as what they are able to do'. The context shapes both choice and aspirations. According to Nussbaum, different capabilities are linked to one another. For example, the dependent status of Indian women, and the fact that they may stay in an abusive relationship far longer than they wish to, is enforced by lack of property rights, literacy, employment-related skills and access to credit.

Sen (1985, p 206) defines agency as 'what a person is free to do and in pursuit of whatever goals and values he or she regards important'. According to Sen, agency is intrinsically valued and exercising agency is directly conducive to wellbeing. In the context of the relationship between agency, resources and achievements, Kabeer (2005) distinguishes between 'passive' forms of agency (action taken when there is little choice) and 'active' agency (purposeful behavior). The other distinction is between effectiveness of agency and transformative agency. Kabeer supports transformative agency, which leads to changes in patriarchal systems. Empowerment indicators and capabilities are closely related (Mahendravada, 2005). Empowered women can make their choices by exercising agency. But in an earlier study (Mahendravada, 2004) it was found that although empowerment programmes increased women's confidence, they did not translate into the actual exercise of choices enabling women to live in the way they want to live. Similarly, although women are capable of political participation, they are constrained by the social and political conditions that prevail in their villages. As expressed by Mahmud (2003), women face a trade-off between the exercise of choice and adherence to existing norms. The trade-offs impose costs up on women that can influence outcomes and behaviours.

NGO interventions and improved capabilities

An important aspect of gender development programmes in India is the involvement of NGOs. The seventh five-year plan was a landmark in the history of the NGO sector as it marked the beginning of official involvement of NGOs in development efforts. Development NGOs were invited to supplement government's micro-level poverty alleviation and basic needs programmes. The Council for Advancement of People's Action and Rural Technology was established in 1986 to support NGOs and help channel the funds for their involvement. According to the Central Statistical Office, there are more than three million NGOs in India and most of them address gender issues in their programmes (Venkatraja and Mahendravada, 2014). The promotion of self-help groups (SHGs) is the empowerment strategy adopted by both the government and NGOs. It is based on the premise that access to financial resources empowers women. The SHG concept was introduced in India on the Grameen model of Bangladesh with a few modifications. The formation of such groups was initially promoted only by NGOs. Later, the Government of India and several state governments made it a policy to promote the formation of SHGs, linking them to local banks to sanction group lending at concession rates. SHGs were found to be effective in giving more intangible benefits to their members in the form of increased confidence, greater mobility and so on (Mahendravada, 2004). The positive impact of NGO interventions on human functionings was reported in a micro-level study in Karnataka (Venkatraja and Mahendravada, 2014). The Human Development Index measured in terms of capabilities in NGO villages was significantly higher than in NNGO villages. Higher positive social externalities of NGO-implemented SHG programmes (Mahendravada, 2004) and the complementarities between NGO and government interventions in the empowerment of women have also been documented (Mahendravada and Joshi, 2012).

Measuring capabilities

Several attempts have been made to operationalise the capability approach. Grasso (2002) did so via the conversion model and identified the linkages between different achieved functionings and wellbeing. Chiappero–Martinetti (2008) used fuzzy sets methodology to capture the vague concepts of the capability approach, while Alkire et al (2013) developed the Women's Empowerment in Agriculture Index to measure empowerment and agency in agriculture.

The present study adopted the methodology proposed by Ibrahim and Alkire (2007), analysing the exercise of agency to understand the extent to which NGO interventions have expanded the agency of women in different domains. Ibrahim and Alkire (2007) proposed four possible exercises of agency that could lead to empowerment.

- empowerment as control (power over): control over personal decisions;
- empowerment as choice (power to): domain-specific autonomy and household decision making;
- empowerment in community (power with): changing aspects in one's life (individual level);
- empowerment as change (power from within): changing aspects of one's life (communal level).

Using the indicators and the questions provided by Ibrahim and Alkire, the study analysed capabilities in the following specific domains:

- Individual
  - Work in private domain
  - Work in public domain
  - Political participation both as contestant and voter
  - Own health
  - Marriage
  - Number of children
  - Protest against violence
- Household
  - Buying and selling of property
  - Selling of produce
  - Children's education
  - Children's marriage

By using the above indicators, Relative Autonomy Index (RAI) was calculated for the women in NGO and NNGO villages. It is the weighted sum of the scores in decision making in different domains and it measures an individual's ability to act on what he or she values. In the earlier studies RAI was applied to different domains in the context of Kerala (Pillai and Alkire, 2007)and Chad (Vaz et al, 2016).

Public policy through five-year plans: a shift from welfare to empowerment

Women's development has been one of the priorities ever since policy planning was introduced in early 1950s. However, there has been a paradigm shift from a welfare approach to an empowerment perspective in tune with global thinking and encompassing approaches from women in development through women and development to gender and development.

The first five-year plan (1951-56) adopted a welfare approach under the women in development framework, and the objective was to provide adequate services to promote the welfare of women so that they could contribute to the welfare of the family and community. The Central Social Welfare Board was set up in 1953 to promote voluntary organisations at various levels to take up women's welfare programmes. The Immoral Traffic (Prevention) Act 1956 was passed during this period. During the period of the second five-year plan (1956-61), the Maternity Benefit Act 1961 and the Dowry Prohibition Act 1961 were enacted. In the third (1961-66) and fourth (1969-74) plans, the welfare of women was grouped with other welfare schemes such as those aimed at elderly and disabled people. Working girls hostels and short-stay homes were introduced during the fourth plan to meet the requirements of working women. The release of the report 'Towards Equality: Report of the Committee on Status of Women in India (1974)' coincided with the end of the fourth plan.[2] The report is considered a historic benchmark and has influenced discussions on women and development. It recognises women as critical inputs for development, not as targets of welfare programmes. During the fourth plan period, the historic Act of Medical Termination of Pregnancy Act 1971 was passed to give reproductive choice to women.

The fifth plan (1974-79) coincided with International Women's Decade. Based on the findings of the Committee on Status of Women, planners realised that constitutional guarantees of equality would be meaningless and unrealistic unless women's right to economic independence was acknowledged. The National Plan of Action (1976) was based on the United Nations World Plan of Action for women. This identified areas of health, family planning, nutrition, education, employment, legislation and social welfare for formulating and implementing action programmes for women and called for planned interventions to improve the conditions of women in India. The Equal Remuneration Act 1976 was also passed to ensure equal wages for men and women.

The sixth plan (1980-85) witnessed a shift from 'welfare' to 'development', recognising women as participants of development and not merely as objects of welfare. The plan adopted a multidisciplinary approach with a special emphasis on health, education and employment. Accordingly, several programmes were introduced to create employment opportunities for women in agriculture, animal husbandry, small-scale industries and so on. The seventh plan (1985-90) aimed to inculcate confidence among women and bring about an awareness of their own potential for development. This plan identified voluntary organisations and educational institutions as important means for reaching people and such institutions were fully involved in launching an organised campaign to combat the evils of dowry and the harassment of women. The Commission of Sati (Prevention) Act was passed in 1987, legally prohibiting *Sati*.[3] During the seventh plan period, in 1986-87, the Ministry of Women and Child Development also launched the Support to Training and Employment Programme for Women, aimed at providing skills that increase employability and the confidence to become self-employed/entrepreneurs.[4]

The eighth plan (1992-97) was a landmark in terms of its identification of the need for appropriate funds for implementing programmes. Special initiatives were launched to complement more general programmes. An important milestone was the passing of 73rd and 74th Constitutional Amendments Act 1972, to encourage women to participate in local governance. The Act provided for 33% representation of women on local elected bodies. During this period, the Pre-Conception and Pre-Natal Diagnostic Techniques (Regulation and Prevention of Misuse) Act 1994 was passed to combat the problem of female feticide based on the identity of the sex of the fetus. During this plan period, the National Commission for Women was formed on the recommendation of the Committee on the Status of Women in India. The commission was constituted on 31 January 1992. Its functions are to review the constitutional and legal safeguards for women, recommend remedial legislative measures, facilitate the redressal of grievances, and advise the government on all policy matters affecting women. India ratified the Convention on Elimination of All Forms of Discrimination against Women in 1993.

The ninth plan (1997-2002) introduced the Women Component Plan as a major planning and budgeting strategy directed at both central and state governments to ensure that 'not less than 30 per cent of the funds/benefits are earmarked in all the women related sectors'. During this period, the National Policy for the Empowerment of Women (Government of India, Ministry of Women and Child Development 2001) was also introduced. The main strategy was 'mainstreaming the gender perspectives' in all sectoral policies and programmes, promoting economic empowerment, social empowerment and gender justice through several policy and gender sensitisation measures.

The tenth plan (2002-07) aimed to empower women through translating the National Policy for Empowerment of Women (Government of India, Ministry of Women and Child Development 2001) into action and ensuring 'survival' protection and the development of children through a rights-based approach. The plan emphasised the introduction of Gender Responsive Budgets. The first Gender Budget Statement was introduced in the 2005-06 budget. All the ministries/departments were requested to highlight the quantum of public expenditure earmarked in budgets for women. The statement, prepared on the basis of the information furnished by the ministries/ departments, outlines the budget provisions for schemes in which 100% provision is for women and for those where the budget allocation for women constitutes at least 30% of the provision.

In the 11th plan (2007-12), gender was a cross-cutting theme, with each sector assessed through a gender lens. The chapter on women and children was entitled 'Women's agency and child rights' to mark the shift from the empowerment of women to recognising women as agents of economic growth and change. The National Mission for the Empowerment of Women was launched on 8 March 2010 by the Ministry of Women and Child Development. The involvement of other institutions such as national and state commissions for women, civil society organisations and Panchayati Raj institutions[5] was sought.

The 12th plan (2012-17) has highlighted the need for ending gender-based inequities, discrimination and violence faced by girls and women by ensuring optimal learning outcomes in primary education, and interventions for reducing under-nutrition and anaemia and providing maternity support. The Sexual Harassment of Women at Work Place (Prevention and Protection) Act 2013 was passed during this plan period to ensure the safety of women in the workplace.

The draft National Policy for Women, released by the Government of India's Ministry of Women and Child Development (2016), clearly identifies the paradoxical situation existing in India at present, stating that 'the growing acknowledgement of gender rights and equality is juxtaposed against increase in reporting of various forms of violence against women such as rape, trafficking, dowry etc'. The policy also acknowledges the expansion of new work opportunities for women alongside continued weak bargaining power in labour market, the increasing number of educated aspiring career women entering the workforce, and the large number of women still working in the low-paid informal sector.

The draft policy recognises the importance of deep-rooted cultural and social beliefs about gender roles and their influence on creating socioeconomic and cultural challenges in the rapidly changing global and national scenario in the new millennium. The policy supports a rights-based approach to creating an enabling environment in which women can enjoy their rights, and promotes the socioeconomic and political empowerment of women to claim their rights and entitlements, control resources and form strategic choices in order to achieve gender equality and justice.

Under the gender and development framework, the draft plan recognised the importance of involving men and boys in targeted gender sensitisation interventions to enable transformative behavioural change towards women. For the first time in any such policy, the role of the private sector in augmenting the required resources is recognised. In line with mandatory corporate social responsibility (CSR) requirements, companies are expected to allocate 2% of their profits to CSR and the draft policy aims to direct at least 10% of the total monies to gender-related development policies.

The recognition that there is a need to shift from welfare to empowerment has changed policy approaches to addressing women's issues. Empowering women by providing the necessary inputs became the priority of both government and non-government organisations, and this led to a paradigm shift in the programmes. Under the new paradigm, programme objectives include improving access to resources, building confidence, promoting gender sensitisation, providing greater access to information, encouraging group activities and so on. While the entry point in earlier programmes was the identification of individual beneficiaries for financial support, the current approach favours community-based organisations. Under this approach, the entry point is the promotion of community-based associations in the form of SHGs, water users' associations, village forest committees, youth Sangha[6] and so on, which are provided both with financial and non-financial inputs in the form of capacity building.

These interventions have seen a tremendous change in the attitude of men and women at the village level where social norms are extremely strong. They provide the necessary inputs to improve the capabilities of women. By improving women's access to monetary and non-monetary resources, and building women's confidence and awareness, these programmes and policies made a positive impact on women's basic capabilities, both internal and external.

The Karnataka study

This section is based on the field study undertaken to understand the impact of NGO interventions to improve the capabilities of rural women in Karnataka, India. Karnataka is one of the states that ranks middle in human development indicators, but with high intra-state variation. Large inter-district variations can be observed within the state, with northern districts performing poorly in gender equity.

The total population of Karnataka is 61 million. This formed 5.05% of the population of India in 2011. The sex ratio of Karnataka is 968, which is above the national average of 940 (2011 census). While the adult sex ratio increased from 964 in 2001 to 968 in 2011, the child sex ratio declined from 973 to 943 over the decade. Overall literacy improved from 66.64% in 2001 to 75.60% in 2011. Male literacy rates increased from 76.06% in 2001 to 82.85% in 2011, while female literacy rates improved from 57.8% to 68.13 % during the same period.

Data analysis

Primary data was collected from the sample respondents located in the Dakshina Kannada and Raichur districts through interviews, and was analysed in various domains for achieved functionings, capabilities (potential functionings) and the value of participation.

Achieved functionings

In order to understand participants' degree of the control over personal and household decisions, respondents were asked who normally makes decisions. If the respondent herself makes the decisions, she has the freedom to choose from the available alternatives. On the other hand, if the respondent's husband or others make decisions without consulting her, she has little choice but to accept the decision whether she wants to or not. This indicates absolute lack of freedom. But in cases where the respondent participates in the decision–making process along with others, she has relative freedom to express her opinions. Responses relating to the participation in decision making in different domains is presented in Table 4.1.

From the data it can be observed that there are considerable differences between NGO and NNGO villages in certain domains. In decisions regarding the distribution of work within the household, the majority of the women from both types of village (36.5% from NGO villages and 46% from NNGO villages) said that others in the family make the decisions and only a few said that they have freedom to decide. This can be atttributed to the joint family system in rural India where the older women in the family decide the duties of the younger women. Regarding the freedom to choose to work outside their home, greater autonomy could be observed for women from NGO villages. The conscientisation and gender awareness programmes introduced by NGOs in their operational area appear to have a positive impact. While 23% of the respondents from NGO villages said that they make decisions by themselves, only 13.5% respondents from NNGO villages said that they did so. In the case of political participation also, there is a significant difference. More women from NGO villages have freedom to decide about political participation. The 73rd and 74th amendments to the constitution of India resulted in 33% of seats in local bodies being reserved for women candidates. In order to effectively make use of this positive discrimination, women should have freedom to choose in this domain. Although only 9.5% women in NGO villages and 2.5% in NNGO villages reported that they make decisions by themselves,

Table 4.1: Distribution of respondents according to participation in decision making (%)

Individual decisions

Different domains	Respondent		Husband/parents		Respondent and husband jointly		Jointly with someone else		Others		No reply	
	NGO	NNGO	NGO	NNGO	NGO	NNGO	NGO	NNGO	NGO	NNGO	NGO	NNGO
Work within household	25.0	27.0	2.5	0.5	35.0	20.0	1.5	6.5	36.5	46.0	–	–
Work outside	23.0	13.5	26.0	31.0	36.5	31.5	0	3.5	14.5	20.5	–	–
Contest elections*	9.5	2.5	9.5	20.5	28.5	26.0	36.0	18.5	17.0	32.5	–	–
Voting decision	52.0	42.5	12.0	19.0	16.5	22.5	13.5	11.5	6.0	4.5	–	–
Own health	36.0	36.5	29.5	26.5	30.5	33.0	3.0	3.0	1.0	1.0	–	–
Own marriage	21.0	15.0	0	0	0	0	12.0	3.0	64.0	75.0	3.0	7.0
Protest against violence	8.0	3.5	11.0	5.5	37.5	28.5	3.0	3.5	4.5	1.5	–	–
Number of children	6.5	3.5	13.0	15.5	73.0	76.0	0	0.5	2.6	0.5	5.0	4.0

Household decisions

Different domains	Respondent		Husband		Respondent and husband jointly		Jointly with someone else		Others		No reply	
	NGO	NNGO	NGO	NNGO	NGO	NNGO	NGO	NNGO	NGO	NNGO	NGO	NNGO
Buying/selling of property	16.5	11.5	26.5	34.5	41.0	19.5	5.5	14.0	10.5	19.0	–	1.5
Selling of produce	6.5	3.5	24.0	20.5	7.0	13.0	0.5	0.0	1.5	0.5	59.5	60.0
Children's education	11.0	9.5	8.0	9.0	76.5	78.1	4.0	2.5	0.5	1.0	–	–
Children's marriage	16.5	11.5	26.5	34.5	41.0	19.5	5.5	14.0	10.5	15.0	–	5.5

Note: * Significant mean difference.

28% reported that they make decisions jointly with their husband and 36% reported that they consult others. In the case of decisions relating to the entire household, like buying and selling household property, selling farm produce and so on, women have very little freedom in all the sample villages. Only 8.5% of women in NGO and 6.3% in NNGO villages reported that they decide on these matters; most of the time the decisions are taken either by the husband or elders in the family. In decisions about children's education and marriage, exercising choices is extremely important as it has implications for girls' access to education and the prevention of child marriages.

Capabilities (potential functionings)

The capability of making independent decisions shows potential functionings. As observed earlier, many women are not able to make decisions independently even in the matters that affect them directly. This may be due to lack of confidence, or to socio-cultural factors like patriarchal norms, caste-specific cultural practices and so on. In the latter case, they are not able to exercise their agency, not because they are incapable of doing so, but because of the social and economic environment in which they live. To understand the potential functionings based on the level of confidence displayed by the sample women, the respondents were asked to express their confidence levels. The findings are presented in Table 4.2. It is interesting to observe that more than 50% of the women in all the villages expressed that they are capable of making decisions.

As far as potential functionings are concerned, there is a significant difference between NGO and NNGO villages in Karnataka. More women in NNGO villages also expressed that they are capable to a high degree provided they are given a chance.

Value of participation

The objective question of participation only tells us about whether women participating or not, not about why they are participating and how much they value such participation. Mere participation does not tell anything about whether the exercise of agency is autonomous or controlled, or how much it is valued. This has policy relevance in the sense that it shows the real effect of women's empowerment programmes on exercising agency. Despite efforts to build confidence, if women are participating only out of compulsion, the participation has no meaning.

Table 4.2: Distribution of respondents according to extent of confidence in taking decisions independently (%)

Individual decisions

Different domains	To high extent		To medium extent		To small extent		Not at all	
	NGO	NNGO	NGO	NNGO	NGO	NNGO	NGO	NNGO
Work within household	49.5	44.5	37.5	43.0	13.0	12.5	–	–
Work outside	38.0	37.5	47.5	36.5	14.5	26.0	–	–
Contest elections*	–	–	60.0	50.0	40.0	50.0	–	–
Voting decision	23.9	21.0	63.7	69.7	12.4	9.2	1.8	0
Own health	50.0	56.9	40.8	41.0	0.5	2.1	–	–
Own marriage	49.2	35.5	48.2	48.2	2.1	2.1	0.5	0.5
Protest against violence	80.8	69.8	17.2	12.1	1.0	14.7	1.0	3.4
Number of children	50.5	47.8	44.1	47.2	4.8	2.8	0.5	2.2

Household decisions

Different domains	To high extent		To medium extent		To small extent		Not at all	
	NGO	NNGO	NGO	NNGO	NGO	NNGO	NGO	NNGO
Buying/selling of property	65.55	51.6	31.0	45.2	3.2	3.2	–	–
Selling of produce	8.2	6.3	73.8	81.3	14.8	10.9	3.3	1.6
Children's education	50.0	45.4	45.5	47.5	4.5	6.0	0	1.0
Children's marriage	46.7	44.0	51.1	53.3	1.1	2.7	1.1	0

Note: * Significant mean difference.

This indicator questions the extent to which a woman feels that her action in each domain is motivated by her own choice, external pressure or the hope that she gets rewarded, for example in the form of greater respect. In self-determination theory, which is the basis for the present methodology, this is characterised as autonomous behaviour and controlled behaviour.

The findings show that majority of the women participate in decision making because they think that it is important. But in the domains of decisions about contesting elections and working outside the home, women reported that they make decisions because they get respect from the people both within and outside the household. There are significant differences between NGO and NNGO villages. A larger percentage of women from NGO villages (38%) said that they exercise agency in their decisions about work outside the home because they think this issue is important. Decisions about protection against violence and number of children are the other two domains where more women in NGO villages than in NNGO villages said that they think participation is important.

Table 4.3: Distribution of respondents according to value of participation (%)

Individual decisions

	No control		External pressure		People approve of me		I think it is important		Reflects deepest value		Not reported	
Different domains	NGO	NNGO	NGO	NNGO	NGO	NNGO	NGO	NNGO	NGO	NNGO	NGO	NNGO
Work within household*	39.0	46.5	–	–	15.0	20.5	46.5	33.0	–	–	–	–
Work outside*	40.5	51.5	5.0	12.5	16.0	6.5	38.0	29.5	0.5	–	–	–
Contest elections*	26.5	53.0	2.5	0.5	39.0	26.5	32.0	20.0	–	–	–	–
Voting decision	18.0	23.5	1.5	00	5.0	10.0	74.5	65.5	0.5	0.5	0.5	0.5
Own health	30.5	27.5	–	–	–	–	68.5	71.0	0.5	1.0	0.5	0.5
Own marriage*	64.0	75.0	28.0	7.5	4.5	7.5	3.5	10.0	00	00		
Protest against violence*	15.5	7.0	–	–	22.5	25.5	47.5	40.5	0.5	0.5	15.0	26.5
Number of children	15.6	16.0	–	–	–	1.0	77.4	60.0	0.5	0.5	6.5	22.5

Household decisions

	No control		External pressure		People approve of me		I think it is important		Reflects deepest value		Not reported	
Different domains	NGO	NNGO	NGO	NNGO	NGO	NNGO	NGO	NNGO	NGO	NNGO	NGO	NNGO
Buying/selling of property*	37.0	53.5	1.0	0.5	14.5	9.0	33.0	19.5	00	0.5	14.5	17.0
Selling of produce	25.5	21.0	–	–	–	–	20.0	38.0	0.5	1.0	54.0	40.0
Children's education	8.5	10.0	–	–	–	–	90.0	89.0	1.5	1.0	0.5	–
Children's marriage	37.0	49.5	00	1.0	00	–	63.0	48.5	00	1.0	–	–

Note: * Significant mean difference.

Factors influencing relative autonomy

Factors influencing the RAI have been estimated to understand how much variation in relative autonomy can be attributed to external interventions and to internal factors like education, age and occupation of the individual. The estimated coefficients with the confidence levels are presented as follows:

RAI = f (institutional intervention, age, education, occupation)
RAI = 5.37 + 1.10 institutional intervention*** + 0.12 age + 0.07 education* + 1.80 occupation**
*** = significant at 1% level
** = significant at 5% level
* = significant at 10% level

The results show the relative influence of institutional interventions by the NGOs. It appears that the presence of an external agency has a strong influence on relative autonomy. The other important variable is occupation. The occupation variable indicating paid employment has significant influence on the relative autonomy of women. Women in paid occupations are more likely to exercise greater autonomy in decision making, which increases their chances of leading the kind of life that they choose. Education is another variable that has a significant influence.

Capabilities to influence community

NGO interventions are aimed at influencing the confidence of women so that they can act as agents of change. According to Sen, agency is socially beneficial and agents advance the goals people value and have reason to value. In the words of Drèze and Sen (1989, p 279), 'it is essential to see public not only as the patient whose well being commands attention, but also as the agent whose actions can transform society'. In order to understand to what extent NGO interventions have an influence on women in improving their confidence and enabling them to consider themselves as agents of change, participants asked on how much they felt that they could influence the community. The results (in Table 4.4) clearly show that more women from the NGO villages feel that they can influence the community, but with some difficulty, because changing the existing social norms takes a long time.

Table 4.4: Distribution of respondents according to capability to influence community (%)

Degree of capability	Karnataka	
	NGO	NNGO
Can influence very easily	–	–
Can influence fairly easily	10.0	–
Can influence, but with a little difficulty	46.5	15.0
Can influence, but with great difficulty	12.5	7.5
No, not at all possible	7.5	40.0
No reply	23.5	37.5
Total	100.00	100.00

Conclusion

The contributions of Mahbub ul Haq (1995) based on Sen's work on human capabilities shifted the focus of understanding development from gross domestic product (GDP) to human development. The first of the United Nations Development Programme's Human Development Reports (UNDP, 1990), which operationalised the concept of human development, defined it as a process of enhancing peoples' choices. The primary focus of the HD approach is on people, opportunities and choices. According to the *Human Development Report 1990*, 'Human development is a process of enlarging people's choices. The most critical ones are to lead a long and healthy life, to be educated and to enjoy a decent standard of living' (UNDP, 1990, p 10). The additional choices are political freedom, guaranteed human rights and self-respect – what Adam Smith called the ability to mix with others without being 'ashamed to appear in public' (UNDP, 1990, p 10). While the critical choices directly enhance human capabilities, the additional choices create conditions to exercise choices.

Public policies play an important role in enhancing both critical choices and additional choices. While public investment in health, education and employment has a direct impact on capability-enhancing inputs, interventions that enhance confidence, improve access to information in a people-friendly manner, ensure human safety and security, help in creating an environment for increasing choices. In this process, NGOs play a complementary role. In the Indian context, the Government of India has been involving NGOs in creating an environment that enhances the capabilities of local communities, especially marginalised sections of society including women. However, there has been a paradigm shift in the strategy adopted: from providing welfare assistance to empowering women. While early policy was operationalised through welfare programmes, the new strategy promotes policies that empower women. These policies are framed with a focus on meeting both practical and strategic needs of women. Addressing the strategic needs is essential for the empowered women to exercise agency. For example public investment to increase girls' access to education gives them opportunities for learning and improves their confidence. But for the confidence to transform into agency, opportunities need to be created. Policies to provide greater employment opportunities, family friendly policies and so on, create the environment for the exercise of agency. This chapter has made an attempt to understand how far these policies have been effective in enhancing the capabilities of women in Karnataka. The study reveals that the policy of involving NGOs in delivering inputs for the empowerment of women has enhanced the capabilities of women in rural Karnataka. There has been an increase in the level of women's participation in decision making at both the personal and household level. This influences the human development of not only the current generation, but also of the future generation, as the choices that women make will have an influence on the intra-household resource allocation and the opportunities given to girls. Given the socioeconomic conditions in India, the policy has contributed to increasing choices for women and has provided them with increased confidence to exercise their agency.

Acknowledgement

This chapter is based on a larger project supported by Indian Council for Social Sciences Research (ICSSR), New Delhi. The author wishes to acknowledge financial support from the ICSSR.

Notes

[1] The Constitution (108th Amendment) Bill, known as the Women Reservation Bill, is a proposed Bill. It aims to reserve 33% of seats in the Lower House of parliament and state legislative assemblies to women. Although it was introduced for the first time in 1996 and passed by the Rajya Sabha (Upper House) in 2010, it has still not been passed by the Lok Sabha (Lower House); see www.thehindu. com/news/national/womens-reservation-bill-the-story-so-far/article6969294.ece.

[2] See http://feministlawarchives.pldindia.org/wp-content/uploads/towards-equality-1974-part-1.pdf? http://feministlawarchives.pldindia.org/wp-content/uploads/towards-equality-1974-part-2.pdf?.

[3] Sati means the burning or burying alive of widows of Hindu religion; see ncw. nic.in/acts/TheCommissionofSatiPreventionAct1987-of1988.pdf.

4 Details about the programmes of the Ministry of Women and Child Development can be found at www.wcd.nic.in.
5 PRIs are rural governance structures. Since 1992 a three tier structure was created for rural governance and the structures at the state level, block level and village level are known as Panchayati Raj Institutions.
6 Youth Sanghas are informal voluntary groups of young men, generally from the same locality and for a particular purpose.

References

Alkire, S., Meinzen-Dick, R., Peterman, A., Quisumbing, A.R., Seymour, G. and Vaz, A. (2013) 'The women's empowerment in agriculture index', OPHI Working Paper 58, www.ophi.org.uk/wp-content/uploads/ophi-wp-58.pdf

Alsop, R., Bertelsen, M. and Holland, J. (2006) *Empowerment in practice: From analysis to implementation*, Washington, DC: World Bank.

Chiappero-Martinetti, E. (2008) 'Complexity and vagueness in the capability approach: strengths or weaknesses?', in F. Comim et al (eds) *The capability approach*, Cambridge: Cambridge University Press, pp 268-309. Available at http://dx.doi.org/10.1017/CBO9780511492587.010 (accessed 15 August 2016).

Drèze, J. and Sen, A.K. (1989) *Hunger and public action (wider studies in development economics)*, Oxford: Clarendon Press, Oxford University Press.

Government of India, Ministry of Women and Child Development (2011) 'National policy for the empowerment of women', available at http://wcd.nic.in/sites/default/files/National%20Policy%20for%20Empowerment%20of%20Women%202001.pdf

Government of India, Ministry of Women and Child Development (2016) 'National policy for women 2016', (draft), available at: http://wcd.nic.in/sites/default/files/draft%20national%20policy%20for%20women%202016_0.pdf

Grasso, M. (2002) *A dynamic operationalisation of Sen's capability approach*, Working Paper Series 59, Milan: University of Milan–Bicocca, available at https://boa.unimib.it/retrieve/handle/10281/22985/29429/A_Dynamic_Operationalization_of.pdf.

Haq, M.u. (1995) *Reflections on human development*, New York, NY: Oxford University Press.

Ibrahim, S. and Alkire, S. (2007) *Agency and empowerment: A proposal for internationally comparable indicators*, OPHI Working Paper 4, Oxford: University of Oxford Press.

Kabeer, N. (2005) 'Gender equality and women's empowerment: a critical analysis of the third Millennium Development Goal', *Gender and Development*, vol 13, no 1, pp 13-24, available at www.amherst.edu/media/view/232742/original/Kabeer%2B2005.pdf.

Mahendravada, I. (2004) 'Social externalities of women's empowerment through microfinancing: a comparative study of two interventions', in I. Guerin and J. Palier (eds) *Microfinance challenges: Empowerment or Disempowerment of the poor*, Pondicherry: French Institute of Pondicherry, pp 303-9.

Mahendravada, I. (2005) 'Capability approach to evaluate women empowerment programmes in India', Paper presented at the Fifth International Conference on Capabilities Approach, Paris, 11-14 September.

Mahendravada, I. and Joshi, S. (2012) 'An enquiry into the complementarity between the Government and NGO interventions in improving the capabilities of Women in Rural India', Unpublished report submitted to Indian Council of Social Sciences Research, New Delhi.

Mahmud, S. (2003) 'Actually how empowering is micro credit', *Development and Change*, vol 34, no 4, pp 577-605.

Narayan, D. (ed) (2002) *Empowerment and poverty reduction: A sourcebook*, Washington, DC: World Bank.

Nussbaum, M.C. (2000) *Women and human development: The capabilities approach*, Cambridge: Cambridge University Press.

Pillai, N,V. and Alkire, S. (2007) *Measuring individual agency or empowerment: A study in Kerala*, Thiruvananthapuram: Centre for Development Studies.

Robeyns, I. (2005) 'The capability approach: a theoretical survey', *Journal of Human Development*, vol 6, no 1, pp 93-117, DOI: 10.1080/146498805200034266.

Sen, A. (1985) *Commodities and capabilities*, Amsterdam: Elsevier.

Sen, A. (1992) *Inequality re-examined*, Oxford: Clarendon Press.

UNDP (United Nations Development Programme) (1990) *Human development report 1990*, Oxford: Oxford University Press, hdr.undp.org/sites/default/files/reports/219/hdr_1990_en_complete_nostats.pdf.

Vaz, A., Pratle, P. and Alkire,S. (2016) 'Measuring women's autonomy in Chad using the Relative Autonomy Index', *Feminist Economics*, vol 22, no 1, pp 264-94.

Venkatraja, B. and Mahendravada, I. (2014) 'Do NGOs impact rural development? An empirical assessment', *Asian Economic Review*, vol 56, no 4, pp 163-76.

FIVE

The contribution to human development of social policies in the Central American Integration System

Guillermo Bornemann-Martínez, Pedro Caldentey and Emilio J. Morales-Fernández

Introduction

Central America is a region well known for its conflicts, poverty and exclusion. Most of the Central American population lives below the national poverty threshold, but the main problem of the region is inequality and exclusion. Although some Central American countries are the poorest in Latin American, their human development indicators reflect the Latin American average and far exceed South Asian and African figures. Besides, indicators are heterogeneous among the members of the Central American Integration System (or SICA, to use the acronym for its Spanish name)[1] on which this chapter focuses.

The struggle against poverty and concern for human development are part of the legacy of social struggle in the region. For instance, prior to the 1950s, policies with human development elements did not inspire anyone. Early signs of a development perspective, based on the accumulation of capital and on prioritising gross domestic product (GDP) growth, were evident in the Central American agricultural exporting model developed by the first generation of economists from the 1950s to the 1970s.

This model was the result of regional imbalance caused by export activities (unequal development between countries and social sectors), and the need to correct it. Public policies emphasised investment in human capital within a context of accumulation of capital influenced by neo-classical growth theories.

The agricultural exporting model had run its course by the time of the Second World War, and in the 1950s the region adopted an import substitution model by promoting the use of local raw materials, planning industrial development and providing trade protection to Central American markets within the framework of regional integration processes. Twenty years later, this model and its policies were rejected due to loss of competitiveness of the region's industrial sector and progressive neglect of agricultural activities leading to increased exclusion and inequality. Repression by military dictatorships in the 1980s and 1990s, triggering social struggles in the Central American region (Valdés Paz and Espina, 2011), also had an effect.

SICA has its roots in the 1950s as a tool for import substitution strategy, the oldest such policy in Latin America. However, the creation of the SICA in 1991 was a joint response to solving the regional conflicts of the 1980s – effectively a Cold War. Esquipulas Agreements (1986-90) designed a peace process free of interference from extrarregional actors and defined a new political stage for Central America based on peace, democracy and development.

SICA is actually a relevant and complex tool for designing and implementing regional initiatives complementary to national policies. The integration of the social dimension of national policies into regional initiatives is an interesting aspect of this, but has had no obvious impact during the decades since the Esquipulas Peace Agreement.[2]

This chapter works on the hypothesis that the theoretical foundations of the social dimension in Central American integration could be a complementary field of policy to improve national efforts. So far, however, regional social initiatives appear to have been inadequate and their impact insignificant. They have not even acted as an enabling environment to incorporate new approaches.

This chapter reviews Central American human development policies to assess the improvements that the adoption of the human capabilities approach would promote in the region. It presents the fundamentals and tools developed by the social dimension of SICA to test the hypothesis that its impact has so far been negligible.

The chapter also examines the progress of national social indicators in the region from the perspective of the effectiveness of policies and from indicators associated with human capabilities. Finally, it makes some suggestions for redefining the social dimension of Central American integration on the paradigm of human development and capabilities approach.

Capabilities approach and human development in Central America national development plans

The objective of this section is to assess the extent of human development and capability approaches in Central American development plans. It also examines how the region has incorporated such inspirational elements into better targeted social policies and assesses the benefits of such advanced approaches.

Development based on the individual and on policies to combat poverty had to wait for the field of human development to mature and consolidate in the early 1990s before being included in government agendas, and in those of politicians and civil society in Central America. The development approach has since then become an essential tool to support policymaking and proposals to reform the state and the services it provides to citizens. It is no coincidence that human development has become a conceptual basis for all national plans in the Central American region.

The evolution of the human development paradigm has been the result of the vital contribution made by different philosophical, anthropological and economic trends during the last quarter of the past century. The contributions of Martha Nussbaum, Amartya Sen, Mahbub Ul Haq, Jean Drèze, Sabina Alkire, Antony Atkinson, James Foster, Francis Stewart and others have also been crucial. Since its consolidation in the annual reports of the United Nations Development Programme (UNDP), the human development paradigm goes beyond the world of multilateral development institutions and it is now part of the fundamentals of public policy in many countries.

The debate now influences national development plans and initiatives in Central America. UNDP initiatives have been particularly important promoters of the human development paradigm in the Central American region. In Nicaragua, in 2013, the Universidad Centroamericana hosted the 11th Human Development Capabilities Association Conference, which is the most important world forum for debating the development and capabilities approach. However, despite the consolidation of the capabilities approach, and according to the judgments of some experts including Sabina Alkire, Ingrid Robeyns, Seeta Prabhu and others, it is still early to take into consideration the capabilities approach as a true theoretical 'corpus' for development. Anyway, what the capabilities approach is proposing is new analysis for tackling the challenges of global society. In 2015, the horizon of Millennium Development Goals (MDGs) increases the need to explore more solid proposals and achieve better outcomes in terms of social justice.

Debate in recent years has been very productive in terms of proposals and new applications in the development field. One of the most important tools to emerge is the Social Progress Index, which helps to gather more precise information that can be used to provide assistance to those who are in poverty and extreme poverty and those who are excluded, as well as migrants and those who are victims of insecurity, bad governance, or lack of opportunities. When researchers focus on these social groups, the tools are available to assess the differences of the indicators, paying special attention to life expectancy, education and opportunities.

Twenty-five years after the publication of the first Human Development Report (UNDP, 1990), the Central American region has undergone important changes in its development priorities. Current political proposals show the intention of moving to a new and more inclusive development model, which includes the design of public policies in a framework that is more open and integrated, taking into account the demands of different social groups in the region.

Every Central American country has approved a development plan inspired to some extent by the human development consensus. In each of the declarations about the vision and conceptualisation of existing human development strategies, we can see features inspired by the human development and capabilities approach. All of these proposals follow a common pattern in terms of reducing poverty and social exclusion. In this regard, national reports focus part of their efforts on improving educational systems for the creation of human capabilities or the creation of formal employment arising from the dynamisation of economic growth. Policy proposals seem to be searching for the virtuous circle that will reduce social exclusion.

With respect to social expenditure in the region, existing development plans led to increase in GDP during the first decade of the century. The regional average is very poor when measured against Latin American figures overall. Costa Rica shows the highest proportion of social expenditure compared with neighbouring countries, even Panama.

The regional context for public policies is a determining factor in effective social spending. The region's countries have attempted to solve social problems with social policy proposals based on utilitarianistic approaches. Despite Central American development plans being sensitive to human development, they concentrate on promoting growth and wellbeing by focusing on meeting basic needs and creating jobs through investment. Income improvement remains the main ingredient in these plans. Furthermore, coordination of these strategies and their evaluation framework has remained under the authority of the ministries of economy or planning agencies, rather than in the hands of social entities in the region.

Discussion of human development and various development experiences has taught us that structural changes have to be made and a certain degree of social and economic development is required in order to overcome poverty and inequality (Valdés Paz and Espina, 2011). In addition to eliminating poverty and social exclusion, social policy should promote changes that transform the social, political and economic structures of the various countries and their reproduction models.

Public policy must take account of the fact that resources and capabilities are complementary but different concepts and elements. It seems pertinent to point out that the central characteristic of human development is the idea of conducting an alternative evaluation of development that places individual capabilities as the primary criterion, and the resources available to society as important but secondary elements. Nonetheless, it also is important to remember that human development is not limited to the study of the capabilities approach, no matter how central.

Two elements that explain the difficulties in applying the capabilities approach to development in Central America and other parts of the world include the need to change this approach into a political goal that, in turn, lays the groundwork for formulating public and social policies.

As regards Central America, it can be stated that the capabilities approach has not gone beyond mere inspiration in the region's development plans. Its implementation is therefore partial and incomplete. Development plans are very much influenced by the language of human development and the capabilities approach, but their strategies are oriented towards the provision of resources and labour market growth. There is a gap between the conceptualisation of capabilities to enable individual participation in any productive activity and the need to change the concept into tools to establish a set of beings and doings.

The multidimensional approach to human development and the capabilities approach involves recognising values as a vehicle for social cohesion and identifying the educational and social elements that influence development. Despite the theoretical debates of recent years, development scholars have not yet been convinced of the importance of values. This area is still an open discussion, but leaving values out of the debate could become a serious methodological problem (Meier and Stiglitz, 2002). Ruttan warned of this (Meier and Stiglitz, 2002) and emphasised his concern for the complexity of the multidisciplinary analysis of culture that some authors summarise by the phrase 'culture matters'; the fact that the scholars and practitioners of development are forced to deal with cultural endowments at an intuitive level rather than in analytical terms should be regarded as a deficiency in professional capacity.

The following are questions arising from this analysis within the context of Central American public and social policies. Is the capabilities approach an effective tool for designing an efficacious social policy? Is it feasible that research spurred by the capabilities approach will produce practical and more effective methodologies to address the most important social problems in Central America? Is it necessary to go beyond traditional approaches, penetrate the shifting fields of culture and values, and think of the kind of capabilities that are required?

Sabina Alkire offers a positive answer to this question, addressing the issue of capacities and the importance of values and culture when she states that: 'There seems to be a confluence of political and intellectual forces seeking to advance development activities in ways not unsympathetic to the capability approach' (Alkire in ENFOQUE Magazine, 2013). However, it is no easy task to put into practice the capability approach. The practice of creating capabilities should not be conceived as a managerialist or technocratic programme with performance indicators (Robeyns, 2008). References can be found to nutrition, health and education in Central American development plans, but there is a gap between formulating goals in these areas and taking a capability route to achieve them. Human development is not limited to achieving basic goals in health, nutrition and education; rather, it should include a wide range of other goals (Robeyns, 2008).

Even assuming that the region has been temporarily and partially successful in its plans to overcome poverty and exclusion, this does not imply the immediate creation of capabilities. The fundamental question raised by the capability approach is what is a person capable of being and doing? That is, what are her opportunities and freedoms? What are the individual's opportunities to choose (Nussbaum, 2007)? These are certainly complex questions for policymakers.

The question we should ask, then, is which key concepts facilitate public policy to serve effectively as a tool to widen capabilities in a variety of cultural contexts. We can build three bridges to link traditional approaches and the capability approach.

The first bridge between the capability approach and public policies is the connection between the individual and society through positive expectations of public policy. Recent social policy in Central America takes into account such positive expectations as the right to be well nourished, the right to health and education, and the right to equal access to justice. All of these are very elaborate functionings. However, the question to evaluate from a capabilities approach is to what extent positive freedoms are fulfilled; that is, whether people are really free from disease (healthy), illiteracy (educated), equal before justice, or psychologically free (from fear, shame, beliefs). The bridge that connects the individual and society can be built from the evaluation of compliance with people's positive expectations in the region. Given the history of violence and exclusion to which the population has been subject in Central America, there is an urgent need to evaluate the gaps in social justice and inequality. It is not mistaken to state that capabilities will be constrained by social injustice.

A second bridge linking the capabilities approach and public policies is the connection between culture and social policy, built on the principles of affiliation and belonging. For instance, migration and social policies are two indissoluble concepts, as seen in Central American migrations. Migration flows – whether permanent or temporary, regional or across borders – mean a progressive weakening of people's sense of belonging to their families. Public policies should be based on an understanding that 'consciousness of affiliation is consciousness of oneself as connected to particular other people and to the larger social world, to one's physical place in the world and to the larger natural world' (Nelson, 2004, p 314).

A third bridge linking the capabilities approach to social policy is the interpretation of the latter as a tool for social reproduction. Nothing is permanent on the social plane. Concepts of family have changed; young people's aspirations and values are different from those of past generations; women have been gaining in social inclusion and prominence; the rights of individuals and social groups have widened; and technology has fostered new ways to participate. This has made public service and other activities more complex.

It is not possible to govern while ignoring or being indifferent to these changes. Social policy and related intervention programmes must go together with social change in order to counteract psycho-social barriers and allow human capabilities and opportunities to emerge.

As capabilities and opportunities expand, changes in individual behaviour are achieved; individual empowerment and concrete activities increase. This in turn strengthens agency and fosters change to help individuals realise their talents, closing a virtual circle of expansion of capabilities and functionings (HDCA, 2013).

In Latin America and, therefore, in Central America, myths, prejudices and beliefs coexist. Poverty and other conditions become so persistent that they underlie ideology transmitted from one generation to another. To the extent that policymakers are able to tackle these issues, the life and functionings of individuals and their families will improve, and opportunities and freedoms will increase. A good example would be a change in the stereotypes and relationships that discriminate against women and prevent them from enjoying equality. To make social progress in this area, an understanding of existing cultural values is required, as well as clearly defined goals relating to the values that need to be changed.

There is no doubt that the 'success' of social policy (or related plans or programmes) depends on many factors. However, the intention is that it acts as a catalyst of social reproduction (objectively and symbolically), that is, as a tool that is appropriate and viable 'for us' to use in order to 'live' (Valdés Paz and Espina, 2011). Ultimately, positive expectations are fulfilled by moving goods closer to services, thus facilitating consumption joined by institutions (formal or informal) and agents (economic or social) that operate simultaneously in shaping the possibilities of individuals and their families regarding the resources they control and their mechanisms for interaction. All of this makes up a social structure. This scenario of possibilities is the breeding ground for capabilities to take shape.

In other words, within the framework of social policy universalising rights, it is also important to create mechanisms for reducing the social distance between those who own more resources (or are more valuable, in relational terms) and those with less capital (or who are less valuable) (Valdés Paz and Espina, 2011).

The following sections are based on this framework and the questions raised here. They seek to analyse the potential of the capabilities approach and produce effective answers to issues ranging from the formulation of regional policies to the challenge of poverty, exclusion and development. To that end, the first section provides a regional perspective of the challenges awaiting response, while the second describes the regional policy framework presented by SICA.

Lights and shades of human development and social policies from a regional perspective

We may ask whether increased spending has been accompanied by efficiency in spending. Up until 2008, social policy focused on meeting the basic needs of some sectors in order to reduce overall poverty and inequality in the region. In this respect, it was generally successful. However, it must be acknowledged that the effectiveness of such policy has been limited and the results achieved have failed to generate either sufficient trust or incentive to maintain spending levels.

It is not easy to analyse the impact of social policies in such complex settings as those of Central America and from a multidimensional perspective. Future challenges demand new methodological proposals and adaptations to facilitate the transition to a more inclusive society. Taking this as a starting point, the current authors developed a proposal for a Market Incorporation Total Index (MITI) and a Social Incorporation Total Index (SITI) (Caldentey et al, 2016), both of which have been designed thinking about the fundamentals of human development.

This approach utilises the complementarity between market incorporation and social incorporation. It is based on the work of Diego Sánchez-Ancochea and Juliana Martínez Franzoni (Martínez Franzoni and Sánchez-Ancochea, 2014), whose analysis we have applied and modified to assess the progress and achievements of social policies in Central American countries.

MISI (Market Incorporation and Social Incorporation) proposes the involvement of people in the generation of wealth and wellbeing conditions through the sustained creation of formal and well-paid jobs (public and private). However, market incorporation has no adequate response to the fact that the salaries of those with higher educational qualifications grow faster than those with lower qualifications; nor does it tackle over-dependence on the market economy or the subsequent exposure to unpredictable risks that are hard for individuals to mitigate against. This is where SITI comes into its own, as a complementary tool for the reduction of disparity and the improvement of wellbeing. Social incorporation would (a) exclude some social groups from direct involvement in the market economy (for example, underage, elderly, ill and disabled people); (b) generate 'security networks' to absorb the economic uncertainty related to the variance of economic cycles; (c) facilitate the incorporation of people into the market economy through the construction and development of human capital; and (d) support the establishment of social rights by the government (Martínez Franzoni and Sánchez-Ancochea, 2014, p 275). SITI is based on the existence of accessible services to the poor and the middle class, and on maintaining adequate levels of social expenditure.

Table 5.1 shows a group of 10 indicators, requirements and policies that can be implemented to increase levels of market and social incorporation. The policies are specific action proposals whose main objective is to achieve social incorporation and incorporation into the market. The indicators are multidimensional measures of incorporation attainment levels, while requirements define the development sense of the indicators and the attainment level desired.

Table 5.1: Market and social incorporation: indicators, requirements and policy dimensions

Type	Indicators	Requirements	Policies
Market incorporation	• Real Gross Domestic Product (GDP) per capita • Distribution of GDP between economy sectors (%) • Formal jobs (paid urban employment) • Real average wages index • Real minimum wages index	• Economic growth • Structured economic change toward economic activities with more productivity • Creation and increase of formal employment • Changes in capital–work relations • Increase in medium and minimum wages	• Measures to promote economic growth, structural change, and specific sectoral policies • Promotion of labour rights and collective negotiation • Sustained growth of medium and minimum wages
Social incorporation	• Investment in health per person (US$ per person) • Public social health expenditure (% of GDP) • Proportion of older people receiving an old-age pension • Investment in education per person (US$ per person) • Public education expenditure (% of GDP)	• Growth of health social expenditure • Increase of percentage of people beneficiary from health social expenditure • Increase of percentage of older people receiving pension • Increase in expenditure on education	• Updating social policies periodically to adapt them to economic changes and social needs • Adjusting universal policies through specific measures • Creating universal measures that provide more equitable access to social protection

Source: Adapted from Martínez and Sánchez-Ancochea (2014, p 278).

Market incorporation indicators

Most researchers and scholars agree on the long-term effect of economic policies on market incorporation, generating new economic activities and improving the output of the existing activities, particularly that of the service sector.

In these terms, the heaviest weight of the tertiary sector on the economy of the country and an increase in its productivity are the drivers necessary to create formal and well-paid jobs (McMillan and Rodrik, 2011). But the productive model changes should be sustainable and balanced to avoid the growth of informal jobs, gradually withdrawing policies that support the activities of low productivity sectors and progressively promoting policies that support the activities of the highest productivity sectors (Pérez, 2010).

Our work analyses five indicators of market incorporation for six SICA members. We then developed the MITI using the most recent indicator values. For each set of data, quartiles have been developed in such a way that the location of one value country in the quartile 1, 2, 3 or 4 receives a score of 1, 2, 3 or 4 according to the corresponding quartile.

Table 5.2 shows the values of five indicators (real GDP per capita, participation in the tertiary sector, paid urban employed population, real average wages index, and real minimum wages index) for each country (Costa Rica, El Salvador, Guatemala, Honduras, Nicaragua and Panama), the classification intervals in the quartiles of each indicator (quartiles 1, 2, 3 and 4), the score assigned to each country for each indicator (Q) and finally the MITI scores.

The MITI scores show high values of market incorporation in Costa Rica (18/20) and Panama (16/20), middle values in El Salvador (10) and Guatemala (10), and reduced values in Honduras (9) and Nicaragua (8).

Table 5.2: Coding dimensions and total index relating to market incorporation

Country	Real GDP per capita (2005 US$ per inhabitant)	Q	Participation in the tertiary sector (% of GDP)	Q	Paid urban employed population	Q	Real average wages index (year 2000 = 100)	Q	Real minimum wages index (year 2000 = 100)	Q	Total index (5 to 20)
Costa Rica	6,031.80	4	67.71	4	70.9	4	122	4	115.7	2	18
El Salvador	3,089.50	3	55.6	3	57.8	2	79	1	102.6	1	10
Guatemala	2,347.10	2	55.5	2	57.9	3			124.2	3	10
Honduras	1,506.50	1	53.3	1	49.4	1	106	2	276.5	4	9
Nicaragua	1,378.90	1	48.5	1	45.6	1	105	1	202.2	4	8
Panama	7,995.10	4	72	4	72.7	4	118	3	109.1	1	16
Quartile 1 Quartile 2 Quartile 3 Quartile 4	(1,378.90, 1,716.65) (1,716.65, 2,718.30) (2,718.30, 5,296.23) (5,296.23, 7,995.10)		(48.50, 53.85) (53.85, 55.55) (55.55, 64.68) (64.68, 72)		(45.60, 51.50) (51.50, 57.85) (57.85, 67.65) (67.65, 72.70)		(79, 105) (105, 106) (106, 118) (118, 122)		(102.60, 110.75) (110.75, 119.95) (119.95, 182.70) (182.70, 276.50)		

Source: Authors' elaboration from Programa Estado de la Nación en Desarrollo Humano Sostenible (2014) and International Labor Organization (2014a, pp 71-81, pp 110).

Social incorporation indicators

Policies that promote social incorporation are measured by separating people's wellbeing from their productive condition and including redistributive measures. These social policies could be universal, contributive or directed. Universal social policies are more efficient (education, health) since they offer similar treatment to all citizens, providing benefits to most of society (middle social classes and those with the lowest incomes) and ensuring a satisfying quality of services, complying with their redistributive objective and favouring the virtuous circle of social incorporation (Huber, 2002; Mkandawire, 2006). Social policies targeting the most vulnerable people are necessary and the most frequent tools used for this purpose are conditional cash transfer programmes.

For the present study, we developed a SITI based on five indicators. We used the most recent values of the indicators, and similar to the MITI, we calculated the quartiles for each index, giving a score based on the location of the value country of one concrete indicator in quartiles 1, 2, 3 or 4.

Table 5.3 shows the five indicators values (investment in health per person, public social health expenditure, proportion of older people receiving an old-age pension, investment in education per person and public education expenditure) for each country (Costa Rica, El Salvador, Guatemala, Honduras, Nicaragua and Panama), classification intervals in the quartiles of each indicator (quartiles 1, 2, 3 and 4), the score assigned to each country for each indicator (Q) and finally the SITI score.

The SITI scores show high values of social incorporation in Costa Rica (20/20) and Panama (18/20), middle values in Honduras (12) and Nicaragua (11), and reduced values in El Salvador (9) and Guatemala (5).

Table 5.3: Coding dimensions and total index relating to social incorporation

Country	Investment in health per person (US$ per person)	Q	Public social health expenditure (% of GDP)	Q	Proportion of older people receiving an old-age pension	Q	Investment in education per person (US$ per person)	Q	Public education expenditure (% of GDP)	Q	Total index (5–20)
Costa Rica	714	4	7.56	4	55.8	4	693	4	7.23	4	20
El Salvador	159	3	4.22	1	18.1	2	116	2	3.04	1	9
Guatemala	80	1	2.4	1	14.1	1	96	1	2.93	1	5
Honduras	101	2	4.33	2	8.4	1	135	3	6.23	4	12
Nicaragua	79	1	4.47	3	23.7	3	69	1	5	3	11
Panama	520	4	5.21	4	37.3	4	313	4	3.76	2	18
Quartile 1	(79, 85.25)		(2.40, 4.25)		(8.40, 15.10)		(69, 101)		(2.93, 3.22)		
Quartile 2	(85.25, 130)		(4.25, 4.40)		(15.10, 20.90)		(101, 125.50)		(3.22, 4.38)		
Quartile 3	(130, 429.75)		(4.40, 5.03)		(20.90, 33.90)		(125.50, 268.50)		(4.38, 5.92)		
Quartile 4	(429.75, 714)		(5.03, 7.56)		(33.90, 55.80)		(268.50, 693)		(5.92, 7.23)		

Source: Authors' elaboration, from Programa Estado de la Nación en Desarrollo Humano Sostenible (2014) and International Labour Organization (2014b, pp 273-79).

Comparative challenges and risks

Figure 5.1 shows a comparative map of the current situation and the extent of improvement in social and market incorporation policies over the period 2000–13 in the Central American countries.

Both indices offer a hierarchy of experiences and indicators that allow us to compare social policies in Central America and to contrast them with the conditions necessary to promote the capabilities approach in public regional policies from SICA.

The combined scores (SITI and MITI) represented in the comparative map show three country clusters:

- countries with high levels of social and market incorporation (Costa Rica and Panama);
- countries making progress in social and market incorporation, but that still have a long way to go (Honduras, Nicaragua and El Salvador);
- the country with the lowest levels of social and market incorporation that needs to define development strategies and policies in two areas in particular (Guatemala).

Figure 5.1 Comparative position of Central American countries in terms of market incorporation and social incorporation

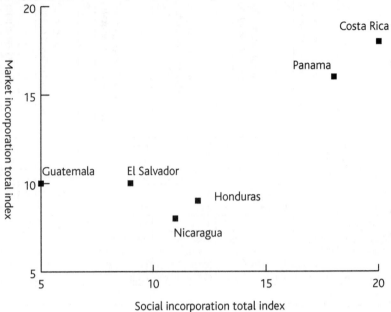

Source: Authors' elaboration from Programa Estado de la Nación en Desarrollo Humano Sostenible (2014) and International Labour Organization (2014b, pp 273-79).

In summary, the scenario for limited growth, inhibiting the creation of formal employment and regular income opportunities in Central America during the coming years, could complicate human development plan proposals.

This chapter is unique in identifying the regional aspects of this problem. Our findings could help to promote horizontal cooperation among Central American countries within SICA. The question is whether Central American integration offers opportunities to improve the design or effectiveness of social policies, and whether it provides the means to incorporate the capabilities approach with more rigour and strength into the conceptualisation and design of social policies. Thus, in the following section we analyse the political framework of regional integration.

The fundamentals of the SICA and its effects

After the conflicts of the 1980s and introduction of the Esquipulas Peace Agreement, Central American countries renewed their commitment to the integration process, replacing the 1960 Central American Common Market with SICA. Despite the very different perceptions of internal and external agents, its development during recent years has been very relevant, and in the period 2004–13 it was one of the most dynamic processes in Latin America (Caldentey, 2014).

Central American integration is the product of an era represented by a debate on the outcomes of the triple transition (political, social and economic) offered in the development framework of the Esquipulas Peace Agreement (Sánchez-Ancochea and Martí Puig, 2014). The peace agreement has been very useful in articulating development processes in recent years but its intensity as a catalyst has declined (Caldentey, 2014). Integration – as with the Esquipulas Peace Agreement – is required to play a key role in the post-Esquipulas development of Central America.

SICA was created as a multidimensional regional integration process and the SICA Social Subsystem is one of its five constituent subsystems. It has its legal foundation in the Tegucigalpa Protocol of 1991, and is enshrined in the Central American Social Integration Treaty of 1995.

The Treaty was signed at the Social Development Summit held in Copenhagen in 1995. According to the Treaty, the SICA Social Subsystem comprises the following bodies: the Central Social Integration Council (CIS), the Central American Social Integration Secretariat (SISCA) or General Subsystem Secretariat, and various regional councils of ministers relating to social issues and their corresponding secretariats.

The Social Integration Treaty helped to correct the deficit of Central American integration assistance in the areas of poverty and basic social needs, and it facilitated some actions of interest in the field of health. However, its legal and institutional tools failed to attract the political leadership and resources necessary to consolidate the social dimension of Central American integration.

The Social Integration Treaty has had limited impact since its introduction in 1995. There are two specific reasons for this, alongside problems relating to SICA's efficiency, which we tackle later. First, in addition to institutionalisation with regard to SICA's social aspects, the treaty was imprecise in its definition of a catalogue of objectives and influential areas of social integration. Second, national CIS representatives formed a heterogeneous group with little political weight and little budget relevance in their national governments.

Social integration is one of the five prioritised regional axes of SICA countries. Social integration institutions have begun to renew their political tools, starting with the approval of the Strategic Approach for Social Dimension of Central American Integration, presented at the Presidential Summit in December 2011. This partially replaces the 2008 SICA Strategic Social Agenda, a strategic planning tool that provided clearer objectives of the subsystem.

The Strategic Approach for Social Dimension of Central America Integration constitutes the political tool that guides and empowers the work of CIS, providing a more complete vision of social integration and the social agenda.

Table 5.4 presents the goals and strategic actions of the new strategy. This approach is more in tune – both conceptually and strategically – with the notion that regional actions will serve as a complementary framework to the social policies of the SICA member countries. The reduction of social inequalities, the promotion of social inclusion, and the regulation of labour markets are a better fit with SISCA's responsibilities, and above all with the responsibilities of each country's CIS representative institutions. SICA countries could respond better with these priorities to the limited tools of negotiation, financing, or implementation of policies and actions from Central American integration.

However, the main contribution of the new strategy exceeds the institutional limits of social integration. It proposes the social dimension aspect of Central American integration as relevant for any dimension of SICA. The social aspect should effectively be of interest to all councils of ministers and SICA secretariats.

Three aspects of the regional framework on social development merit further consideration. First, the goals relating to the social dimension of SICA appear to be consistent with human development and the human capabilities approach. However, these objectives are somewhat diffuse, and lack precise theoretical foundations. The constant revision of the instruments used in social integration reinforces the sense of dispersed goals.

Second, there are challenges in applying the new strategy to regional integration. These difficulties stem from the pressure on governments to reach effective agreements in complex situations that must reflect other dimensions of Central American integration like economic agreement on trade and security.

Finally, there is the classic dilemma of the regional integration: What is the dividing line between national and regional, between competences of governments and regional institutions? How to apply the principle of subsidiarity? Integration demands that regional actions be combined with national actions in a homogenous approach that can help to articulate national and regional policies and make the most of common action in the integration framework.

Table 5.4: Goals and strategic actions of the strategic reconsideration of social integration

Goals	Strategic actions
Reduction of social inequalities	1. Formulation of Central American social development goals 2021 and their baseline jointly with the councils of ministers of the social area.
	2. Formulation of an action plan to ensure its systematic and progressive implementation.
	3. Preparation of the monitoring and evaluation system of the indicators in the Central American Observatory for Social Development.
Promotion of social inclusion	1. Formulation and implementation of national policies and regional lines of social prevention of violence in all its ways, targeting specific groups at risk, including women, children and youths, and with the involvement of key actors linked with this issue so that it is addressed as an interinstitutional and intersectoral process (taking into account education, health, housing, sports and recreation).
	2. Support for the organisation of national social protection systems related to early childhood, including nutrition and food security issues.
	3. Formulation and implementation of one regional strategy supporting the national problems for the promotion of basic social services.
	4. Promotion of border cooperation programmes and projects among countries based on the social development goals.
	5. Implementation of the Territorial Planning Agenda of the Central American Council of Housing and Human Settlement and instruments that ensure the incorporation of the social housing and risk management component with integrality criterion.
	6. Promotion of one regional strategy to strengthen national networks in their capabilities in order to promote the social inclusion of people with HIV-AIDS.
Regulation of integrated labour market	1. Condition of labour market and recruitment of workforce (common work-related standards, work visas or permits that regulate access to services).
	2. Human resources and skills for work (university degree, professional training).
	3. Consideration of mobile population.
	4. Public institutionality (ministers of labour)
Reform and strengthening of social subsystem	Strategic actions at national and regional level, articulation of competencies and budget sustainability.

Source: Consejo de la Integración Social Centroamericana y Secretaría de la Integración Social Centroamericana (CIS-SISCA) (2009).

SISCA has renewed its commitment to tackling the challenges of social integration:

> The promotion of greater complementarity in these public policies involves the strengthening of the coordination capacity of the different actors involved; The adequate strategic and programmatic articulation of services from a

sectoral and territorial perspective; And the development of better technical-operative instruments. (OCADES, 2016, p 10)

The window of opportunity for incorporating the capabilities approach seems clear.

Future prospects and conclusion

Central America has not yet found a suitable response to its social inequalities. Two factors, analysed earlier, awakened in the first decade of the century the hope that the region could finally solve its exclusion problems.

First there were the growth years that Central American countries shared with the rest of Latin America and the positive evolution of some indicators related to exclusion and poverty. As was the case in many Latin American countries, economic growth helped to increase social expenditure in general terms and promote focused development programmes often linked with conditional transfer programmes.

These prosperous years helped governments in the region to approve development plans that explicitly incorporated key commitments to human development policies. National plans incorporated new approaches and interests. The contributions of external actors in the region, including UNDP and Oxfam, have been very important in recent years in incorporating the capabilities approach into the debate on national development plans.

Recognising the processes of expansion or reduction of human freedoms and opportunities is vital to the creation of propitious environments that enable the exercise of full and creative lives. Central America has attempted to test new perspectives and methodological proposals to facilitate the incorporation of the capabilities approach into the social policy of the region. This is a complex process based on the progressive aggregation of multiple approaches.

However, the impact of the progress achieved in the growth years is unclear. There are signs that achievements in poverty and exclusion reduction are being threatened. There are conceptual and practical gaps in the ways countries understand and adopt policies around capacity building. The region seems to be closer to a vision of functions (being healthy and educated) than to one that encourages the expansion of people's freedoms and options.

As Sabine Alkire (Alkire, 2013) points out, the primary evaluation function of the capability approach is precisely to determine the extent of human freedoms or what types of freedoms have been enlarged (or contracted), respectively.

This chapter has applied a regional approach to social policies using the concepts of market incorporation and social incorporation to make a comparative analysis of the behaviour of Central American economies, or order to help to assess the shortcomings of social policies and determine new priorities and tools. The MITI and SITI data confirm the outstanding advances achieved in Costa Rica and Panama. The SITI data suggests a panorama of weaknesses shared among the four remaining Central American countries in terms of social incorporation. However, the figures help to differentiate the case of Guatemala (backwardness and weaknesses compared with other countries and in respect of all the indicators for this index) and the cases of Nicaragua, Honduras and El Salvador (which show some significant differences depending on indicators).

The MITI and SITI tools developed by the authors could contribute to the evaluation of the effectiveness of economic and social policies. The regional approach in an area comprising small and vulnerable countries could create new ways of tackling social challenges, such as poverty, and creating spaces where capacities could emerge. It is not known if something is good until it is tested, although the need to prove is inexhaustible (Alkire, 2013).

The MITI and SITI tools suggested here focus on the relationship between public social policy and the effectiveness of its programmes. They allow us to pay particular attention to the quality of employability by detecting discriminatory policies, access to services and the minimum wage policy, all of which are sensitive to improving the quality of employability.

From this perspective, we can turn plans and actions into development objectives by running social initiatives on the basis of human rights. It is when intentions are inexorably entrusted to the human development paradigm that we can detect gaps (groups experiencing greater vulnerability) and encourage the targeted adoption of social protection programmes that complement social policy.

The MITI and SITI proposals contribute to an inclusive analysis framework, since it achieves an articulated analysis of contributory and non-contributory social protection system and the impact of labour markets in the region.

Likewise, MITI and SITI can also be very useful in accompanying the evaluative instruments of social policy to verify the results of poverty policies that respond more effectively to the lives of families and individuals. The use of indices such as MITI and SITI should stimulate the early development of skills so they are linked to the foundations of a full life and the right to be healthy and educated. They are also connected with decent options and sources of employment. MITI and SITI add information beyond that concerning inequality and social spending; they allow us to focus on the quality of the intervention and, unlike most measures of this kind, are not restricted to an aggregate evaluation.

Behind each intervention exercise of budget execution or social spending, there is still a considerable heterogeneity in assessing efficacy. Spontaneous responses according to the demands of the moment are still very common in Central America. This reflects political intentions with little capacity to maintain the impulse of poverty strategies transcending government terms.

Finally, it is comforting to acknowledge how the vision of development and creation of skills go beyond income and even beyond employability and social protection in Central American plans and programmes. Evidence from different social programmes and social researchers confirms the links between the development of cognitive schemes (relating to family and individuals) and social governance schemes. These contribute to individuals making their own decisions, but at the same time, given their limitations and shortcomings, prevent individuals from visualising long-term opportunities that could help them to live better in the future.

The capabilities approach has helped to spark an interest in human development on the part of global institutions. These days it is even more difficult to address the paradigm of human development without attending to its institutional and political dimension, that is to say, to convert into action 'the development promise' after the exercise of political leadership. It is globally accepted that the impact of development plans depends not only on resources and economic factors but on proper institutional architecture, good quality governance and social and cultural transformations.

These powerful concepts are now part of the concerns and agendas of organisations such as the World Bank and other development agencies. MITI and SITI add to the purpose of facilitating the construction of different levels of social policy aggregation where governance understood as the quality of democracy, rights and security of individuals and communities can be incorporated.

In any case, the inspiring role of the human development and capabilities approach in Central American development is at risk. Three factors explain the difficulties in consolidating its role: the lack of effectiveness of social policies in reducing social inequalities;

the difficulty of converting these complex approaches into concrete objectives and goals; and the weakness of Central American countries in terms of resources and quality of political leadership.

This chapter set out to analyse the framework of regional policies in the SICA to determine if its foundations and tools generate any opportunity to strengthen the influence of human development and the capability approach in social policies in Central America. Our hypothesis, raised in negative terms, has been confirmed. Human development and the capabilities approach are only slightly and unintentionally manifest in the strategic agenda of social integration. The foundations of regional social policies are neither clear nor precise, and this is a main cause of their lack of effectiveness and political impact in SICA countries.

What do we propose in terms of regional policies? We suggest that the strategic approach of social integration in the SICA framework could adjust its focus to the human development capabilities approach in member countries. Drawing on the analysis offered in Table 5.4, the goals of the strategic approach could include the following:

- The categorisation of social inequalities and their reduction (goal1) could be inspired by the conceptual models of human development and the capabilities approach that underlie the Sustainable Development Goals approved by United Nations for 2015–2030. The new global consensus must be inspiring for the specific goals of SICA countries. The Secretariat of Social Integration could develop a set of common goals based on shared indicators that are subject to a monitoring system and regional sphere evaluation.
- The application of the human capabilities approach could facilitate the definition of the promotion of social inclusion (goal 2) and its programmes. The goal would be applied individually but homogenously to inclusion models and tools based on the good practices of the countries with better outcomes (Costa Rica and Panama).
- The multidimensional logic of human development and the capabilities approach could help define social integration goals more precisely, and provide the content for the idea of social dimension in regional integration, which is now limited to the need for regulating integrated labour markets (goal 3). The multidimensionality of development proposals would improve coherence between the economic and social dimensions of integration and between market incorporation and the social incorporation.

The future challenges of Central American countries demand new methodological proposals to facilitate the transition to a more inclusive society. The circumstances of social integration offer some opportunities to promote better and more efficient social policies. Regional policies can be hosts for the necessary bridges between social policies and the human development and capabilities approach.

Note

[1] The following countries are current members of the Central American Integration System (SICA): Guatemala, El Salvador, Honduras, Nicaragua, Costa Rica and Panamá (as of the 1950s); Belize and the Dominican Republic (joining in 2000 and 2013, respectively).

[2] Esquipulas Agreements were signed between 1989 and 1992 as a solution to the regional conflicts inside and among countries with external intervention by the Soviet Union and USA. The historical relevance of Esquipulas lies in its condition of internal solutions, free from the interference of foreign powers.

References

Caldentey, P. (2014) *Los desafíos de la Integración Centroamericana [The challenges of Central American integration]*, Serie estudios y perspectiva 156 [Studies and Perspectives Series 156], ECLAC: Mexico.

Caldentey-del-Pozo, P., Bornemann-Martinez, G. and Morales-Fernandez, E.J. (2016) 'La contribución al desarrollo humano de las políticas sociales en el SICA' [The contribution to human development of social policies in SICA], Paper presented at the 19th World Economy Meeting, organised by the Society of World Economy, Alcalá de Henares, Spain, 1-2 June.

Consejo de la Integración Social Centroamericana y Secretaría de la Integración Social Centroamericana (CIS-SISCA) (2009) Agenda Estratégica Social del Sistema de la Integración Centroamericana (AES-SICA). Versión ampliada. La Libertad (El Salvador): SISCA. Serie Integración Documento No. 5.

ENFOQUE magazine (2013) Journal of the Faculty of Sciences Economics and Business Administration of the Central American University (FCEE) No.19.

HDCA (Human Development and Capability Association) (2013) General Report of HDCA 2013 Conference 'Human Development: Vulnerability, Inclusion and Quality of Life'. Central American University (UCA), 9-12 September, Managua, Nicaragua.

Huber, E. (2002). Models of Capitalism. Lessons for Latin America. University Park, PE: Pennsylvania State University Press.

International Labour Organization (2014a) 2014 Labour Overview Latin America and the Caribbean. Lima (Peru): ILO, Regional Office for Latin America and the Caribbean. Available at: www.ilo. org/wcmsp5/groups/public/---americas/---ro-lima/documents/ publication/ wcms_334089.pdf [Accessed 30 Nov. 2015].

International Labour Organization (2014b) World Social Protection Report 2014/15. Building economic recovery, inclusive development and social justice. Geneva. Available at: www.ilo.org/wcmsp5/ groups/public/---dgreports/---dcomm/documents/publication/ wcms_245201.pdf [30 Nov. 2015].

Martínez Franzoni, J. and Sánchez-Ancochea, D. (2014) 'The double challenge of market and social incorporation: progress and bottlenecks in Latin America', *Development Policy Review*, vol 32, no 3, pp 275-98.

McMillan, M. and Rodrik, D. (2011) 'Globalization, structural change and productivity growth', Working Paper No. 17143, Cambridge, MA: National Bureau of Economic Research, available at: http:// drodrik.scholar.harvard.edu/files/dani-rodrik/files/globalization-structural-change-and-productivity-growth.pdf?m=1435066659.

Meier, G. and Stiglitz, J. (2002) *Fronteras de la economia del desarrollo. El futuro en perspectiva*, Washington, DC: World Bank.

Mkandawire, T. (2006) *Targeting and universalism in poverty reduction*, UNRISD Social Policy and Development Programme Paper No 23. Geneva: UNRISD, available at www.unrisd. org/80256B3C005BCCF9/(httpAuxPages)/955FB8A594EEA0B0C 12570FF00493EAA/$file/mkandatarget.pdf (accessed 30 November 2015).

Nelson, J.A. (2004) 'Freedom, reason, and more: feminist economics and human development', *Journal of Human Development*, vol 5, no 3, 309-30.

Nussbaum, M. (2007) *Las fronteras de la justicia*, Barcelona: Paidós.

OCADES (Central American Observatory for Social Development) (2016) *La complementariedad de la política social y la económica en los sistemas de protección social y las estrategias de salida de la pobreza* [The complementarity of social and economic policy in social protection systems and strategies for the emergence of poverty], Notas para políticas sociales 1 [Notes for social policies 1], Panama City: SISCA, available at: www.sisca.int/centro-de-documentacion/5-ocades/1-publicaciones/serie-de-notas-de-politica-social/ [Accessed 30 Nov. 2016].

Perez, C. (2010) 'Technological dynamism and social inclusion in Latin America: a resource-based production development strategy', *CEPAL Review*, vol 100, no 2, pp 121-42.

Pick, S. and Bornemann-Martínez, G. (2013) 'Agencia y bienestar: el papel de la psicología en la toma de las capacidades humanas de Sen', Hul Haq Lecture presented at the 9th Human Development and Capability Association Conference, Managua, Nicaragua, 8 September.

Programa Estado de la Nación en Desarrollo Humano Sostenible [Program State of the Nation on Sustainable Human Development] (2014) Estadísticas de Centroamérica 2014 [Statistics of Central America 2014]. San José, Costa Rica, available at: www.estadonacion. or.cr [Accessed 30 November 2015].

Robeyns, I. (2008) 'Ideal theory in theory and practice', *Journal of Social Theory and Practice*, vol 34, no 3, pp 341-62.

Sánchez-Ancochea, D. and Martí Puig, S. (2014) *Handbook of Central American governance*, London: Routledge.

UNDP (United Nations Development Programme) (1990) *Human development report 1990*, Oxford: Oxford University Press, hdr.undp. org/sites/default/files/reports/219/hdr_1990_en_complete_nostats. pdf.

PART 2:

Modalities of structure and civil society

SIX

A framework for urban integration: the case of Buenos Aires

*Séverine Deneulin, Eduardo Lépore, Ann Mitchell
and Ana Lourdes Suárez*

Introduction

Latin America is the world's most urbanised continent, with 80% of its population living in urban areas. A third of Latin Americans live in cities with more than one million people (CEPAL, 2014). Argentina does not escape this Latin American characteristic: about 90% of its population is urban, and a third of its overall population – about 15 million of its 45 million inhabitants – is concentrated in the metropolitan area of Buenos Aires.

Latin America has also long been the most unequal continent (Cornia, 2014; Lopez-Calva et al. 2015), and its cities mirror that inequality. In 2010, a quarter of the Latin American population lived in informal settlements. While this proportion has been decreasing since 1990, it has increased in absolute terms, reaching 111 million in 2012 (UN Habitat, 2012, p xii). The Latin American city is characterised by a deep fragmentation between 'the slums and the rest' (Rodgers et al, 2011, p 560). Argentina has followed the same urban fragmentation trend. According to a survey of seven urban agglomerations that contain 60% of the total Argentinian population, there were 1,834 informal settlements in the country in 2013 totalling more than 532 thousand families (TECHO Argentina, 2013).[1] The city of Buenos Aires,[2] whose population numbers three million people, has 41 informal settlements in which more than 200,000 people live (Suárez et al, 2014).

This chapter aims to put into practise the human development approach and put forward capability-promoting policies in the context of urban inequality in Latin America. It responds to the urgent need for social policy alternatives by examining the specific innovative insights that this lens, or novel approach to social policy, can provide to inform interventions aimed at decreasing urban fragmentation and a better distribution of wellbeing opportunities (capabilities) across a given urban territory. It is structured as follows. It begins by discussing the features of the capability approach that are most relevant in the context of the Latin American city, namely its multidimensional and sectoral, institutional and agentic perspective. It then uses the first feature to analyse the dynamic interaction between youth employment and education in informal settlements, and territorial characteristics. It moves on to consider the second feature, analysing the role of civil society organisations in the dynamics of capability expansion in informal settlements. Next, it discusses the agentic feature to examine the role culture and religion can play in fomenting agency and capability expansion. Finally, it summarises some of the features of 'capability-promoting policy' in the fragmented and unequal context of the Latin American city.

A conceptual framework to reduce urban inequality

The 'right to the city' has been a dominant theoretical lens for analysing inequality in an urban context. The idea originated in the late 1960s, in the work of French sociologist Henri Lefèbvre (2015 [1968]), as a response to the growing commodification of urban space, and its exchange value in the property market increasingly taking over its use value. His proposal was for all urban residents to take part in the decisions that affect their lives, and the creation of new urban spaces that would be valued for their use by residents (Brown, 2013). It was not about participation of citizens in formal structures of urban governance, but political participation aimed at transforming the economic processes to replace the exchange value of urban space with its use value (Harvey, 2008; Kuymulu, 2013; Purcell 2013).

The 'right to the city' became prominent in international institutional discourses when the 2010 World Urban Forum took it as its rallying theme, but its original Marxist emphasis on the decommodification of land had given way to greater emphasis on equitable distribution of opportunities to realise human rights and citizen participation in existing governance structures. Policy discussions in relation to equal opportunities for housing, health services, basic infrastructure, education and employment are now shaped by discourses around equity and the Sustainable Development Goals (SDGs).[3] This section argues that the capability approach could be a unifying framework to incorporate the new shift towards equity and sustainable development in the city without losing the original insights of the 'right to the city'.

The capability approach was introduced precisely as a contribution to discussions about equality. Sen argued that the 'capability space' was more appropriate than the space of income, resources or primary goods for thinking about equality (Sen, 1999). Later on, Sen brought his idea of capability to discussions about justice (Sen, 2009), with the normative claim that treating all people as equal implied a distribution of economic and social resources in such a way as to ensure the realisation of a set of basic capabilities for all (Alexander, 2008).

A first feature of framing policies with the capability approach is its multidimensional and multisectoral perspective and its evaluative orientation. It is foremost a comparative framework that helps evaluate whether one situation is better than another (Sen, 2009), whether people in one neighbourhood live better than another or better than its past residents. The capability approach provides a normative framework to assess what a 'better' life could consist of, and provides criteria or evaluation tools to measure what kind of lives people are able to live. Sen proposes a set of basic functionings, or 'beings and doings', to assess how well people are living, such as being adequately nourished, being free from easily preventable diseases, being able to read and write, and participating in the life of the community. There could also be more complex valuable functionings. Frediani (2015) adds, for example, the capability to extend one's house as one capability people who live in informal settlements have reason to value. Some, like Nussbaum (2011), have proposed a specific list of central human functionings to assess how well people live.

To reflect the dynamic of this multidimensional perspective, Wolff and De-Shalit (2007, p 133) have introduced the ideas of 'corrosive disadvantages' and 'fertile functionings'. Often disadvantages (lack of functionings) cluster together to reinforce each other negatively. As the next section will discuss, the very fact of living in one specific neighbourhood can be corrosive and lead to poorer education, lower health outcomes and fewer employment opportunities than in other neighbourhoods. On the other hand, functionings often cluster together to reinforce each other positively. Because of its multidimensional perspective, the capability approach makes possible an analysis of how different wellbeing dimensions affect each other.

A second feature of using the capability approach to frame policy is its institutional perspective. To be free from easily preventable diseases, there needs to be equal access to public healthcare or safe water so that those who do not have the means to pay for a vaccine or water purification have the same opportunities to avoid early death as those born in higher-income families. To be adequately nourished, there needs to be institutions in place that ensure adequate food distribution, with no price distortion, or, in some contexts, public provision of school meals so that all children have equal opportunities to concentrate at school independently of their family situation. Well-functioning institutions of all kinds are essential ingredients of people's quality of life. An unregulated property market, and insufficient provision of low-rent housing, may create homeless families. A corrupt police force that cooperates with criminal gangs may create violent and insecure environments. Lack of coordination between different levels of a government in a given territory, and competition between them because of different political party allegiance, or lack of coordination between state and civil society actors, may lead to poor or insufficient access to basic services.

Given the overarching importance of institutions in the capability framework, Stewart (2013) made the case for broadening the policy evaluation space beyond what individuals can be or do, to include what institutions can be or do – what she calls 'social competencies'. There is a close connection between what institutions can be or do and the relationships among the people who construct or constitute those institutions. For example, the labour market institution does not function well if some of its constituents relate to certain groups of people with prejudice because of where they live. The housing market institution does not function well when some groups relate to the urban space for the sole aim of property speculation without concern for providing affordable housing. When institutions function badly, individual action is often powerless to transform them. This is why building social competences requires collective action so that institutions, such as planning laws and housing market, function well and provide the conditions for all urban residents to enjoy basic capabilities.

A third feature of the capability approach is its agentic perspective. Human beings are not passive recipients of state benefits, or passive victims of badly functioning institutions, they are authors of their lives and shapers of their own environment (Sen, 1999). It is not 'fate' that some people live in areas that are under permanent risk of flooding during heavy rains, or in areas whose ground and air are contaminated. Citizens can take action to change this state of affairs, and demand that the state build proper water drainage systems or provide more efficient waste management, or create a citizen watchdog to monitor environmental regulation compliance of industries operating near the area. Within the capability framework, urban residents are conceived as agents, responsible for creating the economic, social and political conditions for all residents to equally enjoy a basic set of capabilities independently of where they live in the city.

The capability approach does not have a view about specific institutional arrangements that citizens need to create so that all urban residents can equally enjoy a basic set of capabilities, unlike Lefèbvre's right to the city, which advocated direct control of urban policy by residents and elimination of capital maximisation from economic production (Purcell, 2013). It has a more modest utopian horizon. Reducing the number of people who suffer ill health from environmental contamination or increasing access to green spaces would already make cities better or more just, even if no progress has been made in increasing employment opportunities. Nor is the capability approach prescriptive regarding the relationship between representative democracy and capitalist interests. It limits itself to emphasising the agency of all residents to change states of affairs, whether through direct participation or through representative organisations. All residents are responsible to act such that policy decisions create the conditions for equal enjoyment of basic capabilities. In that regard, the capability approach puts a great emphasis on 'public reasoning', which it understands as the organisational ability of people who suffer from a capability deprivation to make their voices heard, as the ability to listen to different viewpoints and see the world from the perspective of another person (Drèze and Sen, 2013)

The next sections discuss in turn each of these three main features of the capability approach in the context of urban inequality reduction policies in Latin America, focusing on the city of Buenos Aires.

Multidimensional dynamics

The opportunities for young people who live in informal settlements to complete secondary school and secure decent employment are closely associated with multidimensional dynamics of deprivation related to residential segregation and segmentation of education services and labour markets. Recent studies carried out in the city of Buenos Aires have shown that the consequences of labour exclusion are heightened when workers live in neighbourhoods of concentrated poverty (Lépore, 2014). Other studies have suggested that the segmentation of educational opportunities confines young residents of informal settlements to poorer educational services than residents of higher-income neighbourhoods (Suárez and Groisman, 2008), and that territorial stigmatisation operates as a mechanism of discrimination in access to formal labour markets (Kessler, 2012). It has also been demonstrated that conditions of concentrated poverty give rise to marginal sub-cultures stemming from collective experiences of disaffiliation sustained over time. These sub-cultures often operate as reference frameworks for what segregated young people do and 'value being and doing', and often generate fatalistic beliefs about their future and their expectations of social mobility (Kaztman, 2001). Thus, what Wolff and De-Shalit (2007) coined as 'corrosive disadvantages' do not solely affect the realisation of wellbeing of young people, but also their subjective perceptions of opportunities for attaining wellbeing.

Linking the capability approach with other perspectives for analysing urban segregation, such as the neighbourhood effects of concentrated poverty, helps us to better understand the multidimensional dynamics of capability deprivation among young people and the consequences for urban integration. The urban segregation approach highlights disparities in the spatial distribution of social and economic opportunities. One of its main theses is that residential segregation acts as a mechanism that reproduces the very urban inequalities of which it is a manifestation (Massey and Denton, 1993). Residential segregation generates 'social isolation of the poor', who have daily contact with equally disadvantaged peers, thus reducing their horizon of possibilities (Kaztman, 2001). It narrows the spaces of interaction between different social groups, increasing educational and labour market segmentation (Kaztman and Retamoso, 2005, 2007), and may also affect the quality of community life and the capacity for collective action, both of which are associated with violence and social disorganisation (Sabatini et al, 2001).

Research on urban segregation highlights two dimensions of the multidimensional dynamics of disadvantage briefly mentioned previously. The first relates to the territorial concentration of poverty and its influence on processes of socialisation and access to opportunities. The second focuses on the integration of these territories into the urban social fabric. A central methodological contribution of this literature has been that of 'neighbourhood effects' (Wilson, 1996). According to this approach, living in a deprived neighbourhood has a negative effect on residents' life chances beyond their individual characteristics. This is particularly the case for children and young people who have been exposed to territorially concentrated poverty for a prolonged period of time. Empirical research has yielded some consistent conclusions with respect to the impact of various social and ecological characteristics of the residential surroundings on indicators such as infant mortality, low birthweight, teen pregnancy, school drop-outs, school attainment, the development of cognitive abilities, child abuse, access to employment and youth criminality (Jencks and Mayer, 1990; Sampson et al, 2002; Murry et al, 2011).[4]

The findings of our research in informal settlements of Buenos Aires highlight the relationship between spatially concentrated poverty and the labour market, and their consequences for the opportunities young people have to be in secure employment and to be educated at the secondary level. It corroborates the influence of the geographical concentration of disadvantages on key indicators of youth marginalisation, taking also into account the effects of the educational and occupational status of family members. In particular, the results of our survey, summarised in the following paragraphs, come from applying logistic regression models to data on a sample of households from the City of Buenos Aires' Annual Household Survey in 2004 and 2012, and a sample of households living in seven Buenos Aires informal settlements collected through the Catholic University of Argentina's Survey of Family Living Conditions in 2011-12 (Lépore and Simpson, 2016).

First, access to formal employment is conditioned by the socioeconomic make-up of the neighbourhoods where young people live. The risk of marginal employment increases significantly when young people reside in informal settlements, independently of other considered factors. In addition to neighbourhood effects, both the educational and occupational status of family members are factors that have a statistically significant influence on young people's employment outcomes. In the case of young people who reside in informal settlements, having parents with a higher level of education is not associated with greater chances of securing formal sector employment. However, participation of a household head in informal employment does increase the risk of young people reproducing these same conditions of occupational informality in a statistically significant manner.

Second, young people's educational attainment is also affected by the effects of spatially concentrated poverty. Living in an informal settlement significantly increases the likelihood of dropping out of school, not attending school and not completing secondary education. The educational environment of the household has a significant effect on reducing the relative risk of educational deprivation. In contrast, the occupational status of household members is not significantly associated with any of these indicators. In informal settlements, when the household's main income earner is in a situation of occupational marginality, the risk of adolescents dropping out of secondary school increases relative to that of adolescents living in households in which the main earner is employed in the formal sector.

Third, residing in an informal settlement contributes to an increased likelihood of a young person neither working nor studying, nor seeking employment, independently of other socio-demographic and economic factors. For young residents of informal settlements, neither the educational climate of the household, nor the occupational status of household members, has a statistically significant influence on institutional marginalisation.

The analysis of these statistical findings suggests that the spatial concentration of disadvantages, combined with labour market segmentation, is a main determinant of urban marginality. Therefore, participation in the marginal labour market among residents of segregated neighbourhoods increases the risk of youth social marginalisation in a significant and cumulative fashion.

This empirical evidence has a number of important implications for social policy. Among others, it draws attention to the insufficiency of conditional cash transfer programmes to tackle the consequences of concentration of disadvantage on the educational and employment outcomes for young people who live in deprived communities. The deficits in educational and employment outcomes are not as much associated with the absence of human capital and family income as with the logic of territorial discrimination and stigmatisation, which prevents disadvantaged young people from accessing opportunities. It also confirms that employment policies directed at increasing employability among disadvantaged young people are often not effective in counteracting the barriers that residential segregation causes in accessing formal labour markets. This is why capability-promoting policies, or policies seeking to reduce disadvantages in unequal urban contexts, imply first of all a comprehensive approach that addresses the dynamics of capability deprivation in a multidimensional and multilevel setting. There is an urgent need to combine housing opportunities with investments in social services, education, transportation, job readiness, training and placement at local and neighbourhood levels. Specifically, in the case of young residents of segregated neighbourhoods, there is a need for mechanisms and incentives that promote in a combined and integrated way educational quality, employment training opportunities and workplace training in the formal economy. From an urban integration perspective, the main challenge is overcoming the residential and occupational circuits of marginality in which young people who live in enclaves of concentrated disadvantaged are trapped. In this respect, international development practices suggest two principal directions: either to lift up neighbourhoods of concentrated poverty through community development, including improvement of public infrastructure, which is also known as 'urbanisation of informal settlements', or help poor people to disperse into socially and economically mixed areas. The next section examines the first option: the role of civil society and community organisations in addressing multiple disadvantages in neighbourhoods of concentrated disadvantage.

Building institutions

Civil society organisations (CSOs) provide an institutional structure through which community members can deliberate, channel common demands, act collectively, and build what Stewart (2013) called social competencies. This section uses the case of the civil society sector of the informal settlements of the city of Buenos Aires to analyse the sector's role in expanding individual capabilities and collective agency in marginalised communities (Mitchell, 2012, 2016). The analysis is based on a civil society organisation survey and a household survey carried out during 2011-12 in seven of the city's informal settlements.[5]

The CSO survey identified a total of 195 organisations operating within the boundaries of the seven settlements, or an average of 1.8 organisations per thousand residents. This means that the organisational density in the settlements is somewhat below the Argentine average of 2.9, but above that of other Latin American countries, such as Brazil, which has an average of only 0.7 (Cao et al, 2011). The scale of civil society activity is comparatively higher when based on the total number of participants. According to the same survey, 3% of residents collaborate as volunteers and nearly half of all residents participate in the activities of at least one organisation. The finding of a dense network of organisations operating in these communities contrasts with the results of some research that has found an erosion of networks of organisations and institutions in segregated communities (Pereira Leite, 2008; Wacquant, 2008).

Six out of 10 CSOs are grassroots organisations[6] and the rest are faith-based organisations, social movements and social service-oriented non-governmental organisations. While the bonds of trust and cooperation among community members were decisive in the creation of grassroots organisations, the construction of alliances with institutions and people from outside of the community have been vital to expanding social connectivity and enabling organisations to gain access to economic resources and diversify their activities. The public sector is the primary source of CSO financing. Eight out of 10 grassroots organisations obtain economic resources from either the city or the national government and many organisations focus their activities on the administration of programmes designed and financed by the public sector.

The principal purpose of over half of the organisations operating in these settlements is the provision of social services, especially food. Nearly a hundred community kitchens operate in these neighbourhoods, providing daily rations of food to around a quarter of all residents. Half of all organisations provide some type of education service, such as after-school programmes, day-care centres, nursery schools and adult literacy programmes. Two out of 10 organisations offer programmes to increase the productive and labour market opportunities of residents, such as job training (in carpentry, auto-mechanics, computing, and so on) and microcredit programmes. The most important health-related activities are drug treatment programmes and workshops on topics such as reproductive health, oral hygiene and nutrition.

There is broad evidence, therefore, that the dense network of organisations operating in these communities contributes to the expansion of individual capabilities (to be well nourished, to be educated, to be healthy, to have opportunities for recreation, and so on) through the provision of social services. The organisations also provide spaces in which community members can interact, socialise and converse, thereby expanding their capability of affiliation. But, to what extent do CSOs provide mediums through which individuals can become active agents in their lives, where through deliberation they can define which goals they value most and collectively work to pursue those goals?

Nearly all of the city's informal settlements have one principal representative organisation that is the main vehicle for advancing the community's collective demands. These organisations, whose origin dates in some cases back to the 1950s, have been instrumental in the transformation of land occupations into neighbourhoods. While their primary demands focused initially on gaining access to basic public services (water, sewerage and electricity), the demands shifted later to obtaining paved roads, streetlights and community health centres and more recently to improving the *quality* of public services and procuring ambulance services. As one resident stated, "The things that have been done are because the people organise themselves. The changes were gradual and always depended on the capacity for organisation of the neighbourhood and the political orientation of the city's government."[7]

While street blockages, occupation of public buildings and other forms of protest have traditionally been the methods most frequently used to voice the concerns of the population, the representative organisations have increasingly expressed their demands through the drafting of formal petitions and judicial and legislative processes. The municipal Law 148, sanctioned in 1998, conferred the responsibility for the diagnosis, planning and control of public policies related to the settlements to a coordinating commission comprised of the city government, social movements linked to problems affecting the settlements (*movimientos villeros*)[8] and neighbourhood representative organisations. After years of legal battles, the city government finally organised formal elections for delegates of the representative organisations in nearly all of the settlements. Civil society leaders, however, have denounced irregularities in the electoral processes and delegates complain that opportunities for the representative organisations to participate in the urbanisation process are extremely limited, despite the fact that a legal framework exists that should guarantee that right. The government has instead prioritised actions to foster direct contact with community members, by setting up 'portable' government offices in the periphery of the settlements and organising neighbourhood assemblies to discuss concrete issues facing the community.

In interviews, organisation representatives also complained about the lack of internal cohesion within the representative organisations, vested interests between delegates and government officials and a lack of transparency in the allocation of lucrative contracts to organisations for the maintenance and provision of public services. All of these factors contribute to lowering confidence in civil society and weaken the capacity to garner community support for collective initiatives. According to household survey, 41% of respondents trust CSOs, 33% trust CSO leaders and only 23% trust the delegates of representative organisations. Moreover, just 6% of respondents indicated that they participate in neighbourhood assemblies and 3% participate in a political party or social movement.

The case shows that while civil society organisations play an integral role in the provision of social services through a relationship of co-production with public sector, their broader role in the processes of integration of the settlements into the city is relatively more limited due to factors intimately related to civil society–state relations, including irregularities in election processes, lack of transparency in the allocation of public resources and the resulting conflict between organisations and the low level of confidence in civil society. True empowerment of community members to work together to obtain common goals requires the strengthening of representative organisations and greater transparency in civil society–state relations. In other words, capability-promoting policies require setting the conditions that enable people to exercise agency in a way that contributes to the good of the community. Given that a large number of CSOs that are active in the settlements have a religious foundation, and given the importance of religious expression in these territories of urban marginality (Suárez, 2015), the next section analyses the role that religion could play in expanding capabilities and building social competencies. It focuses on how religion has contributed to shaping the agency of the residents of the informal settlements of the city of Buenos Aires.

Fostering agency

Religion has permeated and played an important role in the intense seven decades of history of the informal settlements in the city of Buenos Aires. Processes, discussions, events, institutions and people associated with the religious world have left deep footprints in these territories.

In the 1960s and 1970s, the Argentine Catholic Church was shaken by major changes. The Vatican II Council in Rome from 1962 to 1965, and the first Latin American Bishops Conference in 1968 in Medellín, Colombia, opened the way to more committed social religious options. It adopted the 'preferential option for the poor' as an institutional commitment. According to this 'option' or conscious choice, those who live in conditions of poverty are to be the primary concern of the Church's pastoral activities (González, 2010; Dorr, 2012). The informal settlements were a 'privileged place' for that commitment; they opened a way to realise this 'preferential option for the poor' launched by the bishops and widely accepted by many sectors of Catholicism.

A relevant actor in this period was the Movement of Third World Priests (*Movimiento de Sacerdotes del Tercer Mundo*), which took effect between 1967 and 1976, and which had a strong presence in Buenos Aires' informal settlements. The Catholic priest Carlos Mugica was one of its most emblematic and public figures. He had close ties with Peronism – the political movement in Argentina associated with General Perón and labour rights and redistributive policies. He had a major presence in the national media, denouncing the poor living conditions in the city's informal settlements. Mugica came from a wealthy family in Buenos Aires and summoned other priests to live and work in one of the city's biggest informal settlement. His assassination in 1974 at the hands of paramilitary groups shocked the country, marking a milestone in the symbolic burden of these territories, and inspiring many people to work for the poorest in the city.

The figure of these pioneering priests who went to live in informal settlements left a strong mark of commitment, struggle and denunciation that continues to the present day within these territories of urban marginalisation (characterised by lack of government presence, lack of adequate political intervention, deterioration of public infrastructure and increasingly worsening living conditions). Other religious actors, such as religious congregations and committed men and women, followed suit in choosing the informal settlements as a space for social and Christian commitment. Some female congregations in particular led the way by leaving the schools they ran for the privileged in order to live a life of 'insertion' among marginalised communities.

During the last military government (1976-83), several of the religious actors who had been socially and politically engaged were persecuted, and some tortured and killed. In addition to this political persecution, the government of the city of Buenos Aires was determined to eradicate completely the informal settlements in the city. Many organisations resisted this attack and several religious actors had a prominent role in the resistance. Their mantra was the integration of all settlements to the city, and appreciation of the culture of its residents, known as '*cultura popular*'. Both ideas continue to be held in the numerous statements made by the Catholic priests who live today in the settlements of the city of Buenos Aires.

The 'closeness' of the Archbishop of Buenos Aires, Jorge Bergoglio, now Pope Francis,[9] with the residents of informal settlements, and the prioritisation of social and pastoral action among the city's most marginalised areas, was one of the hallmarks of the Bergoglio's model of church governance. He established a more solid and permanent presence of the Church in each of the informal settlement of the city of Buenos Aires; he doubled the number of priests in charge of the ministry in these territories (from 11 in 1998 to 22 in 2012); and he created a special pastoral agency to deal specifically with the problems of the settlements, known as '*Pastoral Villera*'. Bergoglio therefore gave relevance and support to the Church's pastoral and social action in the most marginalised areas of the city. He himself used to visit the city's informal settlements, and walked in its narrow alleyways like a local resident.

Religious buildings such as churches, chapels and houses of religious congregations, particularly of nuns, have become places not only where residents of informal settlements gather to express their faith, but also where many other activities take place and different public services are offered. As the previous section on civil society described, these include serving food for those in need, providing social services, tackling drug addiction, and so on. In short they have become places to pray, celebrate, find help and assistance, and recover. The presence of a church (both Catholic and Pentecostal)[10] that values and positions itself within territories of urban marginality, redirecting the focus of its mission to disadvantaged people, has an important and revitalising effect on people's lives and building the institutional conditions for human flourishing.

From a cultural perspective, manifestations of popular religiosity are privileged channels that express values and ways of being. They are part of informal settlements residents' matrix of meanings, practices and rituals. Popular religiosity plays a large role in shaping their agency by supporting the cosmologic and holistic cultural matrix from which they feed hope and a positive way of facing their lives. Massive processions in honour of a popular saint, rituals in remembrance of dead people, venerations of non-officially recognised religious figures, popular adoration to the Virgin Mary and so on can all be understood as pursuits of recognition, identity and transformation. They do have a social impact, particularly when official Church structures engage in dialogue with them instead of condemning them (as tends to be the case in some places). Many 'popular' religious manifestations have become spaces of 'resistance' in the city's informal settlements. Through its support, the Church helps shape the vital and transforming power that the residents themselves have to be authors of their lives and transform the world around them.

Conclusion

This chapter has explored how the capability approach, as an evaluative conceptual framework with normative redistributive claims, can illuminate policies that promote urban integration in Latin America. It has concentrated on three features of the capability approach: its multidimensional perspective on human wellbeing, the importance it gives to institutions in their instrumental and constitutive role in people's wellbeing, and the centrality of agency in creating the necessary institutional conditions for people to flourish as human beings. It has used the informal settlements of the city of Buenos Aires as empirical ground to demonstrate the emancipatory potential of using the capability approach as analytical lens through with to address disadvantage. It has illustrated how capability-promoting policies can be 'operationalised', and has suggested some ways for policies to become genuine practices of human development that expand people's capabilities and strengthen their agency.

Given the multidimensional dynamics of deprivation, especially how territorial characteristics and employment and educational outcomes negatively reinforce each other, an integral perspective on policy is required. There is little point in initiating employability schemes for disadvantaged young people without addressing at the same time housing or infrastructure deficit and territorial discrimination. Civil society organisations can play a large role in this respect. There also needs to be public action oriented at establishing transparent and inclusive mechanisms of representation between residents and state authorities. While civil society organisations provide an invaluable array of services to local residents of the informal settlements, this is not sufficient. In its recognition of agency as a key feature of policy, with people as subjects and not passive recipients, capability-promoting policies also require taking into account the potential of culture, often intertwined with religion, in enabling residents of informal settlements to be actors of their journey towards more fulfilling and flourishing human lives. This is an underexplored area in the social sciences and would deserve greater attention given that 80% of the world's population is estimated to profess religious beliefs that are core to who they are as human beings. If the capability approach and Sen's idea of justice make significant reference to the characteristics of human beings, which include among others their capacities for reasoning and sympathy (Sen, 2009, pp 414-15), adding the capacity to relate to a transcendental source of value could be an area of significant enrichment for capability-promoting policies.

Acknowledgement

We thank the British Academy International Partnership Mobility Scheme grant number PM150043 for facilitating the writing of this chapter.

Notes

[1]   TECHO Argentina (2013) considered the term informal settlement to denote a set of dwellings with a minimum of eight families, of which more than half lack land titles and access to at least two basic services like water, electricity or sewage.

[2]   The city is the capital of the Federal Republic of Argentina. It has the status of autonomous city since 1994.

[3]   The theme of the 7th World Urban Forum, in Medellín, Colombia, in April 2014, was urban equity in development. See Cohen (2016) for a discussion on the SDGs in context of urban inequality.

[4]   The analysis of 'neighbourhood effects' is not free of methodological difficulties. The literature identifies two central problems with measuring the effects of the

residential context on individual outcomes: selection bias and endogeneity of simultaneity (Sampson et al, 2002).

[5]   These were *villas* 24, 1-11-14, 6, 19 and 3, Piletones and the housing complex Ramon Carrillo. According to the 2010 census, the combined population of these settlements is 106,000, approximately two thirds of the population living in informal settlements in the city. See Lépore et al (2012) for a description of the surveys.

[6]   If all of the people directly involved in the organisation's creation were living in the community at the time it was created, the organisation was classified as grassroots.

[7]   Based on an interview with an organisation leader in Piletones conducted on 12 July 2013.

[8]   In Argentinian Spanish, informal settlements are called *villas miserias*, or *villas*.

[9]   Bergoglio was appointed Archbishop of Buenos Aires in 1998, and was elected Pope in March 2013.

[10]   According to a survey by Suárez (2015), the population in these communities is mostly Christian, like in the rest of the city, but there is a higher proportion of Evangelicals – 16% compared with 3% in the formal areas of the city. Most of these churches are Pentecostals and affiliated to very small, marginal churches located inside the settlements, unlike the Catholic parishes, which are linked to other parts of the city. The survey also highlights a high porosity between church belonging, with many residents attending rituals and events of different churches, and professing beliefs of one denomination, for example, saints in the Catholic Church, and belonging to another denomination.

References

Alexander, J. (2008) *Capabilities and social justice*, Farnham: Ashgate.

Brown, A. (2013) 'The right to the city: road to Rio 2010', *International Journal of Urban and Regional Research*, vol 37, no 3, pp 957-71.

Cao, C., Cecconi, E. and Balian, B. (2011) *La sociedad civil Argentina en el Bicentenario. (2008-2010) (Civil society in Argentina in the Bicentenary)*, Buenos Aires: GADIS, available at http://gadis-asociacion.org/PublicacionesRecientes.asp.

CEPAL (Comisión Económica para América Latina y el Caribe [United Nations Economic Commission for Latin America and the Caribbean]) (2014) *Social panorama of Latin America and the Caribbean*, Santiago: CEPAL, available at www.cepal.org/en/publications/37626-social-panorama-latin-america-2014.

Cohen, M. (2016) 'From Habitat III to Pachamama', *Environment and Urbanization*, vol 28, no 1, pp 35-48.

Cornia, G.A. (ed) (2014) *Falling inequality in Latin America: Policy changes and lessons,* Oxford: Oxford University Press.

Dorr, D. (2012) *Option for the poor and the earth*, New York, NY: Orbis Books.

Drèze, J. and Sen, A. (2013) *An uncertain glory: India and its contradictions*, London: Allen Lane.

Frediani, A. (2015) 'Space and capabilities: approaching informal settlements', in C. Lemanski and C. Marx (eds) *The city in urban poverty*, Cambridge: Cambridge University Press, pp 64-84.

González, M. (2010) *La reflexión teológica en Argentina, 1962-2004 (A theological reflection in Argentina)*, Buenos Aires: Iberoamérica.

Harvey, D. (2008) 'The right to the city', *New Left Review*, vol 53, 23-40.

Jencks, C. and Mayer, S. (1990) 'The social consequences of growing up in a poor neighborhood', in L.E. Lynn and M.G.H. McGeary (eds) *Inner-city poverty in the United States*, Washington DC: National Academy Press, pp 111-85.

Kaztman, R. (2001) 'Seducidos y abandonados: el aislamiento social de los pobres urbanos' ('Seduced and abandoned: the social isolation of the urban poor'), *Revista de la CEPAL*, 75, pp 171-89.

Kaztman, R. and Retamoso, A. (2005) 'Segregación espacial, empleo y pobreza en Montevideo' ('Spatial segregation, employment and poverty in Montevideo'), *Revista de la CEPAL*, 85, pp 131-48.

Kaztman, R. and Retamoso, A. (2007) 'Efectos de la segregación urbana sobre la educación en Montevideo' ('Effects of urban segregation on education in Montevideo'), *Revista de la CEPAL*, 91, pp 133-52.

Kessler, G. (2012) 'Las consecuencias de la estigmatización territorial' ('The consequences of territorial stigmatization'), *Espacios en Blanco. Revista de Educación*, 22, pp 165-98.

Kuymulu, M.B. (2013) 'The vortex of rights: 'right to the city' at a crossroads', *International Journal of Urban and Regional Research*, vol 37, no 3, pp 923-40.

Lefebvre, H. (2015 [1968]) *Le Droit a la Ville* (3rd ed), Paris: Economica.

Lépore, E. (2014) 'Participación laboral y modalidades de inserción socio-ocupacional en las villas de la Ciudad' ('Labour participation and modalities of socio-occupational insertion in the informal settlements of the city'), in A.L. Suárez, A. Mitchell and E. Lépore (eds) *Las villas de la Ciudad de Buenos Aires. Territorios frágiles de inclusión social (The informal settlements of the city of Buenos Aires: Fragile territories of social inclusion)*, Buenos Aires: Educa, pp 95-140.

Lépore, E. and Simpson, S. (2016) *Concentrated poverty and labour markets: Youth marginalization in Buenos Aires's informal settlements*, Working Paper Series on Urban Inclusion and Integration No. 2, Buenos Aires: Catholic University of Argentina, www.uca.edu.ar/index.php/site/index/es/uca/programa-interdisciplinario-sobre-desarrollo-humano-e-inclusion-social/serie-bassp.

Lépore, E., Lépore, S., Mitchell, A., Macció, J. and Rivero, E. (2012) *Capacidades de desarrollo y sociedad civil en las villas de la Ciudad* (*Capabilities for development and civil society in the informal settlements of the city*), Buenos Aires: Educa.

Lopez-Calva L.F., Lustig, N. and Ortiz-Juarez, E. (2015) 'A long-term perspective on inequality and human development in Latin America', *Journal of Human Development and Capabilities*, vol 16, no 3, pp 319-23.

Massey, D. and Denton, N. (1993) *American apartheid: Segregation and the making of the underclass*, Cambridge, MA: Harvard University Press.

Mitchell, A. (2012) 'Las organizaciones de la sociedad civil en las villas de Bajo Flores y Barracas' [Civil society organisations in the neighbourhoods of Bajo Flores and Barracas], in E. Lépore et al (eds) *Capacidades de desarrollo y sociedad civil en las villas de la ciudad* [Capabilities for development and civil society in the informal settlements of the city], Buenos Aires: Catholic University of Argentina, pp 115-87.

Mitchell, A. (2016) 'Civil society organizations in the informal settlements of Buenos Aires: service providers and forces for change', *Voluntas*, vol 27, no 1, pp 37-60.

Murry, V.M., Berkel, C., Gaylord-Harden, N.K., Copeland-Linder, N. and Nation, N. (2011) 'Neighborhood poverty and adolescence development', *Journal of Research on Adolescence*, vol 21, no 1, pp 114-28.

Nussbaum, M. (2011) *Creating capabilities*, Cambridge, MA: Harvard University Press.

Pereira Leite, M. (2008) 'Pobreza y exclusión en las favelas de Río de Janeiro' ('Poverty and exclusion in the favelas of Rio'), in A. Ziccardi (ed) *Procesos de urbanización de la pobreza y nuevas formas de exclusión social (Urbanization processes of poverty and new forms of social exclusion)*, Buenos Aires: CLACSO.

Purcell, M. (2013) 'Possible worlds: Henri Lefebvre and the right to the city', *Journal of Urban Affairs*, vol 36, no 1, pp 141-54.

Rodgers, D., Beall, J. and Kanbur, R. (2011) 'Latin American urban development into the twenty-first century', *European Journal of Development Research*, vol 23, no 4, pp 550-68.

Sabatini, F., Cáceres, G. and Cerda, J. (2001) 'Segregación residencial en las principales ciudades chilenas' ('Residential segregation in the main Chilean cities'), *Revista EURE - Revista de Estudios Urbano Regionales*, vol 29, no 89, pp 5-24.

Sampson, R.J., Morenoff, J.D. and Gannon-Rowley, T. (2002) 'Assessing "neighborhood effects"', *Annual Review of Sociology*, vol 28, no 1, pp 443-78.

Sen, A.K. (1999) *Development as freedom*, Oxford: Oxford University Press.

Sen, A.K. (2009) *The idea of justice*, London: Allen Lane.

Stewart, F. (2013) *Capabilities and human development: Beyond the individual – The critical role of social institutions and social competencies*, UNDP-HDRO Occasional Papers No. 2013/03, Human Development Report Office, United Nations Development Programme.

Suárez, A.L. and Groisman, F. (2008) 'Segregação residencial e conquistas educacionais na Argentina' ('Residential segregation and educational gains in Argentina'), in L. Queiroz Ribeiro and R. Kaztman (eds) *A cidade contra a escola?: segregação urbana e desigualdades educacionais em grandes cidades da América Latina* [Urban segregation and educational inequality in the big Latin American cities. The city against the school?], Rio de Janeiro: Letra Capital.

Suárez, A. L., Mitchell, A. y Lépore, E. (eds.) (2014) *Las villas de la Ciudad de Buenos Aires. Territorios frágiles de inclusión social* [The informal settlements of the city of Buenos Aires: Fragile territories of social inclusion], Buenos Aires: Educa.

Suárez, A.L. (2015) *Creer en las villas. Devociones y prácticas religiosas en barrios precarios de la Ciudad de Buenos Aires* (*Believing in the informal settlements: Devotions and religious practices in the marginal neighbourhoods of the city of Buenos Aires*), Buenos Aires: Biblos.

TECHO Argentina (2013) *Relevamiento de asentamientos informales 2013* (*Inventory of informal settlements 2013*), Buenos Aires: TECHO, available at www.techo.org/informate/techo-argentina-relevamiento-asentamientosinformales.

UN Habitat (2012) *State of Latin American and Caribbean cities*, Nairobi: UN Habitat, https://unhabitat.org/books/state-of-latin-american-and-caribbean-cities-2/

Wacquant, L. (2008) *Urban outcasts: A comparative sociology of advanced marginality*, Cambridge: Polity Press.

Wilson, W.J. (1996) *When work disappears: The world of the new urban poor*, New York, NY: Random House.

Wolff, J. and De-Shalit, A. (2007) *Disadvantage*, Oxford: Oxford University Press.

SEVEN

Culture, equity and social wellbeing in New York City

Mark J. Stern and Susan C. Seifert

This chapter reports on research undertaken to apply the capabilities approach to cultural policymaking in New York City. The authors used previous work in Philadelphia to develop a conceptualisation of social wellbeing based on a multidimensional phenomenon. The project grows out of a belief that cultural engagement is a core capability in its own right. Furthermore, the chapter argues that cultural engagement can facilitate the achievement of other capabilities, what Wolff and De-Shalit (2007) characterise as 'fertile functionings'. Finally, the chapter suggests two amendments to the conceptualisation of capability-promoting policy: one, to consider the role of immediate social context – that is, neighbourhood effects – in assessing impact; and, two, to consider the potential tension between theories of social justice and democratic consent. Before addressing these concerns, we first discuss the political context within which the current research has taken place.

Although New York City's 8.5 million residents barely keep it in the top 20 world cities in terms of population, New York remains a centre for culture and economic life for the United States and the world. The local politics of the city cast a long shadow on trends in the rest of the United States. During the 1990s, mayor Rudy Giuliani was spokesman for the 'revanchist' city in which social elites sought to reassert dominance over seemingly uncontrollable urban populations (Smith, 1996). After the attacks of 11 September 2001, New Yorkers elected billionaire Michael Bloomberg, who presided over the increasing economic division of the city as a wave of displacement drove many poor and working-class families from suddenly 'hot' neighbourhoods. The 2013 mayoral election suggested a new political departure in the wake of the recession and its aftermath. The voters selected a progressive, Bill de Blasio, who made the promotion of social justice the hallmark of his campaign.

New York City has a history of making significant commitments to the arts. The city's Department of Cultural Affairs is the second largest public funding agency in the US, surpassed only by the National Endowment for the Arts. Bloomberg was a supporter of the arts – contributing some of his own fortune to local institutions – but the rationale for policy remained focused on culture's contribution to the economy and its role in promoting tourism (Forman, 2015). De Blasio's cultural affairs commissioner, Tom Finkelpearl, came to the position with a national reputation for promoting an inclusive vision of the connection between culture and social wellbeing (Finkelpearl, 2013). The De Blasio administration's commitment to promoting social equity refocused the city's cultural policy on the social value of the arts for ordinary New Yorkers.

Some theoretical considerations

This chapter makes three conceptual contributions to the discussion of capability-promoting policies: culture as a capability; the importance of neighbourhood context; and the tension between social justice and democratic decision making.

Culture as capability

The fact that cultural engagement has been left off of the 'lists' prepared by Nussbaum and others is surprising (Nussbaum, 2011). One can shoehorn culture into categories like 'imagination' or 'play', but this shortchanges the importance of culture and creativity to people's lives. Its omission is unexpected given the recognition of the 'right to culture' in the Universal Declaration of Human Rights and the 1966 International Covenant on Economic, Social, and Cultural Rights (United Nations, 1966).

Other scholars have noted that culture deserves to be identified as a capability (Sen, 2004; Comim, 2014). We make an even stronger argument, namely, that cultural opportunities have a spillover effect that enhances people's other capabilities – what Wolff and De-Shalit call 'fertile functioning' – by increasing social connection and social and political voice (Wolff and De-Shalit, 2007). Thus, from a policy standpoint, cultural rights may be of strategic importance beyond their intrinsic value.

We have been influenced by the important work of Jonathan Wolff and Avner De-Shalit (2007) in addressing what capability-promoting policy would look like. However, their account is overly state-centred, ignoring the ways in which social context can influence wellbeing. In addition, their advocacy of policies directed primarily at the most disadvantaged neglects the tension between social justice and democratic decision making.

Beyond the state: the importance of neighbourhood context

The capabilities approach focuses on the opportunity of individuals to pursue a particular type of functioning, whether or not they choose to take advantage of the opportunity. The distinction between capability and functioning puts particular focus on the issue of freedom. It is this ability to have a choice between different sets of functionings that differentiates the capability approach from traditional welfare economics. For Sen, this freedom to choose is an additional 'good' that adds to a person's wellbeing (Sen, 1992; Stern and Seifert, 2013a).

Yet, we may ask what institutions are responsible for ensuring that individuals have both access to a particular set of functionings and the freedom to choose. Nussbaum notes that the capability approach challenges us to move beyond negative rights to a positive endorsement of people's right to the material and social conditions that actually provide them the ability to live a life they have reason to value (Nussbaum, 2003).

This perspective highlights, in particular, the role of non-state institutions in enhancing or restricting human flourishing. Nussbaum and Sen, for example, have noted the role of families in constraining the life choices of women. This line of reasoning suggests that individuals' geographic context, what the sociological literature calls 'neighbourhood effects', can exert a powerful influence on individuals' ability to be and do (Sampson et al, 2002; Sampson, 2012).

The tension between democratic participation and social justice

The capabilities approach is premised on four principles: equity, efficiency, participation and empowerment, and sustainability (Alkire and Deneulin, 2009). Based on these premises, Wolff and De-Shalit (2007) conclude that social policy should focus on the wellbeing of the most disadvantaged members of society. There is ample historical evidence that these principles – particularly equity and participation – are often in conflict. The growth of Western welfare states, for example, has been sustained politically by expanding the share of the population that benefits from their programmes. In contrast, efforts to focus policy narrowly on the profoundly disadvantaged have often been politically unsustainable.

Wolff and De-Shalit are willing to make modifications to their focus on the most disadvantaged. They consider whether better-off groups asked to support programmes that help the most disadvantaged have a right to expect benefits from those programmes. However, they reject the argument on its own terms because 'it is premised on a theory of justice that is in conflict with the general approach adopted here' (Wolff and De-Shalit, 2007, p 2260). While they allow that a wider distribution of benefits can be justified to reduce stigmatisation of the poor and thereby increase affiliation, they conclude that 'political expediency should not be allowed to overturn considerations of justice' (Wolff and De-Shalit, 2007, p 2210).

Yet, reducing to political expediency the idea that middle-income groups expect to benefit from capability-promoting policies glosses over a contradiction in their argument. If expediency means 'the opinions of most citizens', Wolff and De-Shalit are arguing that social justice trumps democratic participation. Obviously, this leads us into a thicket too dense for this chapter. We can accept, however, that any social policy that fails to generate support from a large share of the population is unlikely to be sustainable.

Here the US 'war on poverty' during the 1960s provides an example. The conventional historical memory of the war on poverty – that is, Ronald Reagan's conclusion that 'poverty won' – is incorrect. In fact, in less than a decade, public programmes succeeded in reducing the 'official' poverty rate by half. Yet, despite these successes, the policy trajectory was unsustainable. The perception that a narrow group of the disadvantaged were benefiting from the initiative provoked a backlash that culminated in the triumph of Reagan in the 1980 presidential election (Katz, 2013).

Therefore, as we pursue capability-promoting policies, it is wise to keep both democratic consent and social justice in mind but acknowledge that they do not necessarily support one another. We suggest that in the cultural sphere a capability-promoting policy would pursue two complementary but distinct policy goals: assure social equity – that is, ensure that all residents have opportunities for cultural and creative expression; and build from strength – that is, tap existing clusters of cultural resources (not necessarily in the most disadvantaged neighbourhoods) as points of strength from which to leverage the social wellbeing potential of cultural engagement.

Developing a neighbourhood-based measure of social wellbeing

The capabilities approach takes as its starting point the idea that wellbeing is a result of individuals having the actual opportunity (capability) to live a life they have reason to value. Thus, in contrast to more narrow ideas of economic 'welfare', the capabilities approach assumes that wellbeing is a multidimensional phenomenon.

The conceptual issues discussed in the previous section have provided methodological guidance for the project. Our methodology took Stiglitz and colleagues' (2009) report as its starting point. We amended its framework in several ways. First, we identify culture as a dimension of wellbeing and classify cultural engagement as a central element of social connection. Second, because of the importance we give neighbourhood effects in influencing wellbeing, we use census geography as our 'unit of analysis' – ideally, block groups of six to 10 city blocks – rather than national-level measurement. Finally, to examine the impact of culture on social wellbeing, we use a dual perspective that looks at both the right of all residents to cultural opportunities and the relationship of cultural resource clusters to other aspects of wellbeing.

The research design consisted of three elements: the construction of measures of cultural resources at the block group level; the integration of existing data into a multidimensional measure of other aspects of social wellbeing; and fieldwork in a set of New York City neighbourhoods. These ongoing community case studies explore the relationship of culture and the arts to neighbourhood transformation and social wellbeing.

Measures of cultural assets

In New York City, we constructed a cultural asset database that documents four types of cultural assets at the neighbourhood level – non-profit cultural providers, for-profit cultural businesses, resident artists and cultural participants – across the entire city between 2013 and 2015 (Stern and Seifert, 2013b).

The non-profit inventory consisted of more than 4,000 entities, ranging from internationally known institutions like the Metropolitan Opera and the Museum of Modern Art to community and artists' centres of all types, which offer programmes in the arts and humanities – including performing, visual, literary, media and multicultural arts as well as science, history, heritage and folklore – for people of all ages and identities. The for-profit inventory consisted of over 17,000 enterprises across the city, ranging from design firms and art galleries to local music, book and craft stores. For resident artists, we estimated the percentage of the civilian labour force employed in artists' occupations. Finally, we estimated rates of cultural participation based on the administrative records of a sample of approximately 100 non-profit organisations that include approximately 1.3 million cultural participants.

Figure 7.1: Cultural Asset Index, New York City, 2013–15

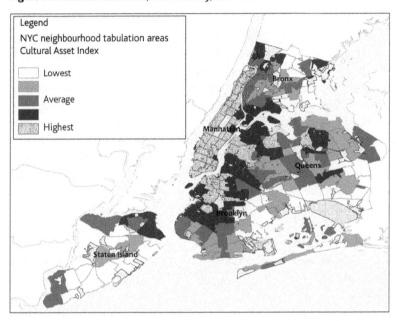

Source: Stern and Seifert (2017).

We combined the four measures into a single cultural asset index (CAI). As expected, the CAI was highest in the city's wealthiest neighbourhoods and those closest to Midtown Manhattan. Because of our interest in the role of culture as a capability in low- and moderate-income neighbourhoods, we calculated a 'corrected' CAI that identifies neighbourhoods with cultural assets that exceed what we would predict based on their location and socioeconomic status – in other words, places of relative strength that could serve as catalysts for change in surrounding areas.

Other measures of social wellbeing

In addition to the Cultural Asset Index, we calculated nine other wellbeing dimensions. These include measures of economic wellbeing, housing burden, healthcare access, and economic and ethnic diversity based on US census data, as well as measures of health, school effectiveness, security, environmental amenities and social connection derived from other data sources. Once the separate sub-indices were calculated, we used another multivariate technique – cluster analysis – to identify parts of the city that have similar profiles across the various sub-indices (Figure 7.2). In New York, cluster analysis resulted in the differentiation of four distinct types of neighbourhoods. At the two extremes, we found neighbourhoods characterised by concentrated advantage and concentrated disadvantage. In addition, a third cluster – Midtown advantage – had a profile similar to that of concentrated advantage. Finally, struggling and diverse neighbourhoods combined some strengths and some dimensions of disadvantage.

Figure 7.2: Social wellbeing clusters, New York City, 2013–15

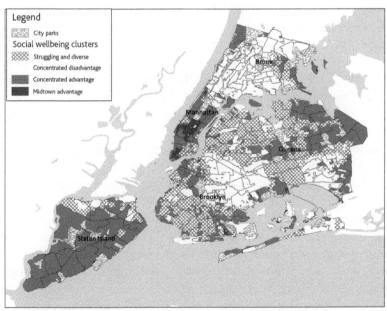

Source: Stern and Seifert (2017).

Research questions and findings

Our study of social wellbeing in New York City sought to determine the relationship between the concentration of cultural assets in a neighbourhood and more favourable outcomes on other dimensions of wellbeing, which we discuss in the following section. In the final section, we propose policy strategies that use culture to enhance social wellbeing and human flourishing in a way consistent with the capabilities approach.

Relationship between different dimensions of social wellbeing in New York City

Wolff and De-Shalit (2007) note the clustering of disadvantages at the level of the individual. Our data suggests that connections between different dimensions of wellbeing are present at the neighbourhood level as well.

As we would expect in a market-dominated society like the US, economic wellbeing remains the key element of social wellbeing in New York City. It indicates the high correlation of different dimensions of material wellbeing across the city's neighbourhoods including income, educational attainment, and labour force participation. Just as striking, however, is economic wellbeing's determinative role in a host of other dimensions of wellbeing. Economic wellbeing goes a long way towards explaining the status of different neighbourhoods on a range of other factors, including housing burden, school effectiveness, health, and access to healthcare.

Also notable is the relationship between economic wellbeing and social connection. The past two decades have seen significant scholarly attention devoted to the role of social capital as an alternative source of resources in a market economy. Our data suggests that while this can be true, in the first instance, social connection is highly dependent on economic wellbeing. Sections of New York that have high scores on economic wellbeing are precisely the same neighbourhoods that have high concentrations of institutional connections and cultural resources. Although correlation coefficients on the order of .4 to .5 do not suggest that economic privilege and social connections are identical, it appears that living in a prosperous neighbourhood often translates into living in a well-connected neighbourhood. The wealthy neighbourhoods of Manhattan and Brooklyn have the highest levels of institutional connection while neighbourhoods in the other boroughs do much worse.

Corrosive disadvantage and fertile functioning

Wolff and De-Shalit (2007) argue that in a good society the correlation of advantage and disadvantage would cease to exist. In the meantime, they are interested in ways in which two or more advantages or disadvantages cluster. When that clustering has a multiplier effect that makes life much worse, they characterise it as 'corrosive disadvantage'. When one capability mitigates the absence of another, they characterise it as a 'fertile functioning'.

We find evidence of both of these features in the New York neighbourhood data. Our health variables provide the clearest evidence of two dimensions of wellbeing interacting to make life much worse. Economic wellbeing is highly correlated with our health variables: health (overall health, chronic conditions, child welfare and birth outcomes) and access to health insurance. As a result, sections of the city that suffer from economic disadvantage often find this compounded by lack of access to healthcare, which increases the risks associated with morbidity and child welfare indicators.

In New York City, culture serves as a fertile functioning. The social connections associated with cultural engagement tend to mitigate the impact of low economic wellbeing on other dimensions of wellbeing. During our initial fieldwork in 'struggling and diverse' neighbourhoods, interviewees affirmed the value of the arts to community life. They pointed to the power of cultural and creative expression to foster dialogue and forge bonds among neighbours and across neighbourhoods, increase residents' access to public space, and give voice to individuals and groups who suffer social marginality or exclusion. If our interviewees' perceptions are correct, we would expect to find evidence that cultural engagement has this type of mitigating effect, particularly in the most disadvantaged neighbourhoods.

Relationship of cultural assets to other dimensions of social wellbeing

To identify the effect of cultural resources on three other dimensions of wellbeing –security, health and school effectiveness – we ran a set of multivariate statistical procedures that controlled for the effects of economic wellbeing, race, and ethnicity. Because of our particular concern with the mitigating effect of culture in low- and moderate-income neighbourhoods, we restricted our analysis to the 40 percent of block groups with the lowest per capita income.

The results of these analyses were consistent with our expectations. First, in no case did cultural assets completely reverse the effects of economic disadvantage. Those sections of the city with the greatest concentration of disadvantage continued to have the worst results for health, school effectiveness and security. Second, however, the presence of cultural assets significantly reduced the impact of economic disadvantage. When we compared low- and moderate-income neighbourhoods with few and with many cultural resources, those with higher concentrations of resources were more secure, healthier, and enjoyed better school outcomes. Certainly the positive influence of cultural engagement –its ability to foster social connectivity and give voice to members of groups who are often silenced – cannot overcome the corrosive impact of economic disadvantage. However, the data suggests that cultural opportunities can mitigate these effects and give residents of poor and working-class communities a chance to live lives they have reason to value.

Toward a capability-promoting cultural policy

How might these findings be translated into capability-promoting policy? Our two major findings are one, that despite the depth of New York City's cultural sector, many neighbourhoods lack significant concentrations of cultural resources, and, two, that another set of neighbourhoods house more cultural resources than we would expect based on their socioeconomic status and distance from Midtown.

Assure social equity: neighbourhoods with few cultural opportunities

Our Cultural Asset Index clearly identifies a set of neighbourhoods with few cultural resources. Typically, these neighbourhoods share three characteristics: high rates of poverty, predominantly African American and Hispanic, and relatively distant from Midtown Manhattan. We suspect that these neighbourhoods are home to a variety of embedded programmes and participatory groups, as well as resident artists and artisans of all disciplines and traditions, engaged in cultural and creative practice. Still, these areas of the city remain relatively disadvantaged with respect to formal cultural programmes, creative businesses and employed artists.

These neighbourhoods, which conform to Wolff and De-Shalit's idea of the most disadvantaged, present a clear case where government should serve as the guarantor of opportunities. Existing institutions have the capacity to address this problem. First, New York City's three library systems include over 2,000 branch libraries located in virtually every neighbourhood in the city. Second, the city's Department of Cultural Affairs funds approximately 1,000 non-profit cultural organisations across the city. Although the overwhelming share of this funding goes to organisations located in economically and culturally wealthy neighbourhoods, the programme could be modified to increase the eligibility of more organisations in highly disadvantaged neighbourhoods (Forman, 2015). Finally, current grantees have connections with thousands of organisations and venues in low-resource neighbourhoods that could be used to expand access in these sections of the city. Taken together, these strategies could provide substantial avenues for expanding cultural opportunities in low-resource neighbourhoods. Indeed, the City of New York in 2016 committed an additional 10 million dollars to funding cultural organisations with an eye towards addressing cross-neighbourhood inequalities.

Build from strength: civic clusters

Our second finding – neighbourhoods that 'exceed expectations' in terms of their cultural resources – provides a different policy opportunity. These neighbourhoods, identified using the 'corrected' Cultural Asset Index discussed earlier, tend to be economically challenged but ethnically diverse. They are the sections of the city that exemplify the mitigating effects of cultural engagement on other disadvantages.

Neighbourhoods with higher concentrations of cultural resources than their economic status would lead us to expect we call 'civic clusters' because they are typically the result of grassroots efforts to build community rather than the focus of market forces. We advocate investment in civic clusters, although they are culturally 'rich', based on the idea of 'building from strength'. This model is adapted from our colleagues at the Reinvestment Fund, a community development financial institution or 'non-profit bank'. The fund's goal is to revitalise urban neighbourhoods by reconnecting them to regional networks of employment, investment and social capital. To do so, they scan disinvested neighbourhoods looking for assets that show signs of vitality, then use these nodes of strength to push outward into areas that are less vital.

Building-from-strength strategies could certainly attract public investment, but they need not stop there. Private philanthropy, which plays a much larger role than government in US cultural funding, is increasingly interested in 'impact investment' to demonstrate the usefulness of its work. An evidence-based rationale for investment in 'struggling and diverse' neighbourhoods would appeal not just to cultural philanthropy but also to foundations that advocate comprehensive community development initiatives. Finally, the vogue for impact investment has now taken hold in the private sector. Neighborhoods that spawn grassroots cultural programmes and enterprises – civic clusters – could be attractive to private investors as well.

This chapter makes three conceptual contributions to capability-promoting policymaking. First, cultural engagement is a capability that contributes to human flourishing in and of itself and also enhances the potential of other capabilities. Second, capability-promoting policies should incorporate 'neighbourhood effects' and community ecology into their conceptual framework as well as their concrete policy analysis. Third, these policies must confront the potential tension between social justice and democracy and employ multiple strategies that can promote both.

Although good policy must be based on a normative commitment to social justice, policymaking remains a practical, not a philosophical, enterprise. Certainly, equity-based policy must address the disadvantages experienced by the worst-off, but it must consider as well the implications of democratic participation and consent. Rather than a surrender to expediency, we should view the multidimensional character of the capability approach – and the arts – as an opportunity to highlight the tension inherent in achieving an equitable and engaged democracy.

References

Alkire, S. and Deneulin, S. (2009) *An introduction to the human development and capability approach*, London: Earthscan.

Comim, F. (2014) 'Building capabilities: a new paradigm for human development,' in F. Comim and M.C. Nussbaum (eds) *Capabilities, gender, equality: Towards fundamental entitlements*, Cambridge: Cambridge University Press, pp 131-54.

Finkelpearl, T. (2013) *What we made: Conversations on art and social cooperation*, Durham, NC and London: Duke University Press.

Forman, A. (2015) *Creative New York*, New York, NY: Center for an Urban Future.

Katz, M.B. (2013) *The undeserving poor: America's enduring confrontation with poverty* (2nd edn), New York, NY: Oxford University Press.

Nussbaum, M.C. (2003) 'Capabilities as fundamental entitlements: Sen and social justice', *Feminist Economics*, vol 92, no 3, pp 33-59.

Nussbaum, M.C. (2011) *Creating capabilities: The human development approach*, Cambridge, MA: Belknap Press of Harvard University Press.

Sampson, R.J. (2012) *Great American city: Chicago and the enduring neighbourhood effect*, Chicago, IL: University of Chicago Press.

Sampson, R.J., Morenoff, J.D. and Gannon-Rowley, T. (2002) 'Assessing "neighbourhood effects": social processes and new directions in research', *Annual Review of Sociology*, vol 28, pp 443-478.

Sen, A.K. (1992) *Inequality re-examined*, Cambridge, MA: Harvard University Press.

Sen, A.K. (2004) 'How does culture matter?', in V. Rao and M. Walton (eds) *Culture and public action*, Stanford, CA: Stanford Social Sciences, pp 37-58.

Smith, N. (1996) *The new urban frontier: Gentrification and the revanchist city*, London and New York, NY: Routledge.

Stern, M. J. and Seifert, S.C. (2013a) 'Creative capabilities and community capacity', in H.-U. Otto and H. Zegler (eds) *Enhancing capabilities: The role of social institutions*, Obpladen: Verlag Barbara Budrich, pp 117-34.

Stern, M. J. and Seifert, S.C. (2013b) *'Natural' cultural districts: A three-city study*, Philadelphia, PA: University of Pennsylvania Social Impact of the Arts Project, available at: http://repository.upenn.edu/siap_cultural_districts.

Stern, M.J. and Seifert, S.C. (2017) *The social wellbeing of New York City's neighborhoods: The contribution of culture and the arts*, Philadelphia, PA: University of Pennsylvania Social Impact of the Arts Project, available at: http://repository.upenn.edu/siap_culture_nyc/

Stiglitz, J.E., Sen, A.K. and Fitoussi, J.-P. (2009) *Report by the Commission on the Measurement of Economic Performance and Social Progress*, Paris: Commission on the Measurement of Economic Performance and Social Progress.

United Nations (1966) 'International covenant on economic, social and cultural rights', GA Resolution 2200A (XXI), available at www.ohchr.org/EN/ProfessionalInterest/Pages/CESCR.aspx.

Wolff, J. and De-Shalit, A. (2007) *Disadvantage*, New York, NY: Oxford University Press.

EIGHT

The third sector and capability-promoting policies

Giuseppe Acconcia, Enrica Chiappero-Martinetti and Paolo R. Graziano

Introduction: research questions and methodology

By adopting the capability approach as a basic framework to analyse social phenomena, this chapter disentangles the role of third sector associations at the local level in increasing social innovative processes by enabling the integration of groups otherwise excluded from the labour market (for example, disadvantaged young people). This participatory research at the micro level focused on two urban areas Giambellino in Milan and Scampia in Naples where the most disadvantaged among the young population are concentrated. In these areas, the unemployed rates are higher than elsewhere in Italy.

In this chapter, we argue that social innovation can be produced by a capability-promoting approach of intermediate actors, bringing about an enhanced capacity of disadvantaged persons to define their aspirations or to be able to aspire. The aim of our research is to show how limited the third sector actors' participation has been both at the meso and micro levels in recent years with respect to policies aimed at contrasting youth unemployment. We try to verify whether this derives from low levels of social innovation on the part of third sector associations or can be attributed to other factors, such as lack of administrative capacity, poor policy design, socioeconomic conditions, youth disengagement and so on. More specifically, we worked on the following dimensions involved in the capability approach: inequality and disadvantages, participation and aspirations.

Inequality and disadvantage represent two key issues in the capability accounting of individual wellbeing and both are meant as intrinsically multidimensional concepts. The capability approach acknowledges that people's available opportunities are affected by both initial endowments and subsequent influential contingencies. Indeed, given one's resources, diverse personal, socioeconomic and environmental conditions can affect differently the extent and type of real opportunities available to people. These sources of variation, in terms of available resources, individual characteristics and heterogeneity of socioeconomic and geographical contexts, play a major role in generating inequality in capabilities as well as in functionings space and should be taken into account when analysing and designing public policy (see Spreafico et al, 2016).

A better understanding of the plurality of both personal and 'environmental' circumstances and how they interrelate can be particularly helpful for detecting potential sources of disadvantage that prevent individuals from fulfilling their own needs and aspirations. An interesting plural definition of disadvantage, directly formulated in terms of functionings and capabilities, has been suggested by Wolff and De-Shalit (2007). They define disadvantage as 'lack of genuine opportunity for secure functionings' (p 182) and consider risk and insecurity as crucial components of disadvantage. They also suggest identifying disadvantages that accumulate over time – what the authors call 'corrosive disadvantages' – and investigating the causal relations across disadvantages in order to understand why and how they take form and persist. In this regard, social policy should be oriented towards de-clustering disadvantages, securing fertile functionings and eliminating corrosive disadvantages.

From a capability perspective, active participation in society is, per se, an important dimension of human life and for empowering people. This is related to the notion of agency as participation refers to the process to act as an agent, to play a role in the society and have voice in the public sphere, and to take part in political life and the decision-making processes (see, for example, Deneulin and Shahani, 2009). More specifically, it has been defined as 'capability for voice', the capability people have 'to express wishes, expectations and concerns in collective decision-making processes and make them count' (Bonvin, 2012, p 15). In this regard, agency and participation are considered of particular relevance in childhood for enhancing the autonomy and agency freedom of young people and enabling them to fully develop their own potential.[1]

Finally, the capability approach is equally interested in people's attitudes, intentions and aspirations. The capacity to aspire, to plan and to construct one's own future is of particular relevance for young people, and family, the school system and the institutional setting play a major role in shaping these aspirations as well as in helping to make them achievable. However, disadvantaged groups may limit their aspirations to a predefined or socially imposed set of (constrained) opportunities or they may not be aware of their full potential or may lack the capacity to imagine their own future.

Recently, participation has also been described as a process of knowledge construction and production, a practice of reflection that requires the direct and active engagement of participants in research investigation. According to Vandekinderen et al (2016), participation should provide an empirical foundation to inform and extend the informational basis of the judgments of justice (Sen, 1990) by a bottom-up perspective and by including the voice and aspirations of young people, particularly in qualitative research. This involves a democratic research process whereby researchers, policymakers and potential beneficiaries of public policy should take part in knowledge production.[2]

Taking into account these key dimensions of analysis, we conducted a qualitative empirical research based on six semi-directive interviews and three focus groups (the first one with 10 participants, the second and the third one with five participants each) within the network of a very active non-governmental organisation (NGO), the *Libera* network (officially *Libera. Associations, names and numbers against mafias*), a community empowerment association engaged in managing confiscated lands owned by mafias. *Libera* is deeply engaged in promoting a culture of legality and anti-corruption. In the Milan case study in particular, one of the *Libera* organisations (*Comunità del Giambellino*, a Milanese neighbourhood organisation) has been a central point of reference for promoting the rights of disadvantaged young people in the neighbourhood, enhancing their relationship with their peers and advocating paths of social inclusion. The organisation has helped many young people to find a job in the formal or in the informal sector and has supported yet others in an effort to enhance their capability to aspire. Together with the focus group, a number of workshops aimed at local unemployed young people have been organised with local trade unions and employment support providers through national and European initiatives (the Jobs Act and Youth Guarantee, respectively). In Naples, *GRIDAS*,[3] together with *Presidio Scampia* and the Scampia movement for unemployed people, is focusing on the needs of workless young people in the district of Scampia, another particularly disadvantaged neighbourhood. All of the interviews and focus groups have been numbered, and the participants in the focus groups are considered to be interviewees (see the Appendix to this chapter).

The methodology adopted has two components: semi-directive interviews and focus groups.

Semi-directive interviews

The six interviewees (two in Milan and four in Naples) are *Libera* coordinators and social assistance professionals engaged in grassroots associations focused on supporting disadvantaged youth in deprived areas. Analysis of the data, collected through the interviews, provided a comprehensive understanding of the lack of youth involvement in public policies definition and development. The interviews were problem-centered and aimed to define the subjects and objects of intervention, evaluate the effectiveness of the activities provided by the associations, and identify the specific needs and demands of unemployed youth at the local level, their level of participation, the structural and social factors influencing policies and young people's capability to aspire in the context of their social background.

Focus groups

For this research we conducted three focus groups targeting young people. As a first step, we involved *Libera* representatives both in Lombardy and Campania. In order to set up the focus groups, we began by contacting and interviewing coordinators of projects involving disadvantaged youth in Milan and Naples. They provided a general framework of the NGO targets and references to specific programmes concerning unemployed young men, women and immigrants in the selected areas of Giambellino (Milan) and Scampia (Naples). These professionals facilitated the contacts with the grassroots associations that we decided to involve in a later stage.

In order to create the focus groups, we then carried out exploratory interviews with social assistance professionals working in two neighborhoods. Representatives of the municipalities participated at preliminary meetings with local associations (for example, *Scampia*) but did not join in with the later participatory research.

The focus groups were organised with the specific aim of understanding levels of inclusion and participation in European programmes at the local level. While conducting the focus groups with the young people, we tried to obtain answers to the following questions. To what extent, especially at the local level, is the effectiveness of third sector associations in activating social innovative processes particularly relevant? To what extent and in what ways do social policies and practices reflect the perspectives of disadvantaged young people in an effective manner? We aimed to take into account respondents' lived experiences and specific backgrounds, in particular the young people's narratives, aspirations, and notions of participation with reference to the case studies in Milan (Giambellino) and Naples (Scampia).

The chapter now presents the empirical results following the three crucial dimensions of the capability approach – inequality and disadvantage; participation; and aspirations – and ends with a conclusion.

Research findings

Inequality and disadvantage

Because of their low level of education and their familial background, interviewees in the Milan focus group experienced a number of discriminatory practices (for example, unpaid work, absence of legal employment contracts, barriers to labour market entry) in their attempt to find a job and they considered themselves to be excluded from the labour market. One participant[4] finished his education at a vocational training school, while others completed at least their lower secondary schooling in Italy[5] or in their countries of origins before moving to Italy.[6] Some respondents[7] highlighted a strong mismatch between school and the labour market and they generally judged their educational path as not useful in finding a job. Three respondents[8] considered the internship provided by their secondary schools as important for their professional life.

The majority of these young people[9] had never worked or had had very precarious jobs. Many of them[10] would accept any kind of job or badly paid, precarious work in order to have some economic independence from their families. One interviewee,[11] an Egyptian national (Christian Copt), had completed a short-term traineeship; another[12] had had an apprenticeship, while others (a Romanian national with German citizenship, an Egyptian national and an Italian national, second-generation Eritrean) [13] were long-term unemployed. Another one had a 'job on call' contract,[14] while two others, a Moldova national and an Egyptian national (Christian Copt), had recently obtained long-term employment.[15]

All these interviewees had grown up in lower-income families. Their parents are all unemployed or on precarious contracts and have low levels of education. In two cases,[16] fathers were employed at the time of the research. In four other cases,[17] the parents were unemployed, even if they had completed their lower secondary schooling.

Many of the Milan interviewees agreed[18] that it was not problematic for foreigners to find a job per se, but that foreign citizenship was detrimental to finding a good job. For some of them, this was the major reason why their peers were forced to leave the neighbourhood: "If they have a job, foreigners are generally paid less than the Italians. If they are illegal immigrants, they often cannot get a job or a contract."

Because of their low level of education, familial background and the fact that they lived in Scampia,[19] interviewees in the Naples focus group experienced a number of discriminatory practices (for example, unpaid work, barriers to labour market entry, lack of high-level job opportunities) in looking for a job and were often excluded from the labour market. Three interviewees[20] finished their vocational training, two completed their primary schooling.[21] Another participant[22] stated that to be involved in a traineeship programme organised by her school she would have had to pay monthly fees that she could not afford.

The majority of the young women in the first Naples focus group[23] had never worked. One of them[24] had had a short-term contract in the previous six months, while another[25] was involved in a training course financed by the Campania Region; one had taken part in a first-stage interview with the local employment support provider in order to accede to the Youth Guarantee programme but she had not been further contacted when we met her.

The five women had grown up in lower-income families. Their parents were all long-term unemployed or on precarious contracts: they had been badly affected by the economic crisis, even after accounting for the fact that disadvantage is perceived as an enduring condition. The brothers and sisters of one participant[26] did not attend secondary or vocational schools, only one of them was employed at the moment of the research. However, the brother and sister of another interviewee[27] had finished their secondary schooling and were working for public institutions or private companies; this participant's father had spent long periods in prison. The father of another woman was a former detainee involved in a regional training programme and working as a fruit seller, and her mother was unemployed.

All these women agreed[28] that their gender was permanently detrimental to their chances of finding a job. For some of them this was the major reason why their peers were forced to leave the neighbourhood: "The only reasonable perspective for a young woman in this area is to be a housewife. This is due to a rooted discrimination towards women's integration in the labour market."

The young unemployed men involved in the activities of *GRIDAS*[29] who took part in the second focus group of the Naples case study are between 23 and 29 years old. Three of them are former detainees. For their low levels of education and their familial background they experienced a number of discriminatory practices when looking for a job and were often excluded from the labour market. Two[30] of them had finished their vocational training, while the others[31] had only completed compulsory schooling (up to 14 years old).

These men were all long-term unemployed. One of them was working on the black market, dealing smuggled cigarettes; another was involved in a regional training programme after a period of detention. Stefano and Raffaele were long-term unemployed with previous experiences of traineeships.

They all grew up in lower-income families and still live in their family home. Many of them[32] would have accepted any kind of job or badly paid precarious work in order to have some economic independence from their families. Two of them[33] had long-term unemployed fathers, brothers and sisters with precarious jobs. The parents of two others[34] had low educational levels and precarious work. Another one[35] was constantly supported by his family who motivated him to keep looking for a job.

They all appeared to be deeply affected by their familial background and their periods of detention. Moreover, they considered it easier to approach criminals and smugglers for their needs. Their specific life experiences meant that they faced additional barriers to finding a decent job. They all highlighted a general mismatch between their educational qualifications and their opportunities for entry in the labour market. However, while they generally did not perceive their low educational level to be the direct reason for their disadvantage, they did consider their familial background as an important factor in the disadvantage they experienced. As one of them stated: "I did not find any alternative to social exclusion. Especially the school did not help me to approach the labour market; neither did my peers nor family."

Participation

The young unemployed Italians and immigrants involved in the activities of *CD Giambellino*, who took part in the Milan focus group, never participated in policymaking processes, and appeared not to be aware of the possibilities offered by the European Youth Guarantee programme. They considered public policies tackling unemployment to be ineffective, and did not believe that employment support providers could help them access the labour market or find a better job. In the words of one of focus group participant: "We did not consider it useful to go to the local employment support provider. The Youth Guarantee [programme] is not effective: we do not have access to a proper job after the first job interviews."

It appeared that some of them had never approached a trade union or even been aware of functions of trade unions. Only one subscribed to FIOM–CGIL (a sectorial trade union). The father of another participant referred to him a local trade union office when he lost his job, but he found no support; another added that she would be unable to subscribe to a trade union because she had no employment history.

These interviewees were involved in the activities of *CD Giambellino* because their families had pushed them to participate in the organisation. Many of them had had some support from the organisation when they had problems at school or had received legal advice. Two of them[36] had been participating in *CD Giambellino* activities for more than 10 years. One interview[37] had begun to get involved in the association when he moved with his family to Italy; another one[38] was being helped by the association to get work in a cooperative; another[39] said that knew about the association because it was located in the centre of the city; and two others[40] often got involved in the charitable activities of the churches near their homes.

Some of them were aware of the resilience of the local black market even during the current economic crisis. For instance, one interviewee[41] said that some of his relatives were forced to pay bribes to local mafia organisations. Another one[42] added that he had been approached many times by local criminals with job offers.

The young unemployed women[43] involved in the activities of *Presidio Scampia*, who took part in the first focus group of the Naples case study, had never participated in policymaking processes. They deemed the Youth Guarantee programme ineffective, along with other public initiatives aimed at tackling unemployment, and did not believe that employment support providers could help them access the labour market or find a better job.

All these women lived with their parents and referred to their families as their major provider of economic assistance. They claimed that the only way of getting a job was through a recommendation from a public institution. This was also the fastest way of accessing subsidies.

These women were involved in the activities of *Presidio Scampia* as a result of taking part in summer camps on land confiscated from mafias. Nevertheless, they had some experience of local black markets, especially since the economic crisis had worsened. Two of them had been approached several times by local drug sellers offering them a job. One of them had been asked to work with local criminals. They all said that if they did not want to become involved in the black market they knew how to avoid it.

The young unemployed men in the focus groups of the Naples case study had never participated in policymaking processes; they appeared highly demotivated, and some of them had given up looking for a job or attending training courses. They did not consider that Youth Guarantee would help them get a job, and they deemed existing public policies aimed at tackling unemployment ineffective. They did not believe that employment support providers offered opportunities to enter the labour market or to find a better job.

Some of these interviewees[44] did not trust trade unions. However, they all had participated in demonstrations on labour rights in the previous six months. One[45] had participated in the movement against the construction of the Chiaiano incinerator. Another had been involved in flash mobs and empty building occupations demanding labour rights, stating that trade unions do not help in the fight for workers' rights.

All these interviewees stated that the economic crisis and anti-corruption policies strengthened the black market rather than reducing it. They added that they regularly received illegal job offers or invitations to take part in the local drug-smuggling activities.

Aspirations

The young unemployed Italians and immigrants involved in the activities of *CD Giambellino*, who took part in the Milan focus group, described a diverse range of aspirations that were not achievable in their current circumstances. They would not ask for economic support from their relatives who often could not help them in any case because they were themselves long-term unemployed. A lack of money for their daily needs seemed to be their first source of concern:

"I avoid to buy what I do not need because I do not want to ask for support."[46]

They expressed a need for more comprehensive and adequate involvement in policymaking processes. They would like to be heard in order to define better public policies aimed at tackling youth exclusion. They highlighted the need for more effective and transparent eligibility criteria for passive social assistance during periods of unemployment: *"We would like more focused and specific youth policies."*[47]

The young unemployed women involved in the activities of *Presidio Scampia*, who took part in the first focus group of the Naples case study, also described a diverse range of aspirations that were not achievable in their current circumstances. They expressed a desire to find a job related to what they had studied. They wanted better job conditions and passive social assistance in periods of unemployment. They aspired to a more transparent and less corrupt labour market. They believed this could happen only with bottom–up change: "I would like to aspire to have a job related to my studies. I would like that my brothers finish their secondary school. Only this can make my future deserving and free."[48] They identified the specific conditions of their neighborhood as detrimental to achieving their aspirations.

The young unemployed men involved in the activities of *GRIDAS*, who took part in the second focus group of the Naples case study, described a diverse range of aspirations that were not achievable in their current circumstances. They all aspired to better jobs. However, they generally appeared very disillusioned and negative about their future. In some cases, they appeared depressed and socially excluded: "I would like to clean up my neighbourhood. This would be a good job opportunity for me."[49]

Conclusion

Our findings illustrated clearly show that disadvantages and inequalities in different spaces usually cumulate and enforce each other. Both contexts (Scampia and Giambellino) can be classified as deprived areas although located in regions (Campania and Lombardy, respectively) and cities (Naples and Milan) with remarkable differences in terms of socioeconomic development.[50] Nonetheless, in both cases, young people with relatively poor family backgrounds face similar trajectories and present a common story of corrosive disadvantages in education and job market opportunities. More specifically, the young people were deeply affected by the inequalities faced by their families, often brought about by low levels of educational attainment and long–term unemployment. The inequalities seem to have increased in the past few years in parallel with the global economic crisis.

Furthermore, the our study fully reflects the twofold definition of participation illustrated in the Introduction, by adopting a participatory method and by hearing the voice of youth and of third sector associations that play an active role in community empowerment programmes. Interviews and focus groups show us that although disadvantaged young people are actively involved in the activities of civil society organisations, and thereby have opportunities to participate socially at the local level, they really have no or little voice in decision-making processes at a higher (regional or municipality) level. This, of course, tells us that a wider remit should be granted to civil society organisations and that more should be done to include disadvantaged young people in the policy implementation of European, national and local programmes. The voice of disadvantaged young people has not been heard by policymakers and generally they do not benefit from existing passive and active policies aimed at tackling unemployment. However, they appeared highly motivated in their involvement in the activities of civil society organisations and had been involved in frequent meetings and initiatives. For these young people, this appeared the only available transformative means of participation or the only way of effecting change in their neighbourhood. What was particularly striking was that several focus group participants did not know about the opportunities available through these organisations. A lack of information, therefore, can also be considered a reason for limited participation and involvement on the part of disadvantaged young people.

The social assistance professionals interviewed were deeply dedicated to enhancing the political awareness of the unemployed young people who took part in association activities, encouraging them to enhance their opportunities to enter the local labour market or make their voice heard by local institutions, and even organising protests and public debates. Many of the young people who took part in our focus group appeared very interested in increasing their knowledge of existing public policies to tackle unemployment and how to access such assistance. However, they seemed completely UNmotivated to pursue their targets.

With regard to aspirations, the respondents in our research seemed to have a capacity to aspire, albeit to different extents, despite their own rather unfavorable personal and contextual circumstances. However, they did not appear to be very confident about the life opportunities available to them in the near future. There is therefore a need for local empowerment schemes that help disadvantaged young people to better channel their aspirations and ensure they are taken into account by local and national decision makers.

The young people involved in this research experienced a number of social inequalities. They appeared to be excluded from higher education, often because of their poor familial background. However, even if they had completed secondary schooling, they were often unable to find a job because the public education system does not facilitate entry into the labour market easily. Most participants had at least one or more family member who had been long-term unemployed, and their peers (sisters, brothers, cousins) were either all unemployed or working in precarious jobs. They all experienced housing-related discrimination, often living in run-down buildings or been forced to live with their families.

They all seemed very negative about their future and their chances of finding a good job, and for this reason they were ready to accept precarious or occasional unpaid work just to get closer to the labour market. On most days, these young people had job offers from drug smugglers or black marketeers. Many of them refuse to participate in the black market even if, especially since the economic crisis, this seems to be the only way of finding a job in their area.

A special source of social inequality is related to the gender discrimination experienced by young women, who, especially in the southern regions, often cannot find a job and are long-term unemployed. Young immigrants experience a range of discriminatory practices, and are usually exploited at work, do not have legal contracts and live in poor or bad housing. Sometimes more than one family is forced to live in the same house. These young immigrants are easily recruited by criminals and smugglers, and are often arrested for petty crimes. The same kinds of discrimination are experienced by former detainees who often are forced to accept unpaid jobs or inadequate labour conditions because of their history.

The capability of these young people to aspire is deeply affected by inequalities they experience. They appeared unwilling to bring these issues to the attention of national and local stakeholders. They often appeared depressed and sometimes their only way to survive was to rely on their family. In some cases, they trusted social assistance professionals with whom they had a long-term connection. This pushed them to take part in the activities of associations like *Libera* that helped them to aspire to a more transparent labour market, fight against corruption and local mafias, take part in social movements protesting about rising unemployment rates, or subscribe to local trade unions.

Generally, the voices and perspectives of these young people have not been heard by policymakers and they have not benefited from existing passive and active policies concerning unemployment. However, they appear to be highly motivated to participate in local association activities and often took part in such initiatives.

Furthermore, it appears that young people's aspirations are currently not addressed by the relevant stakeholders. The young people aspired to better work opportunities, but generally seemed disillusioned and negative about their future. They would like bottom-up change, but this can happen if their narratives are heard and they are empowered to improve their education and work experiences. If they are denied these opportunities, they will continue passively to accept top-down policies without expressing their dissent.

It is also clear that there is insufficient involvement of youth groups in union, third sector and business association contributions to policymaking processes aimed at youth exclusion at the local level. Even at regional official Youth Guarantee workshops, involving relevant local stakeholders, union officials, and representatives from public administrations and third sector organisations, ways of tackling youth exclusion in the labour market are only discussed at senior representative level, and young people are not given the opportunity to have their voices heard. In the Scampia case study, it seems that some of the young people had tried to make such an approach, or had enlisted the help of a relative with connections with local trade unions, but without success. The young people in Scampia and Giambellino had barely heard about the available policies to tackle unemployment. Even if they had had an opportunity to be interviewed for a place on the Youth Guarantee programme by the local employment support provider, they had not been contacted subsequently to begin a traineeship.

At the micro level, there also seemed to be a significant gap between the needs of the young people and existing public policies, and this issue seems not to have been addressed. Disadvantaged young people often need the help of mediators in order to express their needs: according to our interviews, such gatekeeping procedures do not exist within the trade unions or political parties. For this reason, young people have not opportunities to express their dissent and usually lower their expectations of being better placed in the labour market or move to more advantaged areas.

Finally, this chapter has highlighted a series of limitations of existing public policies (in terms of definition, development and, in particular, implementation). It has also identified a lack of targeted policies and sufficient financial resources to tackle youth unemployment. Young unemployed people, especially women, appear not to be sufficiently involved in policymaking. All these limitations are brought about by more complex factors, among them a general lack of job opportunities, the dominance of local mafias, poor integration of young immigrants into the legal labour market, diminished economic resources for the families of disadvantaged young people, a lack of work-oriented courses within the education system, the inadequacy of employment support services networks, a lack of funding for social assistance policies, and a mistrust of young former detainees. The combination of these features make disadvantaged young people more vulnerable than other sections of the society. This makes their voice less likely to be heard by relevant stakeholders, which in turn increases their social exclusion and in some cases depression. Much more should be done to empower these young people, both in terms of participation and aspirations.

Notes

[1] On this subject, see the edited collections by Hart et al (2014) and Otto (2015).

[2] For a review of some recent critiques to participatory methods, see Vandekinderen et al (2016).

[3] Gruppo risveglio dal sonno: 'Awakening group'. GRIDAS (part of the Libera network) is a Scampia-based group of unemployed people. Founded in 2005, it addresses the needs of unemployed people within the district.

[4] Interview 3.

[5] Interviews 4, 5, 9, 10 and 11.

[6] Interviews 6, 7, 8, 12.

[7] Interviews 3 and 9.

[8] Interviews 3, 5 and 6.

[9] Interviews 19, 21 and 23.

[10] Interviews 3, 9 and 10.

[11] Interviews 3, 9 and 10.

[12] Interview 4.

[13] Interviews 6, 7 and 9.

[14] Precarious contract.

[15] Interviews 10 and 12.

[16] Interviews 4 and 5.

[17] Interview 5, 6, 9 and 10.

[18] Interviews 3 to 12.

[19] Interview 19.

[20] Interviews 19 to 21.

[21] Interviews 22 and 23.

[22] Interview 20.

[23] Interviews 19, 21 and 23.

[24] Interview 20.

[25] Interview 21.

[26] Interview 20.

[27] Interview 21.

[28] Interviews 19 to 23.

[29] Interviews 17, 18, 24, 25 and 26.

[30] Interviews 17 and 24.

[31] Interviews 18, 25 and 26.

[32] Interviews 24, 25 and 26.

[33] Interviews 25 and 26.

[34] Interviews 17 and 18.

[35] Interview 24.

[36] Interviews 7 and 8.

[37] Interview 3.

[38] Interview 12.

[39] Interview 9.

[40] Interviews 5 and 10.

[41] Interview 5.
[42] Interview 6.
[43] Interviews 19 to 23.
[44] Interviews 9, 10 and 12.
[45] Interview 17.
[46] Interview 5.
[47] Interview 12.
[48] Interview 20.
[49] Interview 26.
[50] On regional differences in youth education, unemployment and participation in political and social life see Spreafico et al (2016) and Goffette et al (forthcoming).

Appendix: interview list

1. *Libera* coordinator, stakeholder Milan
2. Social assistance professional, stakeholder Milan
3. Male, 18 years, unemployed, Egyptian Copt national (focus group 1, Milan)
4. Male, 21 years, apprenticeship contract (focus group 1, Milan)
5. Male, 20 years, unemployed (focus group 1, Milan)
6. Male, 23 years, unemployed, Romanian national (focus group 1, Milan)
7. Male, 22 years, unemployed, Egyptian national (focus group 1, Milan)
8. Male, 20 years, precarious worker, Moldovan national (focus group 1, Milan)
9. Female, 20 years, unemployed, Eritrean origin (focus group 1, Milan)
10. Male, 21 years, unemployed (focus group 1, Milan)
11. Female, 21 years, precarious worker, Egyptian Copt national (focus group 1, Milan)
12. Male, 20 years, unemployed, Tunisian national (focus group 1, Milan)
13. *Libera* coordinator, stakeholder Naples
14. Social assistance professional, stakeholder Naples
15. Representative of *Presidio Scampia*, stakeholder Naples
16. Representative of Scampia movement for unemployed people, *GRIDAS*, stakeholder Naples
17. Male, 26 years, unemployed (focus group 2, Naples)
18. Male, 22 years, unemployed (focus group 2, Naples)
19. Female, 22 years, unemployed (focus group 2, Naples)
20. Female, 19 years, precarious worker (focus group 2, Naples)
21. Female, 21 years, unemployed (focus group 2, Naples)
22. Male, 29 years, former detainee, unemployed (focus group 3, Naples)

23. Male, 21 years, unemployed (focus group 3, Naples)
24. Male, 27 years, unemployed (focus group 3, Naples)
25. Male, 26 years, unemployed (focus group 3, Naples)
26. Male, 27 years, precarious worker (focus group 3, Naples)

References

Bonvin, J.M. (2012) 'Individual working lives and collective action. An introduction to capability for work and capability for voice', *Transfer: European Review of Labour and Research*, vol 18, no 1, pp 9–18.

Deneulin, S. and Shahani, L. (2009) *An introduction to the human development and capability approach. Freedom and agency*, London: Earthscan.

Goffette C., Vero J., Graham, H., Raeside, R., Chiappero-Martinetti, E., Spreafico, A. and Peruzzi, A. (forthcoming) 'Youth inequality across Europe. Addressing the participation of young people in employment, education and lived experiences' (submitted for a collected volume edited by H.U. Otto).

Hart, C., Biggeri, M. and Babic, B. (eds) (2014) *Agency and participation in childhood and youth: International applications of the capability approach in schools and beyond*, London: Bloomsbury.

Otto H.U. (ed) (2015) *Facing trajectories from school to work. Towards a capability friendly youth policy in Europe*, Dordrecht: Springer.

Sen A. (1990) 'Justice: means versus freedom', *Philosophy and Public Affairs*, vol 19, no 2, pp 111–21.

Spreafico, A., Peruzzi, A. and Chiappero-Martinetti, E. (2016) 'Corrosive disadvantages and intersectionality: empirical evidence on multidimensional inequality amongst young people in Europe', in H.U. Otto, S. Pantazis, H. Ziegler and A. Pots (eds) *Human development in times of crisis: Renegotiating social justice*, London: Palgrave McMillan.

Vandekinderen, C., Roets, G., Van Keer, H. and Roose, R. (2016) 'Social work research as a practice of transparency', *European Journal of Social Work*, vol 19, no 6, pp 1021–34.

Wolff, J. and De-Shalit, A. (2007) *Disadvantage*, Oxford: Oxford University Press.

NINE

Informal workers and human development in South Africa

Ina Conradie

In recent years, scholars and human rights agencies have been emphasising the importance of seeing civil and political rights and economic and social rights as closely related and in fact integrated (Carpenter, 2009; UN, 2011[1]). In South Africa, it is clear that the achievement of political rights has not been sufficient to bring about either comprehensive human development or redress in terms of social and economic inequality.

The anti-apartheid revolutionary and former South African president Nelson Mandela had the following to say on an integrated view of different human rights:

> Today, when we talk of human rights we understand that this discussion should not be limited to the traditional civil and political rights. The international world has gradually come to realise the critical importance of social and economic rights in building true democracies which meet all the basic needs of all people.... In this and in other ways, our Constitution demonstrates the growing globalisation of the struggle for human rights. (Cited in Fukuda-Parr et al, 2015, p 1)

South Africa is therefore a useful context for a case study on how the capability approach could be used to contribute to the complex goal of integrated rights. Why the capability approach? Because it focuses on arguably the most important variable in policy development: the creation of real opportunities for universal wellbeing, with options for individual choices.

This chapter initiates the discussion by asking how the human development approach and the capability approach can be used to inform policy formulation. This is followed by a short background study of poverty and problems in current South Africa. Poverty is connected to the fact that high numbers of South Africans are unemployed, and find themselves in a poverty trap. They are particularly subject to social and economic insecurity, and one way of addressing this might be the provision of innovative forms of social security for informal workers. This chapter therefore reviews such a proposal, based on a transformative model of social protection (Devereux and Sabates-Wheeler, 2004) and on the human development approach and the capability approach, and critically discusses its implications.[2]

The human development approach, the capability approach[3] and social policy formulation

This section explores the nature of the two approaches and the ways in which they can be used for policy formulation. The **human development approach**, initiated by Mahbub ul Haq, can be seen as an approach that aims to provide a policy framework for development based on human development dimensions and indicators. Money, economic growth and the role of 'the market' are seen as crucially important, but as instruments for universal human development, not as ends to enrich a selected group. The redistributive role of governments is therefore seen as a crucial element in development, and social policies as a key instrument for bringing about development and equity. Amartya Sen was one of the scholars who assisted in this formulation, and he was instrumental in shaping the approach, with others, by means of the tools and techniques of the capability approach. Fukuda-Parr (2005, p 303) describes the human development approach as 'the operationalization of Sen's ideas on capabilities'.

Richard Jolly (2003, p 90) sees the human development approach as an alternative and robust paradigm, which he contrasts to the neoliberal paradigm. Fukuda-Parr (2005, pp 312-14) builds on this distinction and contrasts the Washington Consensus with the 'New York Consensus',[4] based on the fact that many United Nations agreements reflect the following human development principles:

- prioritisation of social goals such as health and education;
- economic growth to generate resources for human development;
- political and social reform aimed at greater democracy, human rights, participation and autonomy;
- equity with regard to marginalised groups and women;
- global policy and institutional reform aimed at equal access of poorer countries to institutional resources and power structures.

Haq saw the human development initiative as a radical and new point of departure, and also called human development a new paradigm (Haq, 2003, p17). The human development approach can therefore be presented as an ideological counter-force to dominant neoliberal market ideology, which produces social and economic policy formulation based on largely monetary considerations, including that of austerity in challenging times.

The **capability approach** is described by Sen (2009, p16) as a discipline that focuses on the evaluation of achievements (functionings) and freedoms (capabilities) to do the things a person has reason to value. Alkire and Deneulin (2009a, p 4) identify the approach as being normative, positive and predictive, and see functionings, capabilities and agency as the key terms of the approach (2009b, p 31). Capability scholars furthermore agree that one of the main functions of the approach is to serve as a conceptual framework for policy formulation (Stewart, 2005; Alkire, 2008, pp 28-34; Deneulin and Shahani, 2009; Robeyns, 2011a; Clark, 2012).

Robeyns (2011a) suggests that it might also be useful to take a step back and describe the capability approach more generally in terms of its two normative claims, namely:

> … first, the claim that the freedom to achieve well-being is of primary moral importance, and second, that freedom to achieve well-being is to be understood in terms of people's capabilities, that is, their real opportunities to do and be what they have reason to value.

This would arguably offer a formulation that captures both Sen and Nussbaum's approaches, but could additionally allow for a much broader application of the capability approach than that formulated by the two founding scholars, such as:

> … social criticism, ethnographic studies, policy design in the area of family policies in welfare states, or even – potentially – as part of the design of a revolutionary blueprint of a post-capitalist economic system…. To my mind, the capability approach should be defined in more general and abstract terms, as a theory with a scope potentially as wide reaching as utilitiarianism. Philosophers should consider thinking of the capability approach as 'capabilitarianism'. (Robeyns, 2011a)

In these terms, 'capabilitarianism' would then be a broad philosophical paradigm that could potentially challenge utilitarianism, based on the normative claim of universal wellbeing, to be understood in terms of capabilities.

The impact of the human development approach, with the capability approach as its conceptual component, has especially become clear in recent years. German poverty and wealth reports are using the approach as a framework for national development policies (Arndt and Volkert, 2011), with the Equality and Human Rights Commission in Britain doing so too (Alkire et al, 2009). Burd-Sharps and colleagues (2008) have undertaken the human development 'measure of America' for the American Human Development Report 2008/09, Chiappero-Martinetti and Moroni (2007) have carried out a human development assessment of poverty in Italy, and China has a development approach that translates to the human development approach (Alkire and Deneulin, 2009a, p 7).[5]

Martha Nussbaum's version of the approach, with a set of 10 key dimensions (Nussbaum, 2011), has as its main purpose the establishment of a threshold of human rights for all nations, preferably at the level of the constitution. This focus is therefore a useful one in considering how human rights can be ensured, and which elements should be prioritised. Anand and colleagues (2005) have moreover made an attempt to devise a set of indicators for the 10 dimensions on Nussbaum's list, which arguably makes the use of the list more accessible.

I conclude this section by suggesting a policy toolbox for use within the human development and capability approaches (see Table 9.1). The purpose of the table is to see the different policy strategies as elements of a holistic and integrated approach to human development, as argued earlier. At the institutional level, the tool presupposes a constitution that spells out the entitlements that all citizens of a country should enjoy. This should be followed by human development legislation that gradually builds a set of policies that provide the opportunities for all citizens to realise such entitlements. Lastly, the institutional level has an obligation to provide good and competent governance based on the principles of human development. From the perspective of an individual or a group, these policies should provide capability sets that provide real (and therefore realisable) opportunities to all. The extent to which people avail themselves, or are able to avail themselves, of such capabilities should be evaluated in the assessment of functionings. This should critically lead to an assessment and analysis of capability constraints, which can lead to new policy formulations or new governance practices. To encourage such policies, or to act if they fail, civil society should play a role in the creation of social movements and in the social organisation of civil society, a process that should be constitutionally guaranteed. Civil society organisations and movements should moreover engage in advocacy on behalf of disadvantaged groups.

Table 9.1: The creation of capabilities based on integrated political, social and economic rights

Institutional level	Individual and group/local level
Constitutional human rights: political, economic and social	Individual and collective capabilities or opportunities*
Human development legislation	Assessment of individual and collective functionings
Policies to provide institutional capabilities	Analysis of capability constraints
Human development governance	Social movements in civil society to address capability constraints; advocacy

Note: * See Stewart (2005) and Deneulin and McGregor (2010) for the need to take into account both individual and collective capabilities.

In applying the capability approach to policy formulation, one should concentrate specifically on those aspects of the approach that would enhance social policies. Capability-friendly policies should emphasise the following:

- the provision of a wide range of opportunities for wellbeing, and human development processes to facilitate these (Sen, 2005);
- spaces for human development advocacy (Spence and Deneulin, 2009, p 295);
- capabilities that form real opportunities, in other words realistic opportunities;
- spaces for the exercise of choice, of individuals as well as of groups;
- Spaces for the exercise of agency;
- cognisance of human diversity;
- cognisance of conversion factors that affect the conversion of resources into functionings.

In addition to the above, a useful conceptual tool to keep in mind is that of Richardson (2015), namely to use final ends in policymaking. He urges policymakers to distinguish between what is sought for the sake of what. Increased income for informal workers would be a useful goal for policymaking, but the final end could be thought of as opening up 'valuable ways of being and doing' (Richardson, 2015, p 170). In the capability context, this would mean that people would reflect on what would be a valued life, and would have the capabilities or opportunities to create that valued life, while in the process improving their economic position. The combination of the two aspirations of leading a better life and of doing what is fulfilling can then lead to human development in its fullest sense (compare Conradie, 2013; Conradie and Robeyns, 2013).

This overview of the ways in which the capability and human development approaches can be used for policy formulation is now followed by a short description of South Africa as the context for the social policy discussion.

South Africa's pressing social policy concerns

When the new South Africa came into being with a negotiated settlement in 1994, the African National Congress campaigned with a policy called the Reconstruction and Development Programme (RDP).[6] There had been a long and widely consultative process to which many political and social organisations contributed, as the initiative was widely seen as the human development programme that would bring about justice and equity after years of legislated inequality. Much was in fact delivered in the period after 1994 – a constitution that guarantees democracy and human rights; a large-scale housing programme; water, electricity and other services to many people who had previously had very limited access to these; a reasonably strong public works programme; and a grant system that now pays monthly grants to more than 16.9 million people. The majority of these targeted grants go to parents of children up to 18 years in the form of the Child Support Grant (CSG), which amounts to R370 per month per child. There are also grants for people over 60 who comply with the required income and asset threshold, and similar grants for people with physical disabilities. In spite of this impressive record, these measures were not enough to lift the majority of South Africans out of poverty.

It is important to pause for a moment to consider what South African society looks like at present. There is a population of about 55 million people. Based on a new approach that identified three different poverty lines, it was found that about 29 million people or 53.8% of the population are under the upper bound poverty line.[7] Furthermore, in 2012, only three million African people belonged to the middle class, with an income above R25,000 per annum per person, up from 0.3 million in 1993. The Gini index is 63.4, one of the highest in the world,[8] indicating largely the extent of racial and class inequality despite the gains that have been made since 1994. Lastly, the (contested) official unemployment rate was 25.5% during the third quarter of 2015, while that for young people was 36.1%.[9]

The nature of the 1994 settlement, which favoured non-racial capitalism, meant that only a small elite could be incorporated into the globalised part of the South African economy (Gelb, 2004). The result was the social and economic exclusion of the majority of the population, and the formation of an intransigent poverty trap. This affects mostly African South Africans, who are also trapped in a weak education system, and who therefore find it difficult to find proper work that might allow them to increase their assets, or to improve their education and skills (Adato et al, 2006; Van der Berg et al, 2011).

It is therefore clear that there are numerous social policy issues that need urgent attention. The poverty and inequality that persists in South Africa has led to a range of protests, some of which have been violent. Although protest action has been a constant feature of South African society, with 14,740 protests recorded by the police over a one-year period between 2014 and 2015,[10] such protests seem to be on the increase. Most commentators agree with political analyst Justice Malala that these movements mark a massive political shift in South Africa, reflecting the contention that 'the 1994 democratic breakthrough failed to deliver for the black majority economically'.[11] While this problem is complex and needs indeed to integrate political, social and economic analysis, the question must be asked to what extent the right kinds of social policies could play a role in redressing economic inequality in South Africa, a goal that is both important and urgent.

In 2011, the National Development Plan replaced the RDP. This new plan is outspoken in favouring human development and capability expansion (NPC, 2011). Chapter eleven, on social protection, contains a number of social protection principles that clearly illustrate the plan's human development and capability orientation. According to the authors, social protection should play a role that interlinks economic, social and political objectives. Social protection programmes should further aim to:

- alleviate poverty;
- contribute to self-reliant and sustainable development;
- encourage a culture of saving;
- create mechanisms to activate market opportunities;
- protect the vulnerable;
- prevent the deepening of poverty;
- enhance individual choices and opportunities or capabilities;

- be transformative, and deal with inequality and inequity;
- be developmental, generative, and create new structures for social and economic opportunities (NPC, 2011).

This set of principles is interesting in that they advocate social protection that not only relies on direct redistribution, or social democracy, but also seeks to reactivate defunct economic mechanisms that atrophied during the oppressive apartheid regime. Business opportunities were allocated very selectively before 1994 and there is a need to recreate an entrepreneurial environment and spirit in which the poor can pursue their aspirations. These principles therefore form a sound basis on which to develop social policies in the context of South Africa's persistent poverty and inequality.

The gap in the South African social protection system: social protection for informal workers

South Africa has one of the most comprehensive social security systems in Africa.[12] In South Africa, the CSG plays an important role in combatting poverty among families with children and under a certain income threshold. This programme has been largely successful (UNICEF, 2011, 2012), although May (2016) maintains that there is evidence that a quarter of children under 60 months remain stunted in South Africa. Although CSG is targeted to reach children from poorer families, these families often need the small amount of R370 per month that they receive for every child for other household expenses, such as food for the whole household (UNICEF, 2010, p 100), as they lack other sources of regular income (Neves and Du Toit, 2012; Conradie, 2013, 2014).[13] Leibbrandt and colleagues (2010) maintain that a quarter of the unemployed in South Africa derive income exclusively from the grants of other household members.

For the large section of the South African population that lives within a poverty trap (Adato et al, 2006), there are few opportunities of achieving the capability of livelihood security. If these families have children, they can obtain the CSG, and many mothers use this money to buy something that they then sell in informal markets in order to increase the value (UNICEF, 2012, p 6; Conradie, 2014). For those who do not have children under 18, even this minimal social security provision does not exist. The grants for disabled people and for people on lower incomes above 60 years of age are often also used to supplement household livelihoods. Disability grants of R1,585 per month are paid to adults between 18 and 59 years who have disabilities and who fall below an income threshold,[14] while the grant for people above 60 years of age, which is also aimed at those below an asset and income threshold, pays the same amount. If these grants were used by an individual only, that person's income would be above the poverty line. Usually, however, they are used to supplement household livelihoods, as described previously. Furthermore, contributory social insurance such as that provided for through the Unemployment Insurance Fund, is only accessible to those who are formally employed.

The social security system in South Africa is based on the welfare regime of its former coloniser, Britain. South Africa therefore implemented the liberal welfare regime safety net of the Anglo-Saxon countries (Esping-Andersen, 2006), which provides for vulnerable groups that are excluded from the protection offered to those who work within the market economy, such as children, older people and people with disabilities. Because of the comprehensive uptake of particularly the CSG, 22% of South African households now have a social grant as their main source of income.[15] This includes 12.3 million CSG recipients, 3.2 million recipients of the grant to older persons, and 1.1 million recipients of the grant for people with disabilities.[16]

Adults below the poverty line who are not covered by the grant system arguably form one of these most vulnerable groups in South Africa. If one looks at the broad figures quoted above, it is striking that about a third of the population receives social protection, while more than half of all South Africans live below the poverty line. There is therefore an obvious gap in social protection, and the next question is how many of these vulnerable people engage in informal and survival level economic activities.

Who are the informal workers in South Africa?

Keith Hart first used the term 'the informal economy' in 1970, when he had observed markets in Ghana with both formal and informal properties. People seemed to take the initiative to achieve their goals in spite of bureaucracies and regulations, and formally employed people would often have a stake in informal businesses as well (Hart, 2013). The International Labour Organization uses the term for workers without formal contracts and therefore without contributory social insurance (Hussmanns, 1993). This could include workers in small businesses and people who work for themselves, such as hairdressers, motor mechanics or small-scale informal farmers. The term also covers the category of survival-level businesses. In the real world, , however, it might not be easy to find the dividing line between formal and informal workers, and when it comes to social insurance it might be better for people to define themselves as formal or informal workers. Not everybody in this market will be poor – it is expected that informal workers in South Africa, as elsewhere, would encompass a broad income range. Selected recent labour statistics are given in Table 9.2 below.

Table 9.2: Key labour market indicators (July–Sept 2015)

Indicator	Thousands
Population aged 15–64 years	36,114
Labour force	21,246
Employed	15,828
Formal sector (non-agricultural) Informal sector (non-agricultural) Agriculture Private households	10,930 2,721 897 1,280
Unemployed	5,418
Not economically active	14,867
Discouraged jobseekers Other (not economically active)	2,226 12,641

Source: Stats SA (2015).

According to Table 9.2, there are 2.7 million people involved in informal work of some description in South Africa. If agricultural and domestic informal workers are included, the number goes up to almost five million people. This would mean that about 40% of all workers are informal. Despite that, the informal economy in South Africa only contributes 7–12% of gross domestic product (Altman, 2008, p 15).[17]

It might, however, be that the informal economy is even larger than this. There are, of course, many informal businesses that operate 'off the radar', but unregistered and informal work is a difficult field to research. The category 'not economically active' in Table 9.2 might also contain many informal workers. Even the category 'discouraged jobseekers' is probably incomplete, as many people find it hard to keep looking for work in a context where work is hard to obtain.

Devey and colleagues (2006) surveyed informal workers in South Africa, and found that most of them were 'own-account'[18] workers, although a small number are employees. Almost 90% of them were African. They did not necessarily have one job only, and also changed their activities to meet changes in the market. A small number, 11.8%, had employers who contributed to a pension or retirement fund, and 8% belonged to a trade union. Workers also moved from formal to informal work and vice versa, as opportunities arose (Valodia, 2008).

Whatever the exact profile of informal workers in South Africa, there are clearly many people who attempt to engage in survival-level businesses. Wolfgang Thomas of the Stellenbosch Business School found that 85,000 out of 200,000 households in Khayelitsha run some kind of small business, in other words that 42.5% of the inhabitants are informal workers (USB, 2014).[19] Similarly, Richard Grant carried out a study on the nature of work in the informal areas of Soweto, and found that only 5% of people interviewed had formal work. Unemployment was a big problem, with 37% of household heads not working, and 25% having been unemployed for at least five years. Among the remaining 58%,[20] people either combined formal and informal work (mostly in households), created their own work in survival-level businesses, or did not work while studying or as a result of having retired (Grant, 2010, p 603). In spite of the apparent economic inactivity of the poor, this therefore suggests that there is much informal and survival-level economic activity (Neves and Du Toit, 2012).

We can therefore conclude that informal work is not well understood in South Africa, and that more research should be undertaken in this area. We do know that informal sector economic activities are widely undertaken by those who use them as a survival strategy, and that the livelihood security of these people is precarious and in need of social protection measures. A small number of such workers succeed as informal sector entrepreneurs, but once again there is insufficient research to be able to form a clear picture of what this entails.

A policy proposal for social protection of informal workers in South Africa, based on human development and capability expansion

In developing a proposal to address the lack of social security of informal workers, this section discusses the guidelines considered previously, in combination with those contained in the National Development Plan, and reviewed earlier. This proposal includes in particular the creation of policy mechanisms to activate market opportunities, while at the same time protecting the vulnerable. Furthermore, it contains all the elements that Devereux and Sabates-Wheeler (2004) include in their transformative social protection model:

- **social assistance** to the two poorest quintiles of the population, a protective strategy to enable them to become economically active;
- **social insurance** in the form of a contributory savings scheme, a preventive strategy where retirement savings will be subsidised once, depending on the amount saved over a period;
- **livelihood extension**, a promotive strategy, which will allow people to borrow against their own savings for livelihood-related projects such as business development or education;
- **transformative institutional measures**, to contribute to social justice infrastructure in support all of these components.

The proposal is formulated along the lines of a savings scheme broadly based on the Mbao pension plan of Kenya.[21] This pension scheme is provided by Kenyan private sector businesses, but serves the informal economy. It is based on the novel concept of inexpensive and accessible telephone banking, and of easy and personal access to one's account. All workers may use it, irrespective of income or age, but it particularly allows low-income informal workers to develop a savings culture, and has been highly successful in this regard. In Kenya, where 80% of workers are informal, it created an ideal model for individuals and households to manage their risk profiles. It was jointly established by the Retirement Benefits Authority and the association for informal workers, the Jua Kali Association. It thus provides an opportunity for the creation of micro pensions, in the form of a voluntary, defined contribution, made by individuals according to their own needs and resources (Kwena and Turner, 2013).[22] In South Africa, the success of such a programme would furthermore depend on a non-conditional grant for older people, with no asset restrictions, in order that older people should not be discouraged from saving for their later years (Seekings and Nattrass, 2015, p 148).

Because of the specific context in South Africa discussed above, the Mbao plan is adapted somewhat to create a holistic and comprehensive programme that would help to address the extremes of poverty and inequality in South Africa. First of all a plan of this nature is considered a priority in South Africa, specifically because growth prospects for the immediate future are low and the economic outlook is not positive. This will mean that government has less to spend, but as it will probably mean that employment will not grow, or not grow much, a human development approach would mean that the poor are given priority above other expenditure. This would be in contrast to neoliberal austerity principles, which cut social support to the poor when it is most needed.[23]

Second, we consider it important to incentivise such a programme, in order to encourage wide participation. South Africans are notorious for living in debt[24] and the first condition for asset formation would be to assist people to save. Many South Africans do save, with informal structures called *stokvel*.[25] The national *stokvel* association (NASSAA) claims to have about 800,000 savings groups and savings to the value of about R45 billion, although the research carried out by African Response suggests lower figures. Nevertheless, it is a powerful structure with very low levels of defaulting, and it shows that the poor (and the rising middle class) can indeed save. In possible collaboration with the *stokvel* association, a programme could be devised where people could save as and when they can, as the Mbao members do. Incentives could be that people can borrow at low interest rates from their own and others' savings for asset investments such as the improvement of the education of household members, the establishment or upgrade of a business venture, or for similar concrete asset spending. The main incentive would, however, be that people who have saved regularly and over a period could get a government subsidy, calculated as a percentage of maybe 20% or 25% of the amount they had saved, possibly by the age of 40 or 50. As poor South Africans receive a grant for older persons at age 60, it would have to be before that time, as the poor might consider the grant sufficient for their needs after the age of 60. The poor furthermore often do physical labour, which becomes harder at a later age. In addition, the life expectancy for South African females is 64 years and for males it is 60 years,[26] which means that people might consider 60 too late to receive a payment. It is hoped that the payment of a subsidy based on their contribution would act as an incentive to people below the poverty line to attempt to increase their household income, and to save part of such increased income. People who save would obviously also get interest on their savings, and NASASA is also experimenting with innovative investments in bonds and shares.[27] One might argue that if it had been possible for them to increase their income, many people would surely have done so. It is clearly difficult to operate in the informal economy in South Africa, and for that reason it would be important to support such a programme to the maximum extent possible. Such a scheme should also be supported by different government departments that should concentrate on the creation of capabilities and opportunities specifically for the poor.

It might furthermore be necessary to support the poorest sectors of society, maybe the two poorest quintiles, with small levels of conditional income support to bring them to a level where they can benefit from a programme such as this. If income support is considered, it should be done on the basis of an in-built graduation after a period of a few years, to encourage active involvement and the exercise of agency.

The incentive of being able to achieve the aspiration of improving the household's economic status, and of an eventual financial award, will hopefully encourage many to attempt to succeed where they have failed before, particularly if formal support is offered. At the same time, the open nature of the savings programme, where capabilities, choice, ownership, active participation and joint decision making are key features, has the potential to unlock levels of personal aspirations and functionings that had not been visible before.

As indicated in Table 9.1, it would be vital for the designers of such a policy to analyse the capability constraints faced by those who attempt to realise their aspirations. It would be important to strengthen the bureaucratic structures that will have to offer support and administrative back-up. It would also be important to constantly assess the functionings people gain (an essential component) as the programme is rolled out, in order to adjust the policy. It might be that some aspects of the proposal work well while others do not. It would be a policy in which the Chinese economic strategy of Deng Xiaoping of 'crossing the river by feeling the stones' would be appropriate. Many adjustments are likely to be necessary and the policy is likely to have its risks. But if it succeeds, even marginally, it could play a role in creating new economic structures that could assist in transforming the heritage of inequity and inequality that mars South African society and jeopardises its future.

Conclusion

Because South Africa is a highly unequal society that has still not transformed its racial and class-based inequity, despite an excellent constitution, economic and social policies are urgently needed to fulfil the promises of the political transition of 1994. The South African constitution uses the Rawlsian principle of prioritising the poor, and the extensive (but low-level) social security programme has played a limited role in bringing this about. Nevertheless, if the institutional side of Table 9.1 of this chapter is considered, it emerges that governance is weak and creates continuous capability constraints (Terreblanche, 2012). Moreover, there are also numerous opportunity and capability constraints in the country arising from its colonial and apartheid history. When the poor engage in economic activity, they are often confronted with these enduring obstacles, both concrete and attitudinal, which block progress. It is therefore vital that these constraints be overcome in order to address rising dissatisfaction, poverty and inequality.

Dissatisfaction is on the rise in South Africa, and the fiscus has to deal with many competing claims, among which is the demand for free tertiary education and for better service delivery. Insurance for informal workers is therefore temporarily on the back burner – hopefully not for an extended period of time.

Responding to poverty and inequality will require a wide range of interventions, but in this chapter the focus is on the need to provide social protection as well as economic opportunities and capabilities to the excluded members of South African society, in particular to informal workers. A savings scheme based on mobile phone banking is proposed, with built-in incentives of low-interest loans and a once-off subsidy from government. If this could be undertaken in partnership with savings schemes based on social capital such as the *stokvel* associations in South Africa and Jua Kali in East Africa, already successful in both regions, an incentive might be created for people to use such opportunity structures as are provided by government and society generally in order to become economically engaged. This would be the first step in the process of undertaking risk management for themselves. The savings scheme would be amplified by social assistance to those in the lowest quintiles, by favourable micro loans from their own accounts for livelihood-enhancing expenditure, and by institutional and wide-ranging support services. This proposal would be in line with all the human development principles spelt out in the South African National Development Plan, and would thus also be in line with other social policies in the country.

In the design and operationalisation of the scheme it would be important to keep two goals in mind: that individuals and groups should be able to make choices that will improve their social and economic status, and that the programme as a whole and the choices that disadvantaged participants are able to make will help them to live lives of value. A focus on human development and the creation of meaningful and workable opportunities for the excluded could arguably play an important role in addressing some of the problems experienced in South Africa.

Notes

[1] www.ohchr.org/Documents/Publications/Chapter20-48pp.pdf

[2] Stephen Devereux and I wrote a concept paper on 'Extending social protection to informal workers in South Africa' for the Department of Planning, Monitoring and Evaluation in South Africa in 2015. This paper will shortly be published online. I am grateful to the department for allowing me to base this chapter on some of the thinking in the concept paper. I also appreciate Stephen Devereux's comments on an earlier draft of this chapter.

[3] See Robeyns (2011b) for an argument that the two approaches are complementary but essentially different.

[4] Fakuda-Parr (2005) coins the term to indicate that an alternative to the Washington Consensus is already in place.

[5] Parts of this section were previously used in Conradie (2014).

[6] www.nelsonmandela.org/omalley/index.php/site/q/03lv02039/04lv02103/05lv021

[7] http://beta2.statssa.gov.za/publications/Report-03-10-11/Report-03-10-11.pdf

[8] http://data.worldbank.org/indicator/SI.POV.GINI

[9] www.tradingeconomics.com/south-africa/unemployment-rate, www.statssa.gov.za

[10] http://businesstech.co.za/news/general/126243/this-is-how-many-protests-there-are-per-day-in-south-africa

[11] www.fin24.com/Finweek/Opinion/FeesMustFall-signal-a-massive-political-shift-20151030

[12] The South African social security system nevertheless operates at a much lower level than that of the developed world. The Child Support Grant of R370 per month currently converts to 24 Euro.

[13] It is important to note that the CSG on its own only secures one household member slightly below the food poverty line, which includes no other basic needs (Stats SA, 2015, p 11).

[14] The threshold income for individuals is R69,000 per annum, and they should not have assets exceeding R990,000. For other conditions, see www.gov.za/services/social-benefits/disability-grant or www.gov.za/services/social-benefits/retirement-and-old-age/old-age-pension.

[15] www.gov.za/about-sa/social-development

[16] https://pmg.org.za/committee-meeting/21618

[17] This literature was also reviewed in Devereux and Conradie (2015).

[18] "Own account" workers work for themselves, and run their businesses themselves.

[19] www.usb.ac.za/Common/pdfs/sba_facts/DiversityofBusinessesinKhayelitsha.pdf

[20] That is, the group that is neither formally employed nor unemployed.

[21] I wish to thank Dr Fidelis Hove who introduced me to this pension plan and its possibilities for South Africa.

[22] I shall not review the technical mechanisms of the scheme here, but they can be found in Kwena and Turner (2013).

[23] There are many claims on the Treasury, and such a pro-poor programme will not be uncontroversial.

[24] www.moneyweb.co.za/archive/five-million-south-africans-drowning-in-debt

[25] www.stokvelsa.co.za/, www.bdlive.co.za/business/financial/2015/05/11/a-stokvel-by-any-other-name-is-still-empowering

[26] www.statssa.gov.za/publications/P0302/P03022015.pdf

[27] www.nasasa.co.za

References

Adato, M., Carter, M.R. and May, J. (2006) 'Exploring poverty traps and social exclusion in South Africa using qualitative and quantitative data', *Journal of Development Studies*, vol 42, no 2, pp 226-47.

Alkire, S. (2008) 'Using the capability approach: prospective and evaluative analyses', in F. Comim, M. Qizilbash and S. Alkire (eds) *The capability approach: Concepts, measures and applications*, Cambridge: Cambridge University Press, pp 26-49.

Alkire, S. and Deneulin, S (2009a) 'A normative framework for development', in S. Deneulin and L. Shahani (eds) *An introduction to the human development and capability approach: Freedom and agency*, London: Earthscan, pp 3-21.

Alkire, S. and Deneulin, S. (2009b) 'The human development and capability approach', in S. Deneulin and L. Shahani (eds) *An introduction to the human development and capability approach: Freedom and agency*, London: Earthscan, pp 22-48.

Alkire, S., Bastagli, F., Burchardt, T., Clark, D., Holder, H., Ibrahim, S., Munoz, M., Terrazas, P., Tsang, T. and Vizard, P. (2009) *Developing the equality measurement framework: Selecting the indicators*, Research Report 3, Manchester: Equality and Human Rights Commission.

Altman, M. (2008) *Formal-informal economy linkages*, Pretoria: Human Sciences Research Council, available at www.hsrc.ac.za/en/research-data/ktree-doc/1398 (accessed 4 April 2015).

Anand, P., Hunter, G. and Smith, R. (2005) 'Capabilities and well-being: evidence based on the Sen-Nussbaum approach to welfare', *Social Indicators Research*, vol 74, no 1, pp 9-55.

Arndt, C. and Volkert, J. (2011) 'The capability approach: a framework for official German poverty and wealth reports', *Journal of Human Development and Capabilities*, vol 12, no 3, pp 311-37.

Burd-Sharps, S., Lewis, K. and Martins, E.B. (eds) (2008) *The measure of America: American Human Development Report 2008/2009*, New York, NY: Columbia University Press.

Carpenter, M. (2009) 'The capabilities approach and critical social policy: lessons from the majority world?', *Critical Social Policy*, vol 29, no 3, pp 351-73.

Chiappero-Martinetti, E. and Moroni, S. (2007) 'An analytical framework for conceptualizing poverty and re-examining the capability approach', *Journal of Socio-Economics*, vol 36, no 3, pp 360-75.

Clark, D. (2012) 'Adaptation and development: issues, evidence and policy relevance', in D. Clark (ed) *Adaptation, poverty and development: The dynamics of subjective well-being*, Basingstoke: Palgrave Macmillan, pp 1-31.

Conradie, I. (2013) 'Can deliberate efforts to realise aspirations increase capabilities: a South African case study', *Oxford Development Studies*, vol 14, no 2, pp 189-219.

Conradie, I. (2014) 'Aspirations and capabilities: the design and analysis of an action research project in Khayelitsha, Cape Town', Unpublished PhD thesis, University of the Western Cape, Cape Town.

Conradie, I. and Robeyns, I. (2013) 'Aspirations and human development interventions', *Journal of Human Development and Capabilities*, vol 41, no 4, pp 559-80.

Deneulin, S. and McGregor, J.A. (2010) 'The capability approach and the politics of a social conception of wellbeing', *European Journal of Social Theory*, vol 13, no 4, pp 501-19.

Denuelin, S. and Shahani, L. (eds) (2009) *An introduction to the human development and capability approach*, London: Earthscan.

Devereux, S. and Conradie, I, (2015) 'Extending social protection to informal workers in South Africa: a concept paper', Unpublished paper prepared for the Department of Planning, Monitoring and Evaluation, RSA.

Devereux, S. and Sabates-Wheeler, R. (2004) *Transformative scial protection*, IDS Working Paper 232, Brighton: Institute of Development Studies, available at www.unicef.org/socialpolicy/files/Transformative_Social_Protection.pdf.

Devey, R., Skinner, C. and Valodia, I. (2006) 'Definitions, data and the informal economy in South Africa: a critical analysis', in V. Padayachee (ed) *The development decade? Economic and social change in South Africa, 1994-2004*, Cape Town: HSRC Press.

Esping-Andersen, G. (2006) 'Three worlds of welfare capitalism', in C. Pierson and F. Castles (eds) *The welfare state reader*, Cambridge: Polity Press.

Fukuda-Parr, S. (2005) 'The human development paradigm: operationalizing Sen's ideas on capabilities', in B. Agarwal, J. Humphries and I. Robeyns (eds) *Amartya Sen's work and ideas: A gender perspective*, London: Routledge, pp 303-20.

Fukuda-Parr, S., Lawson-Remer, T. and Randolph, S. (2015) *Fulfilling social and economic rights*, New York, NY: Oxford University Press.

Gelb, S. (2004) *Inequality in South Africa: Nature, causes and responses*, Johannesburg: The Edge Institute, available at www.tips.org.za/files/Gelb_Inequality_in_SouthAfrica.pdf (accessed 16 October 2013).

Grant, R. (2010) 'Working it out: labour geographies of the poor in Soweto, South Africa', *Development Southern Africa*, vol 27, no 4, pp 595-612.

Hart, K. (2013) 'Keith Hart on the informal economy, the great transformations, and the humanity of corporations', available at www. theory-talks.org/2013/06/theory-talk-56.html (accessed 21 April).

Haq, M. ul (2003) 'The human development paradigm', in S. Fukuda-Parr and A.K.S. Kumar (eds) *Readings in human development: Concepts, measures and policies for a development paradigm*, New York, NY: Oxford University Press.

Hussmanns, R. (1993) *Defining and measuring informal employment*, Geneva: International Labour Office, available at www.ilo.org/ public/english/bureau/stat/download/papers/meas.pdf (accessed 16 December 2015).

Jolly, R. (2003) 'Human development and neo-liberalism: paradigms compared', in S. Fukuda-Parr and A.K.S. Kumar (eds) *Readings in human development: Concepts, measures and policies for a development paradigm*, New York, NY: Oxford University Press, pp 82-92.

Kwena, R and Turner, J. (2013) 'Extending pension and savings scheme coverage to the informal sector: Kenya's Mbao pension plan', *International Social Security Review*, vol 66, no 2, pp 79-99.

Leibbrandt, M., Woolard, I., McEwan, H. and Koep, C. (2010) *Employment and inequality outcomes in South Africa*, Cape Town: Southern Africa Labour and Development Research Unit and School of Economics, University of Cape Town, available at www.oecd.org/ els/emp/45282868.pdf (accessed 12 August 2015).

May, J. (2016) 'Child poverty', Lecture on social policy course, ISD, University of the Western Cape.

NPC (National Planning Commission) (2011) *National Development Plan 2030. Our future: Make it work*, Pretoria: The Presidency, Republic of South Africa, available at www.poa.gov.za/news/ Documents/NPC%20National%20Development%20Plan%20 Vision%202030%20-lo-res.pdf (accessed 12 January).

Neves, D. and Du Toit, A. (2012) 'Money and informality in South Africa's informal economy.' *Africa*, vol 82, special issue 01, pp 131-49.

Nussbaum, M. (2011) *Creating capabilities: The human development approach*, Cambridge, MA: Belknap Press of Harvard University Press.

Richardson, H. (2015) 'Using final ends for the sake of better policy-making', *Journal of Human Development and Capabilities*, vol 16, no 2, pp 161-72.

Robeyns, I. (2011a) *The capability approach*, Stanford Encyclopaedia of Philosophy, available at http://plato.stanford.edu/entries/capability-approach (accessed 24 October 2013).

Robeyns, I. (2011b) 'The capability approach and the human development approach: their characterization and relationship', Paper presented at Bielefeld Conference on Human Development Perspectives, Bielefeld, Germany, 26-27 June.

Seekings, J. and Nattrass, N. (2015) *Policy, politics and poverty in South Africa*, New York, NY: Palgrave MacMillan.

Sen, A. (2009) *The idea of justice*, Cambridge, MA: Harvard University Press.

Sen, A. (2005) 'Human rights and capabilities', *Journal of Human Development*, vol 6, no 2, pp 151-66.

Spence, R. and Deneulin, S. (2009) 'Human development policy analysis', in S. Deneulin and L. Shahani (eds) *An introduction to the human development and capability approach*, London: Earthscan.

Stats SA (2015) 'Quarterly Labour Force Survey, third quarter 2015', available at www.statssa.gov.za/?m=2015

Stewart, F. (2005) 'Groups and capabilities', *Journal of Human Development*, vol 6, no 2, pp 185-204.

Terreblanche, S. (2012) *Lost in transformation: South Africa's search for a new future since 1986*, Johannesburg: KMM Review Publishing Company.

UNICEF (2011) *Child Support Grant evaluation 2010. Qualitative research report*, Pretoria: UNICEF South Africa, available at www.unicef.org/southafrica/SAF_resources_csg2012book.pdf (accessed 10 August 2015).

UNICEF (2012) *The South African Child Support Grant impact assessment: Evidence from a survey of children, adolescents and their households*, Pretoria: UNICEF South Africa, available at www.unicef.org/southafrica/SAF_resources_csg2012s.pdf (accessed 10 August 2015).

USB (University of Stellenbosch Business School) (2014) *Khayelitsha small business project: Diversity of businesses in Khayelitsha. Fact sheet 02/2014*, Cape Town: USB, available at www.usb.ac.za/Common/pdfs/sba_facts/DiversityofBusinessesinKhayelitsha.pdf (accessed 12 December 2015).

Valodia, I. (2008) 'Informal employment, labour markets and social protection: some considerations based on South African estimates', *IDS Bulletin*, vol 39, no 2, pp 57-62.

Van der Berg, S., Burger, C., Burger, R., De Vos, M., Du Rand, G., Gustafsson, M., Moses, E., Shepherd, D., Spaull, N., Taylor, S., Van Brackhuizen, H. and Von Vintel, D. (2011) *Low quality education as a poverty trap*, Stellenbosch: Stellenbosch University, available at www.andover.edu/GPGConference/Documents/Low-Quality-Education-Poverty-Trap.pdf (accessed 6 December 2015).

PART 3:

Children, youth and education

The capability approach: what can it offer child protection policy and practice in England?

Brid Featherstone and Anna Gupta

Introduction

The capability approach (CA) has been used to assess individual wellbeing and the evaluation of social arrangements, and to develop policies and practices to effect social change. In recent years, the CA has gained attention and influence in a broad number of public policy areas and across academic disciplines. This chapter explores child protection policy and practice in England, an area of social policy that has hitherto received very limited analysis from the perspective of the CA. It presents an overview of child protection policies and practices, their historical development and their current manifestation in contemporary England, where the political context is dominated by neoliberal policies and an 'austerity' agenda. It then explores what the CA can offer to further our understanding of the impacts of the child protection system. We make recommendations for the development of a more humane and socially just system that promotes children's and their parents' capabilities and rights, and recognises their necessary interrelatedness.

In this chapter we analyse two particular aspects of the child protection system from a capability perspective. We critically examine the ways poverty and parenting are constructed in the dominant discourses and the policies and practices that have developed within this context. In addition, drawing on qualitative research with families who have experienced the child protection system, we explore the impact of interventions on parents, and conclude with recommendations for policy and practice that strives for greater social justice. Prior to analysing these aspects, we present an overview view of child protection policies and practices, their historical development and manifestation in contemporary England.

By using the term 'child protection' in an English context, we are referring to the laws, policies and practices relating to children deemed to be at risk or likely to be at risk of abuse and neglect. We acknowledge, as Waterhouse and McGhee (2015, p 13) do, that 'the same words are used to mean different things at different times and different words may be used to mean the same things'. Differences in use and understanding of the terminology around 'child protection' and 'child abuse and neglect' can be particularly divergent when working across professional and international boundaries (Pösö, 2015). As we explain, the term in the English context has been constructed to refer primarily to 'protecting' children from harm deemed to be caused by parental maltreatment.

The historical and political contexts of child protection policy in England

The way in which a society responds to its most vulnerable children is central to the debate about the relationship between children, families and the state. When and how to intervene in private family life where there are concerns about harm to a child are dilemmas that continually challenge policymakers and child welfare professionals. Compulsory intervention by the state has lifelong consequences and the permanent removal of a child from his or her birth family is one of the most draconian actions a state can take. Alternatively, a lack of timely and appropriate responses to a child at risk of abuse and neglect can result in serious harm or even the death of the child. While the United Nations Convention on the Rights of the Child (United Nations, 1989) provides a set of standards and obligations in relation to vulnerable children, the ways in which governments interpret these requirements reflect the particular historical, social and political contexts of the country (Frost and Parton, 2009).

Over the past two decades, the comparative study of how different countries respond to child abuse and neglect has increased, providing useful frameworks for understanding policy contexts and political influences. A mid-1990s study of child welfare arrangements in nine countries differentiated two general orientations to practice: child protection and family service (Gilbert, 1997). In this study England, the US and Canada were grouped within the child protection orientation, and Sweden, Denmark, Finland, Belgium, the Netherlands and Germany came under the family service orientation. The child protection orientation primarily focuses on parental pathology and deviance requiring investigation and, when necessary, adversarial judicial systems to confer authority. In contrast, the family service orientation perceives the problem as a manifestation of family dysfunction stemming from psychological difficulties, marital troubles and socioeconomic stress, which are amenable to therapeutic interventions. The family service approach promotes more partnership-based practice with parents, including a focus on voluntary arrangements for children in out-of-home care (Gilbert, 1997).

A follow-up study 15 years later, which included the original nine countries plus Norway, found that these approaches had begun to converge (Gilbert et al, 2011). Child protection systems, such as those in the US and England, had adopted features of the family service orientation. At the same time, countries that had been characterised as family service-oriented began to establish policies and practices to respond to increasing concern about abuse to children (Pösö, 2011). In the context of shifting policy orientations that struggled with the complexities and tensions of attempting to achieve a constructive balance between supporting families and protecting children, Gilbert and colleagues (2011) identified a new child-focused orientation. The child is viewed as an individual with a much more independent relationship with the state; an autonomous individual in relation to their family and a social investment for the future of society.

In the first decade of the 21st century in England, the emphasis of the New Labour government was on 'transforming' and 'modernising' children's services, which Garrett (2009, p 140) argues had neoliberalism at its 'dominant or, hegemonic core'. While some elements reflected a shift towards a family service orientation, including universal family support services such as Sure Start, a number of high-profile child death inquiries, notably the Victoria Climbié inquiry[1] (Laming, 2003), preserved the centrality of child protection. Featherstone and colleagues (2014a, p 27) assert that:

> New Labour maintained an uneasy and complex mix of child protection, and a broader focus on social exclusion and children's outcomes in a version of the child-focused orientation outlined by Gilbert et al (2011).

However the death of a child, Peter Connelly ('Baby P'), in 2008 in the care of his parents, and the subsequent political and media outcry, led to a shift towards more authoritarian child protection practice in the last few years of the Labour government. Reactions to the death of Peter Connelly were explicitly used by the Conservative Party as providing clear examples of the 'feckless' and 'dangerous' poor in our 'broken society' and the need for major welfare reform well beyond child protection (Parton, 2014).

In 2010, the Conservative–Liberal Democrat coalition government came into power and following on from the global financial crisis, implemented a tranche of public spending cuts in the name of 'austerity' that have continued unabated to date, under the current Conservative government. In 'austerity' England, many families are having their welfare benefits cut, homelessness is increasing and children's centres and other family support services are closing. At the same time, Conservative politicians and government advisers have, on a number of occasions, spoken about the 'rescue' of children to 'loving' adoptive homes, and a need to speed up this process (Gove, 2013; Burns, 2015).

The policies of the coalition government, Featherstone et al (2014b, p 1736) argue, caused a perfect storm through the 'coming together of a number of developments around early intervention and child protection over the last decades'. This has been supported by use of neuroscience to argue that the first three years of a child's life are critical, and this created a now-or-never imperative to intervene before irreparable damage is done to the developing infant brain (Brown and Ward, 2013), despite this interpretation of the scientific evidence having been widely critiqued (Wastell and White, 2012). Edwards and colleagues (2015) suggest that these claims are justifying gendered, racialised and other social inequalities, positioning poor mothers as architects of their children's deprivation.

What appears to have developed in the context of increasing poverty and inequality, and significant cuts in family support services, is an unforgiving attitude towards parents: improve quickly and within set time limits or your children will be removed from your care.

The current child protection system

The focus on identifying risk as opposed to provision of support is starkly illustrated in the statistical data. The national statistics show that child protection investigations increased by 79.4 % between 2009-10 and 2014-15 (DfE, 2015a). While there was an increase in children placed on a child protection plan (40.4 %) over this six-year period, the much larger increase in investigations meant that the number of children who came under suspicion and were investigated but were not found to be significantly harmed more than doubled from 45,000 to 98,000 (DfE, 2015a). In 2014-15, it is likely that fewer than two in every five investigations led to a child protection plan (Bilson and Martin, 2016). Devine and Parker's (2015) analysis of referral and assessment trends similarly found practices that were preoccupied with detecting abuse, ignored need and frequently left families alienated and frightened.

In England, if, after a child protection investigation, professionals judge a child to be suffering or likely to suffer significant harm, she can remain in the care of her parents and be made subject to a child protection plan or she may be removed from home with the agreement of her parents or, more frequently, via a court order following care proceedings in the family court under the Children Act 1989. The categories under which children can be placed on child protection plans are physical abuse, sexual abuse, emotional abuse or neglect (DfE, 2015b), with the most common category being neglect, followed by emotional abuse. During the period between 2010 and 2015, there was a rapid increase in the number of children being made subject to plans due to emotional abuse (54%) and neglect (28%). In 2015, 78% of children were on child protection plans because of neglect or emotional abuse, and less than a fifth because of physical or sexual abuse (DfE, 2015a). In addition to the increase in the number of referrals and children on child protection plans, new applications to the family courts to remove children from their parents' care have continued to rise over the past few years, with 12,758 applications between April 2015 and March 2016, a 14% increase from the previous year (Cafcass, 2016). Most children unable to return to their birth parents or live within their kinship network are in foster care, although the government's preferred option for children not able to remain within their birth families is adoption, which, unlike most European countries, is most frequently without the consent of parents (Fenton-Glynn, 2016).

Within the literature on child protection, the association between poverty and neglect has long been highlighted (Stevenson, 1998; Baldwin and Spencer, 2005; Pelton, 2015). The official definition of neglect (DfE, 2015b) includes 'a parent or carer failing to provide adequate food, clothing and shelter', factors clearly associated with poverty. The rise in child protection plans for neglect have been occurring alongside a rapid growth in foodbanks and homeless families living in bed and breakfast accommodation (Perry et al, 2014; Gayle, 2015). A study by Bywaters (2015) provides evidence of a clear link between deprivation and a child's life chances in relation to their ability to live with their family of origin. For example, the study found that a child in Blackpool (an area of high deprivation) is 12 times more likely to be the subject of child protection interventions than a child living in Richmond (a very affluent area). Similarly, Hood and colleagues (2016) found that the overall system has become increasingly geared towards protective rather than supportive interventions, especially since the response to the death of Peter Connelly, with deprivation levels continuing to be the key driver of referrals.

While there is acknowledgement that some children will need to be protected from parental harm, including through removal from their parents' care, a growing body of commentators have been calling for reforms in the way the child protection system deals with families where there are need and safety issues, the way in which poor communities are subject to statutory surveillance and control, and the stigmatisation of families who may not be abusing their children but are nonetheless drawn into the child protection process (Devine and Parker, 2015; Bilson and Martin, 2016). In the following sections, we discuss the relevance of the capability approach to evaluating the current child protection system and developing a more humane and socially just system for addressing the needs and rights of English society's most vulnerable children and families.

Poverty matters

The CA offers a framework that clearly establishes the structural basis for poverty and challenges neoliberal ideas that blame individuals for their socioeconomic circumstances. Poverty is regarded as an 'unfreedom' or capability deprivator because it interferes with a person's ability to make valued choices and participate fully in society (Sen, 1999). Poverty is not just about material resources, although these are important, but leads to the deprivation of certain basic capabilities, and these can vary, as Sen (1995, p 15) has argued, 'from such elementary physical ones as being well nourished, being adequately clothed and sheltered, avoiding preventable morbidity, and so forth, to more complex social achievements such as taking part in the life of the community, being able to appear in public without shame, and so on'. The CA places centrally the need to acknowledge both the material and affective consequences of poverty and inequality. Sen (1983, p 159) asserts that shame lies at the 'irreducible absolutist core' of poverty. Shame is individually felt but socially constructed, imposed on people in poverty by dominant discourses and dealings with others, including public services (Walker et al, 2013).

The CA provides a framework for poverty analysis, emphasising its normative or ethical dimension. It stresses the intrinsic importance of people's capabilities, argues for a multidimensional assessment in poverty analysis, and adopts a broad perspective of the many kinds of constraints that can limit people's lives (Hick, 2012). By assigning a role to conversion factors in mediating the relation between commodities and capabilities, the CA takes into account individual heterogeneity and represents a powerful tool to explain situations in which people sharing the same set of resources end up with different capability sets. The CA provides a framework for poverty analysis that avoids the dichotomy of only focusing on material deprivation or individual factors at the expense of structural inequality, and includes an interconnecting of different levels of analysis (micro and macro, individual and context, means and ends) that contribute to our understanding of relationship between structure and agency.

Much of the research on poverty, parenting and harm to children is consistent with the ideas of the CA. Pelton (2015) argues that poverty is the predominant context in which harm and endangerment to children thrive, and is multifaceted, involving direct and indirect relationships. A review of the literature has reinforced the significance of poverty as a contributory causal factor in child abuse and neglect (Bywaters et al, 2016). Poverty differentially affects individual families, with particularly serious consequences for more vulnerable individuals and those without formal or informal sources of support (Hooper et al, 2007). Poverty is most closely associated with neglect and acts both directly through the capacity of parents to maintain the basic conditions for healthy child development, such as food, shelter and warmth, or to buy a variety of forms of support, and indirectly through the stresses created by low income. Poverty is not just incidental but is an influential factor in family relationships on a day-by-day, hour-by-hour basis, in its own right and interacting with other forces such as parental health, substance use and domestic violence (Bywaters et al, 2016). The complex interactions between material aspects of poverty, other forms of structural inequality, and the psychological and emotional experiences of individuals, including long-term lack of respect, opportunity and hope, need to be considered when analysing how poverty affects parents' ability to effectively care for their child. The cumulative effect of adversity can be mitigated by protective factors, both psychological and social (Hooper et al, 2007).

However, within the current policy context for child protection practice in England, consideration of the impact of poverty and inequality is either absent and or actively discouraged. Neoliberal ideas that deny the impact of social structures and promote the belief individuals are responsible for their own functionings dominate. These ideas are exemplified by the former education secretary's statement about neglect:

We are leaving them to endure a life of soiled nappies and scummy baths, chaos and hunger, hopelessness and despair. These children need to be rescued, just as much as the victims of any other natural disaster. (Gove, 2012)

The construction of neglect is one of a problem whereby children need to be rescued from rather than one that their parents can be supported to address. The state's role is therefore primarily to effect the rescue, as in this construction parents are to blame for the neglect and social factors play a limited role, thereby absolving government of responsibility (Gupta, 2015). The response to the problem of child neglect has been to urge social workers to take more children into care, make earlier and quicker decisions, and increase adoption numbers. In addition, social work academics have been criticised for overly focusing on structural inequality, in ways that 'rob individuals of the power of agency and breaks the link between an individual's actions and the consequences' (Gove, 2013).

The absence of attention to poverty and other structural inequalities and the role they play in parenting problems is demonstrated in the report, *Decision-making within a child's timeframe* (Brown and Ward, 2013). This report is part of the Ministry of Justice's 'Knowledge Hub', to be used to inform decisions in the family courts in England, and as mentioned earlier is based on a contested interpretation of the usefulness of neuroscience as the basis for policy. The Brown and Ward report (2013), despite including a section on parental problems that can undermine healthy child development, includes only one mention of poverty and that is as a possible consequence of child maltreatment. Similarly, some key reports on child neglect by organisations including child welfare charities fail to consider issues of poverty and related inequalities, and the impact on families and services of government cuts in welfare spending (Gupta, 2015).

Hooper and colleagues' (2007, p 97) study found that 'a limited conception of poverty, lack of resources to address it, and lack of attention to the impacts of trauma, addiction and lifelong disadvantage on the choices that people experience themselves as having' may contribute to social workers 'overemphasizing agency at the expense of structural inequality'. The findings of this research, although conducted some years ago, have been reaffirmed in studies exploring the perspectives of parents (Gupta et al, 2016a) and are likely to have been exacerbated by austerity policies, as well as the risk-averse culture exacerbated by the political and media reaction to the death of Peter Connelly in 2008. Warner (2015) argues that the media reporting following the death of Peter Connelly served to further the notion of 'other' families living in poverty and of the need to subject 'them' to more intensive moral regulation and social control, and in the process was also constitutive of 'our' middle-class notions of respectability relating to parenting and family life. Garrett (2009, p 537), also drawing on newspaper reports of the 'Baby P' case, highlights the class contempt in the frequent use of the underclass construct and links this to the 'regulatory social agenda of neo-liberalism'.

Sen's (1992) notion of 'informational basis of judgement in justice' emphasises the selection of some sources of information over others and how facts and values are entangled in the design and implementation of public policies (Bonvin, 2014). We would argue that the current discourse framed in terms of individual pathology disregards the substantial body of knowledge on the effects of poverty and inequality and the complex interrelationships between poverty and neglect, and perpetuates the blaming of families and of social workers for not addressing the problem.

The CA highlights that whether individuals have certain capabilities depends not only on individual features like skills and competences, but also on the external conditions in which they find themselves, the norms, institutions and social structures that provide the context and influence their ideas and actions. Our analysis of the child protection system in contemporary England based on the CA would suggest that policies increasing poverty and inequality serve to reduce the 'means' available to families, while cuts to local authority and community-based family support services are at the same time diminishing 'conversion' factors that would enhance capabilities in these adverse circumstances. Families involved in the child protection and family court systems then face a 'triple jeopardy' of punitive practices that fail to recognise the socioeconomic context of their lives (Gupta et al, 2016b). This raises serious questions about social injustice, and the diminution of fundamental 'freedoms', such as Nussbaum's (2011) capability of affiliation, and the human rights of children and families living in poverty in England. This is especially so in the context of adoption, most often without the consent of parents, one of the most draconian actions a state can take.

The CA reinforces the need for more nuanced analyses of the complex interrelationship between the psychological and social impacts of poverty and inequality by policymakers, social workers and other professionals. The focus on internal capabilities gets problematic when they are highlighted at the expense of the external conditions or options necessary for their exercise. When considering the child protection system in England, this analysis suggests the urgent need for a recalibration of the relationship between agency and structure, so that parenting practices by individuals, particularly in relation to neglect, are not reduced to crude assessments of poor choices, but are based on contextualising families' lives, as well as policy and practice responses. While there is a need for the state to impose limits on some parental rights and freedoms in order to protect the capabilities and rights of children (Nussbaum and Dixon, 2012), social institutions also have responsibility to promote children's and parents' right to respect for private and family life in accordance with the European Convention on Human Rights (Council of Europe, 1950). In a CA-informed child protection system, public policy, services and professional practice would be aimed at enhancing the capabilities and human dignity of children and their parents, and recognising their interrelatedness.

Parental perspectives on the child protection system

Much of the research on the child protection system has focused on the experiences and outcomes for children. While studies focusing on children's experiences are essential, relatively limited attention has been given to the perspectives of parents and other birth family members – a gap, we would argue, that reflects the construction of birth parents as blameworthy and 'underserving' in the current system. Not only does this undermine parents' capability for voice, but also restricts opportunities to learn about how the capabilities of parents are promoted or diminished by the intervention of child protection professionals, and how policy and practice could be improved.

Studies involving the perspectives of parents highlight the shaming and blaming nature of the child protection interventions that lead to them feeling dehumanised and stigmatised (Gibson, 2015; Smithson and Gibson, 2016). A qualitative study with parents who have had involvement in the child protection system confirmed a shift from support to policing (Gupta et al, 2016a), in line with quantitative data, including the Bilson and Martin (2016) study. This change is taking place alongside the diminishing availability of services providing early help. As a result, children's services are often viewed as a source of fear rather than one that could provide assistance for families struggling in adverse circumstances. Families in need feel afraid to seek help and have 'nowhere to turn to' (Gupta et al, 2016a). As a family member explains:

> Poverty is living day to day and making ends meet. The money you have is not enough to provide for your kids.

My daughter was bullied at school for her clothes and not having the right fashions; she stopped attending school and I was threatened with prison. I don't like borrowing from family and friends so I asked for help from social services. Then a social worker came around, checked my cupboards and made me feel I had done the wrong thing by asking for help. (Cited in Gupta et al, 2016a, p 2)

The families' experiences reflect the conclusions of Morris and colleagues (2015, p 9) that often limited early help is offered but families 'may face the full wrath of the state if their care is found wanting'. While it is perhaps inevitable that some parents involved in the child protection system will have negative experiences, given that the process may ultimately lead to their child being removed from their care, in an environment where the provision of support is neglected, families often receive no attention until they are in crisis. In a risk-averse climate, this is likely to activate a policing response with shame and blame permeating the process (Gibson, 2015; Gupta and ATD Fourth World, 2015).

Another qualitative study into the experiences of parents who were involved in the English child protection system found that the overwhelming theme of the parents' experiences was that the system was uncaring, inflexible and, for some, harmful to both themselves and their children. The lack of the capability of voice in the process related to a sense that parents were being treated as 'less than human' (Smithson and Gibson, 2016, p 8). Child protection meetings have been singled out in studies involving parents' perspectives as spaces where participants felt particularly powerless and voiceless, as one parent explains:

You sit at the table and listen, but you are not allowed a choice or an input that's going to have any impact. So you are sat there observing what everyone else is doing with your life, and your children's lives on the basis of strangers around the table. It is degrading, humiliating. Everything is taken away from you. (Cited in Gupta and ATD Fourth World, 2015, p 137)

While there is a need for the state to impose limits on some parental rights and freedoms in order to protect children from significant harm, in the context of child protection work, relationships with professionals and how power is exercised on discursive levels and in the interactions between individuals are crucial to the promotion of children's and parents' capabilities. Feelings of acceptance and trust between social workers and families are central for positive engagement (Keddell, 2011). However in a risk-saturated system, feelings of blame and shame dominate and can lead to avoidance and defensiveness, dynamics that inevitably disrupt the potential for effective protective and supportive work with children and families:

> From the beginning, you're already feeling judged. You feel like you're going in the lion's den. You're sat there around a table with people who have been trained to do certain things but you're not trained. You're going in there thinking, "I don't understand what's going on. What have I done wrong?" And, of course, your defence mechanism goes up and you instantly defend your own corner but that sometimes comes across as you being rude, arrogant or not understanding and having a lack of insight. All these posh words come out of their mouths towards you and you feel like you're being attacked. (Cited in Gupta et al, 2016a, p 4)

The CA proposes an understanding of empowerment as the process of expanding an individual's wellbeing freedom, or set of valuable capabilities (Keleher, 2014). 'Expansion of freedom is viewed, in this approach, both as the primary end and as the principal means of development' (Sen, 1999, p xii). Studies involving the perspectives of parents indicate how professionals' use of power *with* rather than power *over* can make a positive difference to their functionings and avoid damaging personal identities that they have reason value (Entwhistle and Watt , 2013). As a parent notes:

> ... social workers are perhaps one of the most intimate relationships [individuals] have with the state, and it's someone who has a lot of power over them ... if that person is not treating them with recognition and respect, what it's doing to their self-esteem, their sense of themselves, regardless of the success of the social work relationship, is actually terribly damaging. It's reinforcing all the negative stuff they're seeing in the media or hear politicians talk.... (www.atd-uk.org/resources/uk)

Smithson and Gibson's (2016) study found that parents could describe positive experiences with social workers, when they were treated in a humane way, yet still experienced being treated as less than human by the system overall. However, for parents who experienced a social worker as uncaring, unsupportive and judgmental the whole process was even more difficult. Just as families' lives need to be contextualised, this highlights the need also to consider how social workers' and other professionals' capabilities to exercise agency in ways that promote parents' and children's capabilities are affected by the organisational structures and cultures in which they work.

Conclusion

This chapter has drawn on the CA to critically analyse child protection policies and practices in England and their impact on family members involved. We have argued that the current child protection system, based on neoliberal ideas that individualises risk and blame and implemented at a time when cuts to welfare and support services are increasing hardship for so many families, is deeply flawed and fundamentally unjust.

What is required is a paradigm shift from a narrow focus on risk and to one that fundamentally aims to promote the wellbeing of children and their families. The CA offers a theoretical framework for the development of policies and practices to support such a paradigm shift aimed at promoting social justice and human flourishing. Parental difficulties would not be ignored, and there will be a need for the state to take protective action in circumstances of significant harm to a child, but this would be in the context of the provision of supportive state services aimed at reducing the deleterious effects of poverty and other forms of inequality on children and their parents.

Capability-promoting social policies in child protection would need to be aimed at different levels of the child protection system:

- At a national level, there needs to be recognition of the impact of poverty and inequality on children's and their families' lives. Serious questions need to be asked and addressed in relation to who are the children who come into care and are subject to child protection interventions and the links to social deprivation. Public debate needs to take place about the social determinants of harm to children and state responsibilities to vulnerable children and families.
- At a national and local level, there needs to be a reversal of 'austerity' policies that result in significant cuts to welfare benefits and community-based family support services – the resources and conversion factors that promote parents' capabilities to adequately

care for their children. Attention should be paid not only to the development of individuals' capabilities, but also to the combined capabilities of poor and other marginalised communities.

- Capability-promoting social policies need to incorporate an analysis of political forces that shape public policy. Attention needs to be paid by policymakers and practitioners to the impact of risk-averse discourses and neoliberal ideas individualising blame on professional practice and families' lives. Social workers and other professionals must take an intersectional approach to understanding how macro-level structural inequalities influence families' lives and professional practice on micro levels with material and psychological consequences. An individual's agency is recognised, but so are the constraints of interlocking structural factors. This approach challenges the child protection narrative that what parents do or do not do is the result of rational choices.

- Attention should be paid to whose voices are privileged in policymaking and practice decisions, with the aim of promoting participation as intrinsically and instrumentally valuable, and learning from successful participatory approaches such as parent advocacy programmes (Tobis, 2013).

- Professionals working within a capability-promoting approach would recognise their ability to promote strengths and enhance capabilities, as well as to diminish and destroy (including power to shame), and have a commitment to promoting human rights, social justice and the dignity of all.

Much further work is required to develop these ideas about the application of the CA to child protection policy and practice, and also to engage with complementary critical sociological and political thinking about power relations and the reproduction of inequality in order to further the development of more humane and socially just child protection policies and practices.

Note

[1] This which was a public inquiry into the death of Victoria Climbié, an eight year old girl from the Ivory Coast who had been known to child welfare and health professionals prior to her murder by her aunt and aunt's boyfriend in London in 2000.

References

Baldwin, N. and Spencer, N. (2005) *Economic, cultural and social contexts of neglect,* London: Jessica Kingsley Publishers.

Bilson, A. and Martin, K.E. (2016) 'Referrals and child protection in England: one in five children referred to children's services and one in nineteen investigated before the age of five', *British Journal of Social Work,* early online publication, 24 May.

Bonvin, J.P. (2014) 'Towards a more critical appraisal of social policies: the contribution of the capability approach', in H.-U. Otto and H. Ziegler (eds) *Critical social policy and the capability approach,* Leverkusen: Barbara Budrich, pp 231-48.

Brown, R. and Ward, H. (2013) *Decision-making within a child's timeframe,* London: Childhood Wellbeing Research Centre.

Burns, J. (2015) 'David Cameron bids to speed up adoption process', BBC News, 2 November, available at www.bbc.co.uk/news/education-34682421.

Bywaters, P. (2015) 'Inequalities in child welfare: towards a new policy, research and action agenda', *British Journal of Social Work,* vol 45, no 1, pp 6-23.

Bywaters, P., Bunting, L., Davidson, G., Hanratty, J., Mason, W., McCartan, C. and Steils, N. (2016) *The relationship between poverty, child abuse and neglect: an evidence review,* York: Joseph Rowntree Foundation, available at www.jrf.org.uk.

Cafcass (2016) 'Care Applications in April 2016', available at www.cafcass.gov.uk/leaflets-resources/organisational-material/care-and-private-law-demand-statistics/care-demand-statistics.aspx.

Council of Europe (1950) *European Convention on Human Rights,* Strasbourg: Council of Europe, available at www.echr.coe.int/Documents/Convention_ENG.pdf.

DfE (Department for Education) (2015a) *Characteristics of children in need: 2014 to 2015,* London: DfE, available at www.gov.uk/government/uploads/system/uploads/attachment_data/file/469737/SFR41-2015_Text.pdf.

DfE (2015b) *Working together to safeguard children: a guide to inter-agency working to safeguard and promote the welfare of children,* London: DfE, available at www.gov.uk/government/uploads/system/uploads/attachment_data/file/419595/Working_Together_to_Safeguard_Children.pdf.

Devine, L. and Parker, S. (2015) *Rethinking child protection strategy: Learning from trends,* Working Paper, Bristol: Centre for Legal Research, University of the West of England.

Edwards R., Gillies, V. and Horsley, N. (2015) 'Brain science and early years policy: hopeful ethos or "cruel optimism"?', *Critical Social Policy*, vol 35, no 2, pp 167-87.

Entwistle, V.A. and Watt, I.S. (2013) 'Treating patients as persons: a capabilities approach to support delivery of person-centered care', *The American Journal of Bioethics*, vol 13, no 8, pp 28-39.

Featherstone, B., White, S. and Morris, K. (2014a) *Re-imagining child protection*, Bristol: Policy Press.

Featherstone, B., Morris, K. and White, S. (2014b) 'A marriage made in hell: early intervention meets child protection', *British Journal of Social Work*, vol 44, no 7, pp 1735-49.

Fenton-Glynn, C. (2016) *Adoption without consent*, Study for the Petti Committee, European Parliament, Brussels: European Union, available at www.europarl.europa.eu/supporting-analyses.

Frost, N. and Parton, N. (2009) *Understanding children's social care: Politics, policy and practice*, London: Sage Publications.

Garrett, P.M. (2009) *Transforming children's services? Social work, neoliberalism and the 'modern' world*, Milton Keynes: Open University Press.

Gayle, D. (2015) 'Number of homeless families housed in B&Bs rises 300% in five years', *The Guardian*, 24 June.

Gibson, M. (2015) 'Shame and guilt in child protection social work: new interpretations and opportunities for practice', *Child and Family Social Work*, vol 20, no 3, pp 333-43.

Gilbert, N. (1997) *Combatting child abuse: International perspectives and trends*, New York, NY: Oxford University Press.

Gilbert, N., Parton, N. and Skivenes, M. (eds) (2011) *Child protection systems: International trends and orientations*, New York, NY: Oxford University Press.

Gove, M. (2012) 'The failure of child protection and the need for a fresh start', Speech on child protection at the Institute of Public Policy Research, 19 November, available at www.gov.uk/government/speeches/the-failure-of-child-protection-and-the-need-for-a-fresh-start.

Gove, M. (2013) Getting it right for children in need', Speech to the NSPCC, available at www.gov.uk/government/speeches/getting-it-right-for-children-in-need-speech-to-the-nspcc.

Gupta, A. (2015) 'Poverty and child neglect: the elephant in the room?', *Families, Relationships and Societies*, early online publication, 15 January.

Gupta, A. and ATD Fourth World (2015) 'Poverty and shame: messages for social work', *Critical and Radical Social Work*, vol 3, no 1, pp 131-9.

Gupta, A., Blumhardt, H. and ATD Fourth World (2016a) 'Giving poverty a voice: families' experiences of social work practice in a risk-averse system', *Families, Relationships and Societies*, early online publication, 1 February.

Gupta, A., Featherstone, B. and White, S. (2016b) 'Reclaiming humanity: from capacities to capabilities in understanding parenting in adversity', *British Journal of Social Work*, vol 46, no 2, pp 339-54.

Hick, R. (2012) 'The capability approach: insights for a new poverty focus', *Journal of Social Policy*, vol 41, no 2, pp 291-308.

HM Government (2013) *Working together to safeguard children*, London: Department for Education.

Hood, R., Goldacre, A., Grant, R. and Jones, R. (2016) 'Exploring demand and provision in English child protection services', *British Journal of Social Work*, vol 46, no 4, pp 923-41.

Hooper, C., Gorin, S., Cabral, C. and Dyson, C. (2007) *Living with hardship 24/7: The diverse experiences of families in poverty in England*, London: Frank Buttle Trust.

Keddell, E. (2011) 'Reasoning processes in child protection decision making: negotiating moral minefields and risky relationships', *British Journal of Social Work*, vol 41, no 7, pp 1251-70.

Keleher, L. (2014) 'Sen and Nussbaum: agency and capability expansion', *Ethics and Economics*, vol 11, no 2, pp 54-70.

Laming, H. (2003) *The Victoria Climbié inquiry report*, London: The Stationery Office.

Morris, K., White, S., Doherty, P. and Warwick, L. (2015) 'Out of time: theorizing family in social work practice', *Child and Family Social Work*, early online publication, 7 October.

Nussbaum, N. (2011) *Creating capabilities: The human development approach*, Cambridge, MA: Belknap Press of Harvard University Press.

Nussbaum, M. and Dixon, R. (2012) *Children's rights and a capabilities approach: The question of special priority*, Public Law & Legal Theory Working Papers No. 384, Chicago, IL: University of Chicago Law School.

Parton, N. (2014) *The politics of child protection: Contemporary developments and future directions*, Basingstoke: Palgrave Macmillan.

Pelton, L. (2015) 'The continuing role of material factors in child maltreatment and placement', *Child Abuse & Neglect*, vol 41, pp 30-9.

Perry, J., Williams, M., Sefton, T. and Haddad, M. (2014) *Emergency use only: Understanding and reducing the use of food banks in the UK*, London: Child Poverty Action Group, Church of England, Oxfam GB and The Trussell Trust.

Pösö, T. (2011) 'Combatting child abuse in Finland: from family to child-centred orientation', in N. Gilbert, N. Parton and M. Skivenes (eds) (2011) *Child protection systems: International trends and orientations*, New York, NY: Oxford University Press, pp 112-30.

Pösö, T. (2015) 'Research in child abuse and neglect: a Finnish perspective', in L. Waterhouse and J. McGhee (eds) *Challenging child protection: New directions in safeguarding children*, London: Jessica Kingsley Publishers, pp 89-99.

Sen, A. (1983) 'Poor, relatively speaking', *Oxford Economic Papers*, vol 35, no 2, pp 153-69.

Sen, A. (1992) *Inequality reexamined*, New Delhi: Oxford University Press.

Sen, A. (1995) 'The political economy of targeting', in D. Van de Walle and K. Nead (eds) *Public spending and the poor*, Washington, DC: World Bank, pp 11-24.

Sen, A. (1999) *Development as freedom*, Oxford: Oxford University Press.

Smithson, R. and Gibson, M. (2016) 'Less than human: a qualitative study into the experience of parents involved in the child protection system', *Child & Family Social Work*, early online publication, 4 February.

Stevenson, O. (1998) *Neglected children: Issues and dilemmas*, Oxford: Blackwell.

Tobis, D. (2013) *From pariahs to partners: How parents and their allies changed New York City's child welfare system*, Oxford: Oxford University Press.

United Nations (1989) *United Nations Convention in the Rights of the Child*, London: UNICEF UK, available at www.unicef.org.uk/Documents/Publication-pdfs/UNCRC_PRESS200910web.pdf.

Walker, R., Kyomuhendo, G.B., Chase, E., Choudhry, S., Gubrium, E.K., Nicola, J.Y. and Ming, Y. (2013) 'Poverty in global perspective: is shame a common denominator?', *Journal of Social Policy*, vol 42, no 2, pp 215-33.

Warner, J. (2015) *The emotional politics of social work and child protection*, Bristol: Policy Press.

Wastell, D. and White, S. (2012) 'Blinded by neuroscience: social policy, the family and the infant brain', *Families, Relationships and Societies*, vol 1, no 3, pp 397-414.

Waterhouse, L. and McGhee, J. (2015a) 'Introduction: challenging child protection and safeguarding children', in L. Waterhouse and J. McGhee (eds) *Challenging child protection: New directions in safeguarding children*, London: Jessica Kingsley Publishers, pp 9-18.

ELEVEN

The capability approach and a child standpoint

Sharon Bessell

Introduction

Policy is focused on the identification of actual or anticipated problems and on responses to those problems. It refers to 'the principles that govern action about means as well as ends and it, therefore, implies change: changing situations, systems, practices, behaviour' (Titmuss, 1974, p 138). Social policy, which is the focus of this chapter, can be defined as 'the actions taken within a society to develop and deliver services for people in order to meet their needs for welfare and wellbeing' (Alcock, 2008, p 2). Determining the actions that should be taken to enhance welfare and wellbeing is by no means a straightforward task. In developing social policies, policymakers are faced with the complexities, diversity and messiness of people's real lives, lived within complicated webs of interpersonal relationships and within broader macroeconomic and social structures.

Scholars and practitioners of policy have long debated how policy is, and should be, developed and analysed. On the one hand, evidence-based policy is presented as objective and value-neutral – a means of allowing policymakers to manage economic and social affairs in 'an apolitical, scientized manner such that social policy is more or less an exercise in social technology' (Schwandt, 1997, p 74). In some quarters, such an approach is considered essential if policy is to accurately identify the problems that demand action, and to ensure that the resulting action is scientifically based and unbiased. On the other hand, the interpretivist turn in policy analysis has recognised that policymaking is deeply normative. Interpretivist policy analysts have challenged the notion that policy is made only on the basis of data resulting from econometric modelling and longitudinal and experimental research, which is devoid of values (Sanderson, 2002). Rather, they suggest that policymaking is necessarily embedded in the values, norms and politics of a society and its political, social and economic systems. Dryzek (2002, p 214) has aptly described policymaking as 'a process of deliberation which weighs beliefs, principles, and actions under conditions of multiple frames for the interpretation and evaluation of the world'.

Following in the interpretivist tradition of discursive analysis, this chapter begins with a recognition that social policy is a normative enterprise, seeking not only to 'develop and deliver services for people in order to meet their needs for welfare and wellbeing', as Alcock (2008, p 2) posits, but to do so in ways that privilege particular ideas and values. This chapter demonstrates the ways in which strongly held values around egalitarianism and ensuring that people have a reasonable opportunity to make what they want of their lives – colloquially described as having a 'fair go' – have shaped social policy settings since the beginning of the Australian nation state. While recognising that these, like all values, are often contested and framed in competing ways, I argue that a 'fair go' resonates with a capability approach, with synergies between the expansion of capabilities and freedom to live the life one values and Australian ideas of egalitarian individualism. However, a closer analysis of the key elements of Australian social policy over time reveals a relatively narrow focus on paid employment as the primary means of achieving social and individual wellbeing. As a result, social policy has been highly gendered and, importantly for the purposes of this chapter, has resulted in the under-development of social policy on issues that children value – particularly time with parents. Having examined the values that underpin dominant approaches to social policy in Australia, this chapter argues that a child standpoint, illuminated by research with children, provides a means of rethinking social policy in ways that are genuinely inclusive of children and able to expand the capabilities of all, regardless of age.

The capability approach and social policy

The capability approach is valuable not only in framing the policy problem to be addressed, but also in offering a useful analytic lens through which to assess the representation of policy problems and responses. Importantly, the capability approach provides a means of making explicit the normative dimensions of policymaking (Robeyns, 2003, p 62). Van Hulst and Yanow (2016, p 97) describe the process of policy framing as drawing 'certain features of an intractable policy situation together, thereby both rendering them more coherent and graspable and diverting attention from their ambiguities and uncertainties'. By prioritising the expansion of people's capabilities, the capability approach positions human development (rather than economic growth or income maximisation) as the objective. The capability approach takes as its basic premise the idea that the aim of public action and policy – be it on poverty reduction, social policy or distributive justice – should be to expand the freedom people have to engage in beings and doings that are valuable to them (see Alkire, 2005, p 117). In his conceptualisation of capability freedom, Sen (1985, 1990, 1992) is particularly concerned with the expansion of capabilities among those who are deprived. Significantly, the capability approach provides a way of moving beyond income as a means of determining quality of life, wellbeing, or levels of deprivation to focus on the freedoms that enable people to make the choices that matter to them (see Alkire, 2005). Thus, improving the lives, welfare and wellbeing of people, particularly those who are deprived or marginalised, becomes the central feature of policy in ways that are both 'coherent and graspable'.

While the capability approach renders visible and prioritises the expansion of capabilities that people have reason to value, there remain ambiguities and uncertainties about how to determine what those capabilities are. These ambiguities and uncertainties have led critics of the capability approach to dismiss it as unworkable (see Rawls, 1999, p 13) or lacking specificity. Yet, during the past two decades there has been a remarkable expansion in thinking about how capability freedom can be conceptualised and operationalised. In particular, Nussbaum's (2000) work on creating a list of capabilities has been significant in furthering debates on how capabilities are to be determined, despite critiques that question the appropriateness of a theoretically derived set of capabilities (Sen, 2004). While there remain unresolved ambiguities and uncertainties around the capability approach, lively debates have ensured transparency around the nature of those uncertainties, which is not a feature of all policy frames.

Egalitarianism and a 'fair go' as central to underpinning Australian identity

Ideas are central to understanding the ways in which policies are framed, discussed, negotiated and contested (see Cox, 2001; Béland and Hacker, 2004; Béland, 2005). Ideas matter, not only within formal policymaking processes, but to broader public discourse around social issues and the expectations that citizens have of their governments. Ideas are deeply bound up with people's identities and sense of right and wrong; they often evoke deep emotions and loyalties (see Goldstein and Keohane, 1993, p 8). Understanding approaches to social policy in Australia necessitates an understanding of the ideational foundations on which that social policy has been built.

Australian self-image is underpinned by ideas of egalitarianism and mutual support, often described colloquially as 'fairness' or ensuring that everyone has a 'fair go'. While divisions based on class, race, gender and religion have existed throughout Australia's history, Kapferer and Morris (2003, p 90) argue that they have been 'suppressed or transmuted as part of the Australian national presentation'. Australian national identity emerged as 'an imagined resolution of difference as sameness, or unity of project', with Australians represented – and self-representing – as 'egalitarian and classless' (Kapferer and Morris, 2003, pp 90-1). Fairness and equality have been central tenets of the egalitarian ethos that has underpinned Australian national identity.

Ideas of fairness and equality are instrumental in shaping the popular imagination of what it is to be Australian. As Marian Sawer has observed (2008, p 45), 'A heroic past becomes part of the genealogy of the present.' Values of egalitarianism were already deeply embedded in representations and self-representations of Australia prior to 1901, when six self-governing British colonies united to form the Commonwealth of Australia. As early as 1859, novelist Henry Kingsley described Australia as a 'workingman's paradise' (cited in Greig et al, 2003). Throughout the late 1800s, Australia became known as enabling (white) working *men* to throw off the class strictures of Europe in order to create their own futures (see Greig et al, 2003). If ideas of egalitarianism and fairness pre-existed the establishment of the Commonwealth of Australia, those values are often presented as having been forged into the essence of Australian national identity by the experiences of the First World War, only a little more than a decade after federation. The most celebrated achievements of Australia's first wartime experience as a nation are not military victories but the exhibition of characteristics of mateship, mutual support and decency in the face of extreme adversity. Kapferer and Morris have described the ways in which the mythology surrounding Australian soldiers in the First World War and in later wars came to represent a 'society of equals who possessed as inner qualities the capacity to govern themselves. Thus, the need for hierarchical orders of power and control was made redundant' (Kapferer and Morris, 2003, p 91).

A commitment to fairness and equality in situations of desperation is represented by other authors (see Edwards, 2002, p 57; Leigh, 2013) as quintessentially Australian. It is a representation of 'Australianness' that has been embraced by both the left and the right. Economist and Australian parliamentarian, Andrew Leigh, captures a powerful imagining of Australian values when he describes 'a belief in equality [as] a golden thread through Australia's history, even at times when the gap between rich and poor has widened'.

An egalitarian ethos, manifesting as a stated commitment to fairness and equality, has been a device for both inclusion and exclusion within Australian society. Significantly, while values of fairness and equality appear to be universally applicable, and are presented as such, they often play out in particularly masculinist terms. Indeed, the historical focus on the significance of these values during wartime highlights the ways in which men have experienced them – and demonstrated them towards other men. Mateship, the interpersonal relationship generally considered as encapsulating values of egalitarianism and fairness, is a particularly male construct. Men across socioeconomic status refer to one another as 'mate', a practice described by Leigh (2013, p 3) as a 'universal leveller', but one that does not level gender divides within society. Women rarely use the term mate, and are called mate (particularly by men) on even rarer occasions. In practice, the application of deeply held values of fairness and equality – often described as Australian egalitarianism – is shaped by both gender and race (see Greig et al, 2003).

Egalitarianism and a fair go in the distribution of resources

Saunders (2004, pp 4-5) describes a normative commitment to 'fair' distribution of resources as a defining feature of popular and political discourse in Australia since the mid-19th century. In the last two decades of the 19th century, reconceptualisations of liberalism, influenced by the English philosopher T.H. Green, became influential in the colonies that, 20 years later, would federate to become Australia (see Sawer, 2008). Drawing on Green, the idea of freedom was recast: no longer 'freedom from' but 'freedom to'. This recasting shifted from negative to positive freedom, emphasising the importance of individuals having the freedom to develop to their full potential, supported by a state committed to promoting fairness (Sawer, 2008, pp 45-6).

As the ideological and normative foundations for the new Australian state were laid, the idea that the state must proactively create the conditions for a fair society took hold in some quarters. As Castles (2001, p 539) has observed, the role of the state was not to create a social democratic welfare system of universal provision, but to ensure that 'those who were waged were able to maintain a decent life for themselves and their dependents without further intervention by the state'. Thus, particular emphasis was placed on the necessity of ensuring that (male) workers received fair wages, in order to provide decent living standards for themselves and their families. Values of egalitarianism combined with values of individualism to create an ideological commitment to the state creating the conditions for equality, then letting individuals act unfettered to make the most of those opportunities – in Kapferer and Morris' (2003) characterisation, a commitment to 'egalitarian individualism'. This has played out in the centrality of workforce participation and fair remuneration to social policy in Australia.

The Commonwealth of Australia Constitution Act 1901 (section 51, xxxv) provides for the federal Parliament to legislate in areas of 'conciliation and arbitration for the prevention and settlement of industrial disputes extending beyond the limits of any one State'. In 1904, the Commonwealth Court of Conciliation and Arbitration was established to arbitrate on industrial disputes providing an institutional basis for a deep normative commitment to minimum wage and a safety net for (male) workers. These dual objectives would become central pillars of Australian social policy throughout the 20th century.

While contested, and sometimes rejected, by key political actors, liberal ideals of positive liberty, enabled through fair employment conditions and a minimum wage, have underpinned Australia's social policy throughout the 20th century. Central to this has been the idea that the state has an obligation to create the opportunity for 'freedom to'; that is, opportunity to achieve potential despite the circumstances of birth or social class. Industrial arbitration and wage regulation have been essential to this, leading to what Castles (1985) described as a unique model of the 'wage-earner's welfare state'. The objective of arbitration was not to respond to those who had fallen into poverty, but to prevent poverty through a combination of full (male) employment, living wages sufficient to support a family, and reasonable conditions of work.

From the 1940s to the 1970s, Australian social and labour policies were shaped by the objective of full adult male employment (women, as wives and mothers, were by definition excluded) (see Harris, 2001). Harris (2001, p 13) describes the 1940s as a period of reframing, when 'self-interest and competition were questioned and found wanting'. The economic circumstances of the time allowed the policy of full employment to become a reality. The narrative of social welfare policy shifted from providing relief, via charitable beneficence, towards those unable to gain employment to the idea that the unemployed had a social right to assistance from the state (Harris, 2001, p 14). While an economic reality of full employment had provided the strongest element of Australia's social safety net after the Second World War, by the late 1960s the risk of poverty among households with an unemployed breadwinner was extremely high, particularly where there were dependent children. Intervention from the Whitlam Labour government in 1973 sought to address the shortfall by standardising pensions and unemployment benefits at 25% of average weekly earnings (Harris, 2001, p 15). Interventions to create the conditions for positive freedom to be achieved were extended beyond the 'working man' to marginalised groups who had previously received little attention in policy discourse. Yet, labour force participation, renumerated by fair wages rather than the welfare state, remained the means by which a decent standard of living could be achieved.

Accompanying ideas of fairness and equality are questions of how fairness is best achieved through policy. As discussed, the Australian welfare state is premised on the idea that government has a role to play in actively promoting fairness. However, this does not extend to the government having a role in fostering *full* equality. Australia's welfare state is based on liberal, rather than social democratic, principles. The aim of the welfare system has been to support those in need, with an expectation that those who are able to support themselves do so rather than rely on the state. Kapferer and Morris' (2003) characterisation of Australia's 'egalitarian individualism' is pertinent to characterising the contemporary Australian welfare state in the early 21st century.

Peter Whiteford (2011, p 2) notes that Australia's contemporary social security system is significantly different from other liberal welfare regimes, which are financed by employer/employee contributions:

> By contrast, Australia's flat-rate payments are financed from general taxation revenue, and there are no separate social security contributions; benefits are also income-tested or asset-tested, so payments reduce as other resources increase. The rationale for this approach is that it reduces poverty more efficiently by concentrating the available resources on the poor ('helping those most in need') and minimises adverse incentives by limiting the overall level of spending and taxes.

Whiteford demonstrates (2011) that Australia's levels of taxation are low among members countries in the Organisation for Economic Co-operation and Development (OECD), with a highly progressive taxation system resulting not from high taxes on the wealthy, but from those in the lowest income groups paying low taxes relative to similar groups in other OECD countries. Strongly targeted redistribution of the taxation revenue is a central pillar of Australia's welfare state, with Australia spending less on social security benefits than any other OECD country, but redistributing more to the lowest 20% than any country other than Denmark (Whiteford, 2011, 2015).

It is also important to note other elements of the Australian social policy and social security environment: the old-age pension has been in place since 1909 and is currently available to those over the age of 65 (approximately 14% of the population in 2013), with about half of those eligible actually receiving the pension; universal healthcare has been consistently in place since 1984; and child benefits have formed an important element of social policy since the 1980s (see Castles, 2001). Paid employment in fair conditions for reasonable remuneration has been central to the Australian welfare state, but has been accompanied by a broader set of social security provisions.

In recent years, the long-held commitment to positive freedoms, egalitarianism and redistribution designed to promote a fair society have been strongly challenged. From the early 1990s, Australia's system of arbitration came under threat from both sides of politics, as Australia wound back industrial regulation in a drive for global competitiveness. This had a negative effect on the wages, conditions of work and job security of many low-skilled and vulnerable workers. In parallel, already limited benefits for groups outside the labour force were subject to stringent means-testing measures or were wound back. In 2005, the conservative Liberal–National coalition government introduced 'Welfare to Work' measures, based on the idea that 'increased participation in work from all Australians capable of work, including welfare recipients, increases individual wellbeing and is needed to help improve our future standard of living' (cited in Brady and Cook, 2015, p 1). Social contribution, including that of sole parents with young children, was reframed entirely in terms of paid employment. The policy reforms, particularly in relation to parenting payments, moved away from long-held values around expanding positive freedoms and egalitarianism towards strong emphasis on individual – not social – responsibility. Moreover, long-held values around the importance of fair working conditions and remuneration were eroded. Ten years after the introduction of Welfare to Work policies, Brady and Cook (2015, p 2) found 'little evidence that these reforms have had positive impacts on parents' and children's overall wellbeing, and suggestive evidence that they have had negative impacts on subjective and financial wellbeing'.

More recently, there has been a further shift away from government commitment to creating opportunity for all. In 2012, then federal treasurer, Joe Hockey, led a call that was repeated across the federal government for 'an end to the age of entitlement'. Hockey argued:

> Government spending on a range of social programs including education, health, housing, subsidised transport, social safety nets and retirement benefits has reached extraordinary levels as a percentage of GDP.... The social contract between government and its citizens needs to be urgently and significantly redefined. The reality is that we cannot have greater government services and more government involvement in our lives coupled with significantly lower taxation. As a community we need to redefine the responsibility of government and its citizens to provide for themselves, both during their working lives and into retirement.

Hockey's comments, which echoed the views of his conservative colleagues in government, misrepresent the nature of social policy in Australia and signal a further ideological shift away from a uniquely Australian welfare state based on ideas of egalitarianism.

To what extent does Australia have a capability-promoting approach to social policy?

On one level, Australia's approach to social policy – particularly prior to the 1990s – has strong resonance with a capability approach. The emphasis on fair working conditions and remuneration recognises not only income, but income that is sufficient to enable the realisation of positive freedoms. Castles (2001, p 539) has pointed out that until the late 1980s, Australia's wage dispersion was more equal than in most other countries as a result of an arbitration system designed to maintain fair wages. This points to a level of social justice in distribution that is central to Sen's (1992) conceptualisation of capability.

Values of individualism and of egalitarianism also resonate with a capability approach that 'puts human agency (rather than organizations such as markets or governments) at the centre of the stage' (Drèze and Sen, 2002, p 6). Egalitarian individualism, described by Kapferer and Morris (2003), sits comfortably with concepts of both social justice and ethical individualism, while rejecting methodological or ontological individualism (see Robeyns, 2005, pp 108-9).

Yet, there are important ways in which Australian social policy fails to demonstrate a capability-promoting dimension. The positive freedoms and creation of opportunities embraced as fundamentally Australian values have influenced social policy in somewhat narrow ways. As discussed, workforce participation on fair terms has long been seen as the most effective means of providing individual and family welfare and wellbeing. However, the failure to address the gendered divisions within the workforce – including a disturbingly persistent gender wage gap – indicates the shortcomings of this approach. Given the patriarchal origins of concepts of egalitarianism, it is perhaps not surprising that gender equality within the workforce has been halting, but given the centrality of workforce participation to the welfare state this is problematic. The centrality of work, both in people's lives and as a means of ensuring individual and familial welfare, also raises challenges in achieving capabilities in other areas of life. Work–life balance is lower in Australia than the OECD average, while 13.4% of Australians work in paid employment for 50 or more hours per week.

The shortcomings of Australia's approach to social policy, when analysed through a capability lens, have become more acute since the 1990s, as Australia has increasingly moved towards a residual model of social welfare (Harris, 2001). As a result, a range of indicators question ongoing commitment to the long-held value of a 'fair go'. The Australian work-based welfare state is neither adequately responding to the problems of structural poverty nor expanding the capabilities of those living in poverty. A 2014 report on poverty in Australia (ACOSS, 2014) found that 13.9% of all people are living below the poverty line (defined as 50% of median income). This figure increases to 17.7% for children under the age of 18 years, with over 23% of children under the age of 15 living in poverty. While poverty is particularly prevalent among the unemployed (61.2% of people who are without work live below the poverty line), one third of people living below the poverty line are in paid employment. More women than men live in poverty, with poverty especially prevalent among single mothers and their children (ACOSS, 2014).

The extent of child poverty in Australia, and policy reforms that have had deleterious impacts on low–income families, particularly single-parent families, raise important questions about the impact of current social policy on *children's* capabilities. The remainder of this chapter focuses on the value of a child standpoint in identifying capabilities, before discussing the capabilities that children, collectively, identify as valuable.

Capabilities from a child standpoint

There is considerable, and growing, interest in the value a capability approach might bring to both the study of childhood(s) and to policies and practice seeking to support children to reach their full potential. Recent research has also explored the relationship between a capability approach and children's participation and agency (for example, Hart et al, 2014). Iervese and Tuttolomondo (2013, p 244) have identified a focus within the capability approach on 'the future realisation of children's capabilities and increased interest in the development of capabilities during the present stage of childhood'.

Here, I seek to turn some traditional approaches on their head, by asking what children's views on what makes a valuable life bring to theorising and public action from a capability approach. Rather than focusing on how to develop children's capabilities, I draw on work that has developed within social studies of childhood over the past two to three decades to explore the implications of thinking (or rethinking) concepts of egalitarianism, a 'fair go' and individualism from a child standpoint. At the heart of the discussion that follows is the assumption that children are experts in their own lives and have the capacity to engage in considered reflection on what might improve – and what diminishes – their lives and the lives of those around them. This assumption is not without controversy. Modern, Western conceptualisations of childhood have positioned children as being *in the process* of gaining the competency that is considered to characterise adulthood. Waksler (1986, p 74, emphasis in original) has argued that this has resulted in adults taking for granted that 'children *as a category* know *less* than adults, have *less* experience, are *less* serious, and are *less* important than adults'. Alanen (1990) has argued that such ideas of childhood – and of children – are reflected in – and reflect – social theory, whereby 'the child' is defined not by what he or she is, but by what he or she is not yet and what he or she will be in the future (as an adult). The child, according to Alanen (1990, p 16), is generally depicted in social theory as 'pre-social, potentially social, in the process of becoming social', but not as a social being with the capacity to exercise agency.

Taking a child standpoint is one means of challenging and shifting a 'pre-social' view of children. Drawing on feminist theory, I take a child standpoint as a means of recognising that an individual's social location frames their reality, bringing some features of reality into prominence and obscuring others (Swigonski, 1994, p 390). As Swigonski argues (1994, p 390), 'standpoint theory begins with the idea that the less powerful members of a society experience a different reality as a consequence of their oppression'. My aim here is not to suggest that there is an objective 'truth' that can be discovered from children's perspectives, but to argue that social situatedness both shapes and reflects different realities (Stoetzler and Yuval-Davis, 2002). By listening to – and learning from – children's perspectives, we are able to bring to our analysis of how capabilities can be expanded – and how capability deprivation can be addressed – a set of experiences and priorities that are often marginalised because children are assumed to be in the process of becoming social beings rather than being social agents.

If a child standpoint has potential benefits in enriching the aims and nature of public action to enhance capabilities, it also reflects a political project that directly seeks to challenge children's subordinate social status. As Roberts (2008, p 263) argues, 'listening to children is central to recognizing and respecting their worth as human beings, drawing a direct relationship between being listened to and the human dignity that is foundational to the concept of human rights'.

(Re)conceptualising a 'fair go' from a child standpoint

This final section considers Australia's approach to social policy and the focus on paid employment from a child standpoint. It draws on research undertaken with 108 children aged between seven and 12 years in six urban sites in eastern Australia.[1] The research, which took place over a period of four years, sought to gain insights into children's views on what makes a strong and supportive community (see Bessell with Mason, 2014). Our methodology drew on participatory principles and was underpinned by a rights based approach; that is, a deep commitment to respecting children's rights and dignity within the research process and to creating spaces for genuine engagement (see Bessell, 2013, 2015). Our aim was not to observe children or to extract information, but to work with children to co-construct knowledge and to understand society from a child standpoint. In doing so, we gained deep insight into what children value not only about their communities, but about their lives more broadly. This, in turn, provides a lens through which to consider both capability freedom and the idea of a 'fair' society from a child standpoint.

Participatory research with children provides a means of illuminating the values that children, collectively, as a generationally distinct group within a social order, consider important to the normative aspects of developing policy. Importantly for the purposes of this chapter, participatory research with children offers the potential to understand what egalitarianism and fairness mean for children. Participatory research with children also offers the potential of contributing to the development of a 'list' of capabilities from a child standpoint. Here there are possibilities for moving beyond a philosophically developed set of capabilities towards a bottom-up approach that reflects the experiences and priorities of specific groups, particularly those – such as children – who are generally excluded from debates about the capabilities that might be the focus of public action. My aim here is not to develop a single or immutable list of capabilities, but to determine the capabilities that are recognised as valuable to specific (marginalised) groups and to question to extent to which those capabilities are facilitated or obstructed by social policy.

Ideas of fairness were fundamentally important to the children who participated in this research. However, their framing of 'fairness' was not always in harmony with the dominant (male) adult-constructed ideas discussed above as underpinning social policy in Australia, within which workplace participation is central. Significantly, children were particularly concerned with the treatment of those who are outside the workforce, and a dominant theme was concern for people who are homeless. The presence of homeless people within their communities was, for most children, a powerful manifestation of a lack of fairness and opportunity.

When children spoke of their parents' work, fairness was an important theme. Three aspects of fairness were consistently raised by children: the financial situation of the family, conditions of work, and hours worked. Children's lives were structured by the realities and demands of their parents' work in fundamentally important ways. Children living in economically disadvantaged families were particularly aware of their parents' working conditions and the ways in which those conditions shaped their own lives and their familial context. These children were acutely conscious of the fact that their parents' wages were insufficient to meet the family's needs. In the most financially disadvantaged families, children described their parents being unable to pay bills and sometimes rent, and often struggling to buy food. Children described their own strategies to protect their parents from further financial pressures and stress – most commonly by refraining from asking for money to engage in sports or other activities, including school activities. Here, a child standpoint is in line with the value of fair remuneration that has underpinned Australian social policy since the early days of federation, but which has been increasingly eroded since the 1980s and the shift away from industrial arbitration.

Children's sense of unfairness at their family's precarious financial situation was exacerbated when they knew their parents worked in conditions that were unsafe or insecure. Children described the impact of stressful working conditions on their own lives and on the family's wellbeing more generally. Significantly, the children who participated in this research were born after the winding back of Australia's arbitration system and of a range of social security benefits. The work environments they described as unfair are characteristic of Australia in a wage earners' post-welfare state era.

Our research found parents' working hours to be a major concern from a child standpoint. The resource children considered most important – and often most absent from their lives – was time with parents, and particularly time with fathers. Australia can be described as based on a one-and-a-half (rather than dual) earner model, whereby fathers tend to work full time and mothers part time. Most children who participated in our research wanted more time with both mothers and fathers. Many children described their mothers as being present, but very busy, as they juggled paid employment and household responsibilities. Moreover, fathers were often absent because of work, and many children described their fathers as being tired or stressed at the end of the working day, and unavailable to them. Consistently, children described as unfair and unreasonable the perception of employers and of a workplace-based social system that parents' time at work is more important than time with their children.

Significantly, policy discourse in Australia has paid very little attention to parents' time with their children. When time has been considered, it has been in the context of debates around public support for childcare in order to facilitate mothers' re-entry to the workforce. Children's time with fathers has been almost entirely absent from the policy agenda. The combination of a wage-earner welfare state and the legacy of the male breadwinner model continues to dominate, often implicitly, policy settings and public debate, at the same time as the protections once afforded to workers are being wound back. Fathers' time with their children has received little consideration within the dominant policy and social discourse. The increasing entry of women into the workforce since the 1970s has resulted in efforts to integrate women into the labour market, rather than rethinking the approach to work–family balance. Moreover, policy initiatives around Welfare to Work that seek to force single parents (usually mothers) to re-enter the workforce through restrictions on welfare benefits ignore entirely issues of child–parent time. Across these policy issues we see a striking disconnect between a child standpoint and adult-centred, work-centred policies.

When considered through the lens of the capability approach, child–parent time can be conceptualised as important in at least two ways. First, time with parents is identified by children as a resource they have reason to value. Second, time with parents is essential to children as a social conversion factor. Children in this research described the value they place on actively engaging in their communities, for example through developing strong relationships with neighbours and others, and participating in and contributing to community events. In the Australian context, however, the opportunity for children to act independently of their parents is extremely limited. When parents were unavailable to facilitate children's engagement in their communities, children were far more likely to describe feeling both isolated and disconnected from those communities.

From a child standpoint, the emphasis on adult (particularly male, and increasingly female) workforce participation as the foundation of Australian social policy – but increasingly with fewer protections around working conditions and hours and levels of remuneration – has the effect of limiting rather than expanding children's capabilities. This is particularly evident in relation to children's social achievements. Significantly, the importance of child–parent time to children (as a resource they have reason to value) and to society (as collective benefit resulting from the realisation of individual capabilities), is illuminated – and its value made explicit – when considered through a capability lens.

Conclusion

This chapter has sought to demonstrate the value of the capability approach in illuminating the normative values on which social policy is based and in assessing the policy settings that result. More significantly, however, the chapter has sought to demonstrate the importance of considering capabilities that are valued not only by those who are most likely to have voice and influence, but by those who are silent or silenced. Importantly, children – while often presented as beneficiaries of social policy – rarely have the space within which to articulate the capabilities they have reason to value. As argued here, Australian social policy has been built on ideas of fairness, but has privileged particular interpretations of what a 'fair go' is and for whom. From the perspective of children, fairness looks rather different from the (male-focused) adult-led definitions that have shaped policies. Developing a child standpoint through participatory research with children is one important means of bringing to the fore the capabilities that children have reason to value. In doing so, a child standpoint has the potential to contribute to both capability-promoting and child-inclusive policies.

Note
[1] This research was funded by an Australian Research Council Linkage Grant, LP900106.

References
ACOSS (Australian Council of Social Services) (2014) *Poverty in Australia*, Strawberry Hills: Australian Council of Social Services.

Alcock, P. (2008) *Understanding poverty* (3rd edn), Palgrave: London.

Alanen, L. (1990) 'Rethinking socialization, the family and childhood', in P.A. Adler, P. Adler, and N. Mandell, *Sociological Studies of Child Development, volume 3*, Greenwich, CT: JAI, pp 13-28.

Alkire, S. (2005) 'Why the capability approach?', *Journal of Human Development*, vol 6, no 1, pp 115-35.

Béland, D. (2005) 'Ideas and social policy: an institutional perspective', *Social Policy and Administration*, vol 39, no 1, pp 1-18.

Béland, D. and Hacker, J.S. (2004) 'Ideas, private institutions and American welfare state "exceptionalism": the case of health and old-age insurance, 1915-1965', *International Journal of Social Welfare*, vol 13, no 1, pp 42-54.

Bessell, S. (2013) 'Child-centred research workshops: a model for participatory, rights-based engagement with children', *Developing Practice*, no 37, pp 21-24.

Bessell, S. (2015) 'Rights-based research with children: principles and practice', in R. Evans and L. Holt (eds) *Methodological approaches and methods in practice, volume 2*, Singapore: Springer.

Bessell, S. with Mason, J. (2014) *Putting the pieces in place: Children, communities and social capital in Australia*, Canberra: Australian National University, available at http://cpc.crawford.anu.edu.au/publications.

Brady, M. and Cook, K. (2015), 'The impact of welfare to work on parents and their children', *Evidence Base*, no 3, pp 1-23.

Castles, F.G. (1985) *The working class and welfare*, Sydney: Allen & Unwin.

Castles, F.G. (2001) 'A farewell to Australia's welfare state', *International Journal of Health Services*, vol 31, no 3, pp 537-44.

Cox, R.H. (2001) The social construction of an imperative: why welfare reform happened in Denmark and the Netherlands but not in Germany, *World Politics*, vol 53, no 3, pp 463-98.

Drèze, J. and Sen, A. (2002) *India: Development and participation*, Oxford: Oxford University Press.

Dryzek, J.S. (2002) 'Policy analysis and planning: from science to argument', in F. Fischer and J. Forester (eds) *The argumentative turn in policy analysis and planning*, London: Taylor and Francis.

Edwards, L. (2002) *How to argue with an economist: Reopening political debate in Australia*, Cambridge: University Press Cambridge.

Goldstein, J. and Keohane, R.O. (1993) 'Ideas and foreign policy: an analytical framework', in J. Goldstein and R.O. Keohane (eds) *Ideas and foreign policy: Beliefs, institutions, and political change*, Ithaca, NY and London: Cornell University Press.

Greig, A., Lewins, F. and White, K. (2003) *Inequality in Australia*, Cambridge: Cambridge University Press.

Harris, P. (2001) 'From relief to mutual obligation: welfare rationalities and unemployment in 20th-century Australia', *Journal of Sociology*, vol 37, no 1, pp 5-26.

Hart, C.S., Biggeri, M. and Babic, B. (eds) (2014) *Agency and participation in childhood and youth: International applications in schools and beyond*, London: Bloomsbury.

Hockey, J. (2012) 'The end of the age of entitlement', *Sydney Morning Herald*, 19 April, available at www.smh.com.au/national/the-end-of-the-age-of-entitlement-20120419-1x8vj.htm.

Iervese, V. and Tuttolomondo, L. (2013) 'Youth participation outside the classroom', in C.S. Hart, M. Biggeri and B. Babic (eds) (2014) *Agency and participation in Childhood and youth: International applications in schools and beyond*, London: Bloomsbury.

Kapferer, B. and Morris, B. (2003) 'The Australian society of the state: egalitarian ideologies and new directions in exclusionary practice', *Social Analysis: The International Journal of Social and Cultural Practice*, vol 47, no 3, pp 80-107.

Leigh, A. (2013) *Battlers and billionaires: The story of inequality in Australia*, Carlton: Black Inc.

Nussbaum, M.C. (2000) *Women and human development: The capabilities approach*, Cambridge: Cambridge University Press.

Rawls, J. (1999) *The law of peoples*, Cambridge MA: Harvard University Press.

Roberts, H. (2008) 'Listening to children: and hearing them', in P. Christensen and A. James (eds) *Research with children: Perspectives and practice* (2nd edn), New York, NY: Falmer Press.

Robeyns, I. (2005) 'The capability approach: a theoretical survey', *Journal of Human Development*, vol 6, no 1, pp 93-114.

Sanderson, I. (2002) 'Evaluation, policy learning and evidence-based policy making', *Public Administration*, vol 80, no 1, pp 1-22.

Saunders, P. (2004) 'What is fair about a "fair go?" [There are many different definitions of "fairness"]', *Policy: A Journal of Public Policy and Ideas*, vol 20, no 1, pp 3-10.

Sawer, M. (2008) 'Changing frames: liberal and feminist perspectives on Harvester', *Dissent*, Autumn/Winter, pp 45-9.

Schwandt, T.A. (1997) 'Evaluation as practical hermeneutics', *Evaluation*, vol 3, no 1, pp 69-83.

Sen, A.K. (1985) 'Well-being agency and freedom: the Dewey Lectures 1984', *Journal of Philosophy*, vol 82, no 4, pp 169-221.

Sen, A.K. (1990) 'Development as capability expansion', in K. Griffin and J. Knight (eds) *Human development and the International Development Strategy for the 1990s*, London: Macmillan.

Sen, A.K. (1992) *Inequality reexamined*, Cambridge, MA: Harvard University Press.

Sen, A.K. (2004) 'Elements of a theory of human rights', *Philosophy & Public Affairs*, vol 32, no 4, p 315.

Stoetzler, M. and Yuval-Davis, N. (2002) 'Standpoint theory, situated knowledge and the situated imagination'. *Feminist Theory*, vol 3, no 3, pp 315-33.

Swigonski, M. (1994) 'The logic of feminist standpoint theory for social work research', *Social Work*, vol 39, no 4, pp 387-93.

Titmuss, R.M. (1974) 'What is social policy', in S. Leibfried and S. Mau (eds) *Welfare states: Construction, deconstruction, reconstruction*, Cheltenham: Edward Elgar.

Van Hulst, M. and Yanow, D. (2016) 'From policy "frames" to "framing": theor a more dynamic, political approach', *American Review of Public Administration*, vol 46, no 1, pp 92-112.

Waksler, F. (1986) 'Studying children: phenomenological insights', *Human Studies*, vol 9, no 1, pp 71-82.

Whiteford, P. (2011) 'How fair is Australia's welfare state?', *Inside Story*, available at http://insidestory.org.au/how-fair-is-australias-welfare-state.

Whiteford, P. (2015) 'Inequality and its socioeconomic impacts', *Australian Economic Review*, vol 48, no 1, pp 83-92.

TWELVE

Capabilities and the challenge to inclusive schooling

Franziska Felder

This chapter proposes an ethical model of inclusion that views inclusion as social participation. It thus opposes ideas of inclusion such as those commonly found in systems theory, for example, where it is understood in purely instrumental-functional terms and on a societal level (Luhmann, 1984; Stichweh, 2009). From the perspective of systems theory, inclusion is merely a binary question of being 'in' or 'out'. There are no processes of inclusion and no communities as interpersonal associations that include or exclude. This chapter aims to offer an alternative to this vision, arguing that we can refine our understanding of what we view as 'full' or 'substantive' inclusion. Against the background of a purely functional, explicitly non-normative understanding of inclusion, it offers a normative model of inclusion that relates itself to a broad theory of human flourishing and individual and societal development embraced by the capability approach.

The proposed model is based on two intuitions. The first of these – inclusion understood as a *social* phenomenon, as already mentioned – can be thought of in both communal and societal terms.

In the communal perspective, people interact as specific others. The associated forms of inclusion are directly interpersonal and the forms of recognition that are thus established, and also express inclusion in a sense, are horizontal and interpersonal as well. Friendship is a paradigmatic form of communal inclusion. It is formed and supported by the mutual feelings of trust and affection among all partners (two or more people).

In the societal perspective, people are abstracted from their subjective feelings, interests and characteristics, and are considered as abstract others, typically as citizens. In this case, inclusion is mediated by institutions, for example when authorities design and construct a building that is accessible to everyone, including wheelchair users and blind people. This form of inclusion is mediated institutionally because it is not acted out between specific persons (as in communal inclusion), but instead reflects the attitudes of a particular authority and thus of the state, in a certain manner, and applies these attitudes to abstract others, such as the users of a building.[1]

In addition to these distinct forms of interpersonal, communal inclusion and institutionally mediated societal inclusion, there are naturally many intermediate forms. The separation of interpersonal, communal inclusion and societal inclusion is analytical. In real life, both forms are expressed, usually in mixed form. This becomes evident in school settings, for instance. On the one hand, teachers enact a role prescribed by the state, thus serving as mediators of societal inclusion in their societal function as teachers (which is expressed in a range of deontic powers, as specific rights and obligations). As part of this role, teachers are expected to adapt their attitudes and conduct to the deontic powers adhering to their function. For instance, they are obligated, for reasons of fairness, to treat all children equally, without displaying particular sympathy for individuals. But after all, teachers are 'only human' (in the colloquial phrase) and thus they also have subjective interests, feelings and needs. Good teachers are also expected (albeit in a weaker sense, as a moral expectation) to teach their material in a motivated and personally engaged manner, while also regarding each child as a unique individual with specific needs and interests. It is therefore somehow expected that they will exercise their role *and* authentically interpret and embody it – that is, with interest, feelings and motivation. These two aspects form the basis of their professionalism. However, they can only achieve this if they regard the class and the individual children as forming a community, in which they, as teachers, are also aware of being independent, particular beings, specific people with feelings and interests.

The second intuition in the model proposed here is that inclusion is concerned with freedom, insofar as – over the course of a lifetime – people should also have the freedom to choose the contexts of inclusion, to affirm such contexts, and to have a say in their design. We can observe that inclusion in the nuclear family at the start of life is neither voluntary (children are simply born into their families), nor associated with much possibility of affirmation. The scope of consultation and co-determination remains highly limited in children who are not yet autonomous, such as babies. However, this involuntariness should not apply beyond those highly dependent phases that are ontogenetically determined. Reflecting on the entire life of a person, we do not consider inclusion that is largely imposed from the outside to be either 'substantive' or 'full'. This is where the capability approach comes into play. This chapter argues that the capability approach can articulate and analyse this intuition of the freedom to be included, thus enhancing our concept of 'full' or 'substantive' inclusion.

The chapter then aims to apply this proposed model to the topic of inclusive schools. The design of inclusive schooling poses an urgent challenge. Article 24 of the United Nations (UN) Convention on the Rights of Persons with Disabilities explicitly stipulates that education must be inclusive and schools must be designed in an inclusive manner (UN, 2006). States that have signed and ratified the Convention, nearly 170 so far, are thus legally obligated to provide an inclusive education system. This chapter offers some thoughts on how to design inclusive schools based on the model proposed.

Different perspectives on inclusion

The two aspects of inclusion in the model proposed – recognition and freedom – have different perspectives. The first deals with the 'how' of inclusion, while the second focuses on the 'what' of inclusion. These two aspects interact dialectically – that is, the meaning and role of each aspect in the context of a full, normatively valuable concept of inclusion can only be assessed against the background of the other aspect. 'Full' or 'substantive' inclusion does not encompass inclusion that is voluntarily chosen and affirmed, but ultimately based on disrespect (for instance, through feigned care and attention), or inclusion that is based on recognition but without being voluntarily chosen or affirmed (for instance, when the recognising person is affirmed, but not the context of inclusion as such).

The context of schooling poses a great challenge, as compulsory schooling is not voluntary by nature: scholastic inclusion thus constitutes 'forced inclusion', to some extent, at least with regard to its provision of educational content. But the argument still applies that scholastic inclusion that is not affirmed by the participants (in particular, children, teachers and parents), and is not supplemented internally through the voluntariness of intersubjective contact, must also be considered 'incomplete', 'partial' or 'non-substantive', just like inclusion in which participants interact according to prescribed roles, but remain emotionally detached or cold. Such inclusion may indeed be physical, and it may also be embedded structurally or institutionally (in a paradigmatic sense, via rights, such as those set out for education in Article 24 of the UN Convention on disability rights [UN, 2006]), but this still does not constitute 'full' or 'substantive' inclusion, as it is not realised or experienced interpersonally.

Let us now address in turn these two aspects of inclusion, beginning with social intentionality and recognition.

Social intentionality and recognition

This first aspect is associated with two assumptions. First, the form of inclusion available to a person depends on the attitudes or actions of another person, a group or an institution. Only in this sense can inclusion be understood as a social phenomenon. This intuition is best understood in negative terms, against the background of that which does *not* fit the concept of inclusion. If a couple of people are taking the train from A to B, we do not necessarily assume this to be an instance of inclusion. It is not considered inclusion if the people simply happen to be sitting in the same train. However, we do think of a train trip as an inclusive moment when the individual group members know one another and their aims are socially interconnected. This in turn means that intentions – motives or feelings – must be shared, that these are based on a sense of identification with others (to be more specifically defined), and that this results in cooperation, in both a broad and a narrow sense. Inclusion only occurs when this is the case. In other words, in order to emphasise social meaning and the sense of sharing and commonality inherent in any substantive concept of inclusion, we must assume that attitudes and actions are socially intentional. Only in this way can we understand the 'we' addressed through inclusion and implied in 'social participation'.

Meanwhile, although social intentionality is indeed a necessary part of inclusion, it does not suffice to establish inclusion as a value in the full and positive sense. In order to consider it a positive social phenomenon, a second point is crucial: the attitudes and actions that comprise inclusion must offer *recognition* (Ikäheimo, 2003). In other words, we include others in a positive sense when we treat them with attitudes of recognition or undertake action jointly with them. These horizontal aspects of recognition may be mediated intersubjectively as well as institutionally (Ikäheimo, 2014). For example, teachers can recognise the achievements of students from within their institutional role as teachers, thus demonstrating institutionally mediated horizontal recognition. The earlier example of the train trip, by comparison, indicates intersubjective horizontal recognition. A group of friends plans a trip. On the morning of the trip, they all meet at the train station and then travel together from A to B. The intersubjective recognition among the travellers is not based on any institutional roles they might hold as individuals, but rather solely on psychological states, attitudes and other processes of an intrasubjective or intersubjective nature. In contrast, institutionally mediated horizontal recognition relates to subjects as the holders of particular roles that comprise deontic powers such as rights and obligations. Here, the exact attitudes of individuals and their relations to one another are of secondary importance. Recognition in this context is primarily a matter of acts and omissions, having less to do with attitudes.

To understand the relationship between recognition and inclusion, it is helpful to specify what we mean by recognition. In a normative sense, this refers to the recognition of persons and not (as in 'acknowledgement') the recognition of norms or rules. If we understand recognition as being directed at persons, we can distinguish four different modes of recognition: in the form of interpersonal relationships such as love and friendship; as individual regard (axiological dimension); in the form of respect (deontological dimension); and as social esteem (contributive dimension). With this differentiation, I follow the recognition theorist Axel Honneth (1994), while also adding thoughts from Heikki Ikäheimo (2014) and Susanne Schmetkamp (2011), who have both drawn key distinctions in this respect – Ikäheimo by distinguishing between interpersonal and institutionally mediated recognition (and thus also forms of inclusion), and Schmetkamp by identifying the form of regard as a second mode of intersubjective recognition.

For Honneth (1994), love is the first form of recognition. This form described as 'love' is intersubjective, as it must be established between individuals, and it also covers the axiological dimension of values and care. Recognition in the form of love and care is concerned with the basic needs of people in close personal relationships. It is thus particularly directed at specific individuals and helps to secure self-assurance. For the topic of inclusion, the strong ontological significance of this form of recognition is based on the human need for care and the experience of being cared for. This particularly applies to the start of human life. People cannot survive or thrive if they do not receive love and attention from close caregivers (Spitz, 1945). There is also much evidence to suggest that this reliance on caring, interpersonal contact remains a constant throughout human life and as a part of adult experience.

Of course, this form of recognition is not purely subjective, in the sense of depending solely on the subjective attitudes and actions of the persons involved. An 'intersubjective' relationship is always embedded in objective conditions and dependent on those conditions. These are elements that must be understood as essential or important for the relationships among people (Ikäheimo, 2014). From this perspective, teachers also function as an environment for students in the classroom, at least to the extent that they clearly represent role models for orienting students in their dealings with peers (Huber, 2011). However, this 'attitude atmosphere' also depends, although not exclusively, on how much teachers care for children in an unconditional sense. This significance of caring relationships, more narrowly defined, is also evident at the level of peers. Many studies have indicated that a sense of relatedness among peers, and a dense social network in general, are vital for the existence of strong social inclusion in terms of social participation and cohesion. This impact also extends to learning motivation and outcomes (Furrer and Skinner, 2003).

The second form of recognition is respect, which is usually expressed through rights, and helps to secure dignity and self-respect. As Joel Feinberg (1970) argues, rights allow their holders to stand proud in interactions with others. Rights that express respect also grant power to limit the actions of others or expect certain actions from them. They are thus associated with aspects of both negative and positive liberty (Berlin, 1969). Following Thomas H. Marshall (1950), it can be noted that, historically, each new generation of rights has resulted in greater inclusion and better equality for rights holders, to create fully fledged members of society. This also applies in the case of the UN Convention on disability rights (UN, 2006), which states (and thus recognises) that human rights should be granted in full to people with disabilities.

The third form of recognition is social esteem, which helps to secure a feeling of self-worth. Recognition in the form of social esteem relates to people as the carriers of particular characteristics and capabilities. Ikäheimo (2014) calls this the contributive dimension, as it serves to recognise people (or rather, characteristics of people) that make a valuable contribution to our life. As people are cooperative beings by nature, this form of recognition depends on the form of shared purposes. What this contribution actually refers to, however, is frequently debated, offering a target for disputes and challenges. What is esteem and where is it directed? What does it mean to esteem a person for his or her contribution to the good of others? And does this esteem only consist of instrumental esteem? In other words, does it only refer to characteristics that are a means to an end, such as those enabling someone to earn a lot of money, pay high taxes, and thus contribute to the community indirectly? Does this mean that other characteristics that are not instrumental – such as genuine, unselfish care for others – are devalued? Ikäheimo believes that a person can be esteemed in more than just an instrumental sense. This non-instrumental esteem is expressed as gratitude, for example as a sincere response to the altruistic actions of others. According to Ikäheimo, this is the aspect of esteem that first reveals the independence of a third form of recognition.

As already suggested, we can also invoke a fourth form of recognition that is important for the context of inclusion and especially crucial for the inclusion of people with disabilities – that is, regard. In this context, the key consideration is that a good society must also show sensitive regard for the characteristics of its (co-)members as *specific* others in order to ensure that all people can participate in social life as moral equals (Schmetkamp, 2011). This also includes specific, individual regard. Like love, it safeguards the basic conditions of personal identity, but it cannot be conflated with love, as it is not directed at the person as a whole. Instead, it only focuses on specific characteristics, such as disabilities.

Being included is thus a form of recognition, and recognition specifically demonstrates inclusion. We can specify this in four ways. The individual is included through love as a particular other with specific needs and interests, and through regard as a person with a specific background and characteristics, such as disabilities. The other is also included as an abstract other, an equal among equals, in the form of respect, as expressed through rights. And finally, contributions that add to communal or societal value, through achievements and benefits, are also recognised in the form of esteem.

The capabilities required for the recognition that underlies inclusion, in its various forms of expression, can be termed 'capabilities for affiliation', with reference to Martha Nussbaum. 'Capabilities for affiliation' are socially integrated capabilities. This means that they are both an individual ability and a social condition (and are thus tied to both internal and external conditions for freedom). On the one hand, a 'capability for affiliation', according to Nussbaum, means 'being able to live with and toward others, to recognise and show concern for other humans, to engage in various forms of social interaction; to be able to imagine the situation of another' (Nussbaum, 2000, p 79). On the other hand, it also means 'having the social bases of self-respect and non-humiliation; being able to be treated as a dignified being whose worth is equal to that of others' (Nussbaum, 2000, p 79).

Thus, in a narrower sense, 'capabilities for affiliation' enable interpersonal, communal inclusion and are tied to forms of interpersonal recognition in the form of love or regard. But they also express other aspects of societal inclusion that are covered by the second form of recognition: the deontic dimension of respect, as primarily realised through institutional rights. Being able to appear as an equal among equals, a person whose dignity is valued as much as that of others, points to the presence of the external conditions of 'capabilities for affiliation', and thus socially conditioned freedom. 'Capabilities for affiliation' therefore combine the four specified forms of recognition, and express these as individual abilities *and* as social conditions: as the ability to attend to others in an empathic, loving and caring way, and also as a social basis for being able to interact with others as a respected, esteemed person. The social dimensions of 'capabilities for affiliation' already suggest the second aspect of inclusion – that is, freedom – that is needed to make inclusion 'full' or 'substantive'.

Freedom or capabilities

The second aspect of inclusion is based on the assumption that inclusion – even if not originally voluntary in every case – must nonetheless be affirmed by all participants in the social context. In addition, inclusion must involve the expression of (at least minimal) self-determination. If I belong to a chess club, but I have no interest in chess, this form of inclusion and the resulting recognition (for example, to be recognised as a good chess player) are not 'full' and 'substantive'. And it is also hard to consider as 'full' or 'substantive' any kind of inclusion that is so externally determined that it covers every aspect of life.[2]

For communal forms of inclusion, this assumption seems to me undisputed. Friendship, for instance, is not a 'true' friendship if it is only affirmed or labelled as such by one person in the relationship. Friendship also clearly has to do with freedom; it can only be considered friendship if it is voluntarily chosen and maintained, and if it is based on affection and care – not, for example, on a sense of duty or to keep up appearances. Somewhat less obvious is the assumption that inclusion has to do with the freedom of choice and affirmation, as well as co-determination, when we think of societal forms of inclusion. For instance, do individuals cease to be citizens if they fail to exercise their citizens' rights and do not vote? This would seem strange at first glance. Ultimately, such citizens do not lose all of their rights, at least in a democracy, if they decide, for example, not to vote, and thus express their dissatisfaction with the political conditions in their country. Similarly, we would not say that a society falls apart if it is denounced by an individual (as in the case of friendship). Nonetheless, societal inclusion must at least be affirmed in a weak sense, and thus by individuals as citizens, in order for 'full' and 'substantive' inclusion to apply from a societal perspective. And above a certain threshold, when a substantial number of citizens no longer actively participates in societal processes (for example, by ceasing to vote), a democracy can no longer be considered functional.[3] In a functioning democracy, the state as an institution must succeed in being accepted and affirmed by the citizens of a society, at least in a weak sense. It seems safe to assume that a state that does not manage this will be undermined from within.[4]

But how can we define more precisely the understanding of freedom expressed through inclusion? The capability approach has made an important contribution by drawing attention to the significance of freedom (also specifically for the inclusion of people with disabilities). The capability approach has emphasised that certain people (including those with disabilities) need more goods than others in order to have the same life opportunities. This is the aspect that emphasises freedom as an outcome, being able to live a life of one's choosing. This relates to the notion of co-determination and its preconditions. Meanwhile, the capability approach has also stressed the significance of freedom as freedom of choice. It makes a difference whether or not people choose their particular life circumstances. Two situations may look the same externally even if one originated in freedom and the other arose without a choice. Sen illustrates this difference through the example of fasting and starving. In both cases, people go without food, but in one case this state is achieved voluntarily, perhaps for purposes of spiritual-mental purification, while in the other case there is no opportunity to eat.

In this context, according to Amartya Sen and Martha Nussbaum, capabilities represent the substantive freedoms enjoyed by a person, consisting of opportunities for choice and action (usually connected). Sen writes that 'a person's "capability" refers to the alternative combinations of functionings that are feasible for her to achieve. Capability is thus a kind of freedom: the substantive freedom to achieve alternative functioning combinations' (Sen, 1999, p 75). This therefore does not refer only to the capabilities of a person in the sense of internal abilities, but also to freedoms consisting of a combination of internal abilities and the opportunities offered by the social, political and economic environment. Nussbaum calls these substantive freedoms 'combined capabilities'. These must be differentiated from two other forms of capability: 'basic' and 'internal' (Nussbaum, 2000). All three forms may be applied to the topic of inclusion, both with regard to personal capabilities and the necessary environmental conditions. So let us take a closer look at what Nussbaum calls 'basic', 'internal' and 'combined' capabilities.

'Basic capabilities' are innate to humans. People are born with them. Even if these inborn abilities do not constitute needs in the true sense, they do reflect needs. These abilities, simultaneously reflecting needs, also include social abilities. For example, studies by the developmental psychologist Michael Tomasello (2009) show that the ability to engage in social cooperation is innate to human beings. According to Tomasello, specific human cognitive abilities can only be understood as socio-cognitive abilities. These are biologically based forms of identification with others that emerge at a very early age in dyadic interactions with parents and close caregivers. At the end of the first year of life, or when a child begins to plan its own actions, this leads to an understanding of others and the self as active subjects. This therefore involves intersubjective identification and comprehension that is innate to human beings, but requires a social environment in order to develop fully. According to Tomasello's hypothesis, now supported by sound empirical evidence, children display a biologically founded form of identification with others, and on this basis develop simple forms of higher-order intentionality starting from around the age of one. They understand themselves and others as intentional subjects that relate to the world through perception and action. This simple form of higher-order intentionality enables identification with and through cultural learning from others. And it leads almost automatically to social intentionality and thus to cooperation and (cooperative) communication.[5] These foundations of recognition were mentioned at the beginning of the chapter. Here, they also appear as the foundations of freedom.

'Internal capabilities', the second layer of capabilities, build on 'basic capabilities', but in order to develop they require social stimulation, interaction and institutions, such as education and parenting. Language is a typical example of an internal capability that is derived from 'basic capabilities', but requires a learning environment for its development. This applies at a higher level for many other capabilities developed over a lifetime that could be described as more abstract or detailed. Thus, the ability to read, play chess, or use a computer are also internal capabilities. These capabilities should not be regarded in isolation, but always in interrelation and interaction with their environment. This means that they can be either developed or hindered depending on whether the environment is supportive or obstructive. Unlike true 'basic capabilities', they do not develop naturally in an evolutionary process that already exists ontogenetically in human beings. In their development and expansion, the environment brings with it the aspect of freedom, revealing the full meaning of capabilities: not abilities in the sense of skills, but opportunities for realisation, or 'combined capabilities'.

But how are the individual and social conditions of the freedom to be included, described by Nussbaum as 'basic', 'internal' and 'combined' capabilities, connected with the necessity of affirmation in contexts of inclusion? What is meant by 'affirmation' in the first place? Perhaps this is represented by what Harry G. Frankfurt has termed 'care' (understood as an individual capability). Frankfurt writes:

> A person who cares about something is, as it were, invested in it. He identifies himself with what he cares about in the sense that he makes himself vulnerable to losses and susceptible to benefits depending upon whether what he cares about is diminished or enhanced. Thus he concerns himself with what concerns it, giving particular attention to such things and directing his behaviour accordingly. Insofar as the person's life is in whole or in part devoted to anything, rather than being merely a sequence of events whose themes and structures he makes no effort to fashion, it is devoted to this. (1982, p 260)

Affirmation in the sense of 'care' is essentially self-reflexive and is therefore tied to a capacity for action and self-awareness. It refers to identification and thus intentionality, and in the case of inclusion also to social intentionality, and identification and connection with the aims of others. This concerns both 'basic' capabilities – that is, innate human capabilities for social intentionality (as demonstrated by Tomasello's research) – and 'internal' capabilities, in other words, the ability to demonstrate empathy or solidarity, which must be learned and applied in a social environment. But it also concerns 'combined' capabilities, and thus environmental factors, conditions of 'external freedom'. A positive, stimulating environment – in which, for example, each individual is empathically open to others – supports and enables 'care', and thus the affirmation of contexts of inclusion.

If we then connect the ideas about 'care' according to Harry Frankfurt with the aspect of recognition, the following picture emerges. From a deontic perspective, caring refers to the affirmation of norms, authority and respect, as well as the rights and obligations of others as equal partners. In axiological terms, caring means showing empathic attachment to oneself and others, for example in the form of friendship, love or individual regard. And in contributive terms, caring means paying attention to others' achievements and thus their contributions to the common good, and recognising these contributions as valuable.

The capability approach also highlights the special significance of the other key aspects of freedom expressed in inclusion. I have already addressed the first fundamental aspect. The ability to freely choose contexts of inclusion is of key importance for a person's life beyond the ontogenetically determined phases of dependency in the first years. The main point is the quality of this choice, that is, not only the outcome, but also the process and thus the question of how this choice originated. The capability approach has always particularly stressed this significance of participation and self-determination.

Freedom must here be thought of in social terms, as freedom that is necessarily tied to the freedom of others and thus to cooperation and a sense of 'we'. To be a member of a community of free beings (invested with dignity and respect) means having co-authority over the community's norms and values. This freedom regarding norms and values is also expressed through interpersonal, particular inclusion: we all, as partners in friendship, determine what friendship *specifically* means for us. The meaning of this socially conceived freedom, as expressed in inclusion, is found in social interaction, in social intentionality as a precondition for recognition. Here, we also see the dialectical relationship between recognition and freedom.

We can now apply some of these thoughts to the example of inclusive schooling, at the same time offering an application-oriented conclusion.

Application and conclusion: inclusive schools

I have based my model on two intuitions. Inclusion can be understood as a social phenomenon that can be expressed both in an interpersonal, communal–particular fashion, and in an institutional, societal–universal fashion. The necessary actions, ideas and motivations underlying inclusion may only be understood as recognition when we speak of inclusion as 'full' or 'substantive'. Meanwhile, 'full' or 'substantive' inclusion also requires freedom, that is, the ability to choose and affirm contexts of inclusion, and to have opportunities for co-determination. When speaking of 'capabilities to be included', we must keep in mind the aspects of both recognition and freedom. Just as the freedom available for inclusion can only be used on the basis of true recognition, the dimensions of recognition suggested by inclusion, when viewed over a lifetime, can only be 'substantive' and 'full' if they are associated with freedom.

What changes must therefore occur in order to make schooling inclusive in this 'full' or 'substantive' sense? First, we need to change our idea of inclusion. Instead of viewing inclusive schooling as an 'all or nothing' concept, as it usually appears in public discussions, inclusion should be regarded as a gradual phenomenon. People may be included in many forms and contexts, through varying forms of recognition, and may enjoy various types of freedom in and through these methods. Inclusion is therefore a complex and ceaseless work in progress. The bad news is that inclusion can always fail and it is constantly fragile. It features interpersonal and institutional facets that are mutually conditioned and reinforcing. It is not possible to guarantee that inclusion will be secured institutionally or even maintained interpersonally once and for all, as it is too dynamic and multifaceted. The good news is that inclusion comes in degrees and nuances. This also applies for the 'difficult cases' of inclusion, such as children with severe disabilities: a child with multiple severe disabilities may not always prefer to be taught in the same classroom with other children. Indeed, perhaps this child would thrive better in other forms of institutional care. This is also a way for the child to be included. The success of inclusive schooling cannot be measured solely through institutional contexts *per se* (although such considerations are important, as they have a 'gatekeeping' function), but rather through the forms of recognition they express and the freedoms they make available to people. When it comes to choosing contexts of inclusion, we should thus be guided by the following questions. Is this genuinely the person's own choice, that is, not externally determined? This question is not straightforward, particularly in the case of minor-age children who are not yet fully autonomous. But efforts should still be made to identify the genuine desires of each child, including those of children with cognitive and mental disabilities. A second, related, question is whether the child can affirm his or her inclusion (whether in a special school or a regular school) even without having freely made this choice originally. Here, the focus must be on the child's future and wellbeing. This aspect is among those clearly expressed in the capability approach. It has less to do with the current states of being expressed in 'functionings', but rather with the freedoms made available, that is, 'capabilities'. The goal should be a good life. This consists not only in momentary subjective wellbeing, but also in positive development in the longer term, with a view towards the future.

Another relevant question is whether the child can have co-determination over the details and arrangements of his or her life contexts. We should ensure that children are not simply subject to external determination (for instance, regarding therapy and treatment), but that they are consulted in important matters related to their schooling. This naturally applies for all children. Only in this way can inclusion transcend the individual level to become one that concerns us all and reflects a sense of 'we'.

Schooling poses a specific challenge for the inclusion of children because, on the one hand, schools are structurally tied to 'institutional forced inclusion', and on the other hand, they must offer a learning and practice environment for voluntary inclusion supported by sympathy. In the face of strong constraints and external determination, which particularly do not favour intersubjective, communal forms of inclusion, this involves the difficulty of trying to promote the affirmation and co-determination of inclusion. Is this possible, and if so, how? In other words, how can we create an atmosphere of inclusion that accommodates recognition and freedom when the context itself at least partially contradicts this?

Here, it is worth specifying again what we mean by an 'atmosphere of inclusion'. First, an 'atmosphere of inclusion' supports and enables love or friendship and regard (from an axiological perspective), respect (from a deontic perspective) and social esteem (from a contributive perspective). Second, despite the extensive institutional 'forced inclusion' involved, it is necessary to create islands, moments and methods that offer voluntary co-determination and consultation, thus enabling children to affirm their inclusion (and that of all others in the class). More specifically, this is an atmosphere in which each individual child can be appreciated as a special human being, with his or her needs taken into consideration, and treated with dignity and respect. It is an atmosphere in which children can experience themselves as self-determining, and in which empathy and participation are encouraged and given opportunities for expression in the sense of 'combined capabilities'.

This is achieved indirectly by creating an 'atmosphere of solidarity', which is a collective task (not only to be accomplished by teachers). It is also achieved directly when teaching uses and promotes the opportunities for social co-determination, and the learning of empathy and 'care'. Empirical research has shown that teachers play a key role in this context, although they cannot be considered solely responsible for the success or failure of inclusion. For example, empirical studies by Anne Jordan and her colleagues (Jordan et al, 1997, 2009) showed that teachers' ideas about disability, and the question of whether they felt responsible for children with disabilities, were crucial both for the social inclusion of such children and for their learning success. Teachers who primarily viewed disability as an impairment and an unalterable fate appeared to be less willing to advocate for those students. Consequently, these children were more poorly regarded by their classmates and also had significantly poorer learning results. To some extent, teachers therefore function as the mediators of academic and social learning, as role models for how other people – in this case, children – are to be treated. Teachers who believe in the potential of each child, in their moral equality and uniqueness, have a good foundation for creating an atmosphere of inclusion in the classroom.

The capability approach invites us to see human life and human development as essentially social in nature. Having access to goods like education shapes our individual identity and development. Relying on a 'thick' moral psychology and notions of a good human life, the complex interrelationships between structural, institutional and interpersonal as well as personal aspects of inclusion and ultimately inclusive schooling becomes evident. In focusing on what people can actually do and be, the capability approach offers a normative tool in analysing and criticising inclusive education. Yet, the capabilities approach to inclusive education, apart from its basic idea of enhancing people's freedom, is still waiting for its implementation true to the ideal. The difficulties of implementing it have different sources. Not only is it difficult for highly differentiated educational systems to make the transition from being segregative to being inclusive; some functions of schooling – for instance, the selection function of matching student's performance with their career tracks by means of exams and certifications – seem to be in sharp tension with the ideals of inclusive education. Even deeper, however, lies another problem. We still do not have a clear idea about what we actually mean by inclusion. It is hoped that this chapter has shed some light on how we can gain more insight into the ideal of inclusion.

Notes

[1] Of course, there are also other forms of societal inclusion, for example when citizens interact horizontally as abstract beings, as in the case of elections. Such forms of societal inclusion must be differentiated from vertical means used by the state to include its citizens, as in the earlier example of designing buildings and public transport to be accessible to everyone.

[2] For this reason, we hesitate to describe the inhabitants of dictatorships such as North Korea as being 'included' in their country, or as citizens of their country. In dictatorships, people may not express their essence with self-determination or contribute to decision making about their common fate as a nation.

[3] Here, it must be noted again, I am not arguing that inclusion is impossible without being affirmed or chosen. I am only arguing that such inclusion is not 'full' or 'substantive' in terms of normative substance and value.

[4] Conversely, it is also the case, of course, that 'full' inclusion means that all citizens have a voice, and can also express that voice. Democracy, as an institutionalised form

of societal discussion, does not only encompass rights. It also includes obligations for citizens to include themselves actively in society.

5   Humans display a higher form of intentionality than other highly developed animals, including the great apes. The latter are capable of perceiving one another as active agents, but people are able to see others as cooperative partners, thus developing a concept of collective intentionality. The difference can be illustrated using the example of a football match. Apes are able to watch a match with others whom they regard as co-spectators. Humans, however, can play together on a football team or, in other words, direct their attention to a *single* match as co-players along with 10 other people.

References

Berlin, I. (1969) 'Two concepts of liberty', in I. Berlin (ed) *Liberty*, Oxford: Oxford University Press.

Feinberg, J. (1970) 'The nature and value of rights', *Journal of Value Inquiry*, vol 4, no 4, pp 243-57.

Frankfurt, H. (1982) 'The importance of what we care about', *Synthese*, vol 53, no 2, pp 257-72.

Furrer, C. and Skinner, E. (2003) 'Sense of relatedness as a factor in children's academic engagement and performance', *Journal of Educational Psychology*, vol 95, no 1, pp 148-62.

Honneth, A. (1994) *Kampf um Anerkennung: Zur moralischen Grammatik sozialer Konflikte* [The struggle for recognition: The moral grammar of social conflicts], Frankfurt am Main: Suhrkamp.

Huber, C. (2011) 'Lehrerfeedback und soziale Integration. Wie soziale Referenzierungsprozesse die soziale Integration in der Schule beeinflussen können' [Teacher's feedback and social integration: is there a link between social referencing theory and social integration in school?], *Empirische Sonderpädagogik*, vol 3, no 3, pp 20-36.

Ikäheimo, H. (2003) *Analysing social inclusion in terms of recognitive attitudes*, Social Inequality Today, Sydney: Macquarie University.

Ikäheimo, H. (2014) *Anerkennung [Recognition]*, Berlin: De Gruyter.

Jordan, A., Lindsay, L. and Stanovich, P.J. (1997) 'Classroom teachers' instructional interactions with students who are exceptional, at-risk and typically achieving', *Remedial and Special Education*, vol 18, no 2, pp 82-93.

Jordan, A., Schwartz, E. and McGhie-Richmond, D. (2009) 'Preparing teachers for inclusive classrooms', *Teaching and Teacher Education*, vol 25, no 4, pp 535-42.

Luhmann, N. (1984) *Soziale Systeme. Grundriss einer allgemeinen Theorie [Social systems]*, Frankfurt am Main: Suhrkamp.

Marshall, T.H. (1950) *Citizenship and social class and other essays*, Cambridge: Cambridge University Press.

Nussbaum, M.C. (2000) *Women and human development: The capabilities approach*, Cambridge, MA: Cambridge University Press.

Schmetkamp, S. (2011) *Respekt und Anerkennung* [*Respect and recognition*], Paderborn: Mentis.

Sen, A. (1999) *Development as freedom*, Oxford: Oxford University Press.

Spitz, R.A. (1945) 'Hospitalism: an inquiry into the genesis of psychiatric conditions in early childhood', *Psychoanalytic Study of the Child*, vol 1, no 1, pp 53-74.

Stichweh, R. (2009) 'Leitgesichtspunkte einer Soziologie der Inklusion und Exklusion' [Guiding ideas of a sociology of inclusion and exclusion], in R. Stichweh and P. Windolf (eds) *Inklusion und Exklusion: Analysen zur Sozialstruktur und sozialen Ungleichheit* [*Inclusion and exclusion: Analysis of social structure and social inequality*], Wiesbaden: VS Verlag für Sozialwissenschaften.

Tomasello, M. (2009) *Why we cooperate*, Cambridge, MA: MIT Press.

UN (United Nations) (2006) *Convention on the Rights of Persons with Disabilities*, Geneva: United Nations.

THIRTEEN

Early childhood educational curricula: implications of the capability approach

Antoanneta Potsi

Introduction

This chapter endeavours to explore the potential of a capability-promoting policy in early childhood education (ECE). More specifically, reference to Martha Nussbaum's list of basic human capabilities, developed as a relatively definite standard of minimal justice, and an adequate frame for capability-promoting policy in Early Childhood Education (ECE) and especially in the curriculum development will be considered (Richardson, 2015). These central capabilities, defined as the minimum human entitlement, are deeply rooted in the normative principles that govern ECE, and provide a general framework for policymaking and policy evaluation.

The significance of ECE is generally accepted and many countries are exploring the educational needs of the young with a special focus on those who are economically and socially disadvantaged (OECD, 2006). ECE offers a chance for the establishment and support of the kind of habitus that supports the long-term means of fulfilling one's potential. Indeed, ECE can improve children's long-term life chances and their long- and medium-term outcomes (see, for example, Wright et al, 2000; Magnuson et al, 2004; Duncan et al, 2012). Thus, another aspect is that educational systems can also reproduce social inequalities. As Wiborg and Hansen show (2009), even in relatively wealthy and welfare-rich countries such as Norway, growing up in a poor household means you are more likely to be poor as an adult. This type of economic disadvantage is persistent and difficult to address. Added to this, confounding factors come into play such as the association between being a migrant child, living in a poor neighbourhood and being unlikely to attend an ECE institution, and a lower likelihood that a high-quality ECE institution will be available in the local community.

Furthermore, factors that contribute to disadvantage tend to compound and cluster (Bask, 2011), resulting in cumulative disadvantage over time.

Universal access to ECE for all children is advocated as a way to reconcile work and family life and to promote the socioeconomic integration of vulnerable groups in society. The United Nations International Children's Emergency Fund (UNICEF) concludes that this increasing government interest in early childhood services occurs because they offer an apparent opportunity to break into the cycle by which disadvantage tends to reproduce itself, and because no nation today can afford to ignore opportunities for maximising investments in education in a competitive economic environment increasingly based on knowledge, flexibility, and lifelong learning skills (Dahlberg and Moss, 2005). As a consequence, ECE programmes appear to have grown more academically demanding. They are regarded as a preparation for academic learning and as a remediation for the effects of poverty, since childhood is considered a decisive phase in the reproduction of deprivation and social inequality, and deficiencies during this critical life period may well have long-term effects on later life.

Policies emphasise the aim to shape the future life chances of children, especially those growing up in socioeconomically distressed situations and circumstances (Lister, 2003). 'Children are the future' is frequent mantra, especially in political speeches. The urgent demand to prepare the children for the future and the challenges of the future economy is also found in national and international policy documents and more specifically in curricula. Sardar (1986) refers to the process of educating a child holistically, as advocated in most current curricula prescribing the ideal of a 'good education' for children. By this measure, an image, notion and vision of the future is required that will equip the child with the relevant insights and skills to think critically and creatively about the future and to engage positively in shaping it. This emphasis on childhood's futurity tends to overshadow understandings of children as agents of change in the here and now, often excluding them from democratic negotiation about preferences and futures. Therefore, children are, more often than not, regarded and treated as adults in the making or human becomings, and they lose their social status as participatory citizens.

ECE curricula sketch the concept of a good start in life based on the positioning of the agreed norms and values of a specific cultural setting. From this political framework, the aims, learning objectives and skills are set for the next generation of a specific culture. Policymakers have invested a lot of attention in the description of the kind of learning that is expected at this life stage. As Wood and Hedges (2016, p 388) argue, within contemporary policy frameworks, the ECE curriculum document has become the site through which content, coherence and control are articulated, as a means of aligning preschool and compulsory education policy, and ensuring that children achieve educational and school-readiness goals that in turn contribute to longer-term economic and sociopolitical goals. In this context, education is regarded as an economic investment with measurable outcomes compared with other investments through cost-benefit analysis[1] and as a result children are experiencing an intensification of workload with a focus on marketable skills and an emphasis on technical competence and performativity as a guarantee of future prosperity. Instrumental views of the curriculum put an emphasis on its serving an extrinsic aim or external purposes such as producing citizens who will benefit society. This can be contrasted with the view that the curriculum should serve the intrinsic aim of providing a value in its own right, so that it is seen as self-fulfilling and providing experiences that are worthwhile (Soler and Miller 2003).

This chapter offers a critique to these reductionist and instrumental views, and advocates for an alternative vision of a capabilit-promoting ECE curriculum that aligns with Nussbaum's list of basic human capabilities and her emphasis on offering a relative standard of minimal justice in ECE settings. From this perspective, the focus should be each individual child's capability development, which will enable her or him to realise a life she or he has reason to value. In recent years there has been growing international interest from people working in diverse sectors and fields of formal, informal and non-formal education in the potential of the capability approach to contribute ideas, policies and practices (Unterhalter et al, 2007). Education is a central arena in which to apply the capability approach as a normative and valuative framework that assures human rights, strives for the respect of human dignity and creates the conditions in which people can live flourishing lives. To date, the investigation of the potential of the capability approach to ECE and curriculum development has been marginal and there is a lack of knowledge of what the capability approach would and could mean in curriculum policy practice.

Early childhood education curricula

ECE programmes appear to have grown more academically demanding over the past 25 years. This might be a consequence of the general move to restructure all levels of education, which, in many countries, took place in the 1990s, with the implementation of national curricula; the setting of teaching and learning targets, national assessment tests, and new inspection procedures; and a whole discourse on performativity (Tsatsaroni et al, 2003).

Within this time frame, a significant number of curricula have been planned and carried out in many countries all over the world, and these have been accompanied by numerous discussions on their effectiveness as well as their implementation in the ECE setting. A significant number of works relating to the preparation as well as the formulation of early childhood curricula can be found in current research. In addition, it is notable that since 1996, there has been a tendency for ministries of education and/or welfare within the member states of the European Union to reform their early childhood curricula on a national level (for example, Norway: 1996; Sweden: 1998; UK/Scotland: 1999; UK/England: 2000; Greece: 2001, 2003, 2011; France: 2002; Finland, Denmark, and Germany: 2003). This wave of curriculum reforms has occurred in combination with other reforms such as the extension of working hours (all-day kindergarten).

Curricula sketch the concept of a good start in life based on the positioning of the agreed norms and values of a specific cultural setting. Curriculum development is an ideologocal, political, selective and partial process, often with an ethnocentric focus where the values, ideals and norms of a specific legitimate culture are illustrated. Apple (1982) argues that the curriculum needs to be linked to a whole array of proposals for centralisation of cultural and economic control and accountability that extend well beyond the school. For Apple (1988), a curriculum takes particular social forms and embodies certain interests that are themselves the outcomes of continuous struggles within and among dominant and subordinate groups; and it is certainly not the result of some abstract process, but evolves through the conflicts, compromises and alliances of identifiable social movements and groups. Andersen and Hansen (2012) refer to Bourdieu's theorising on cultural capital, according to which the culture of the most powerful classes serves as a legitimate culture that can be mastered to varying extents. Students who have been inculcated in these cultural forms from childhood will have the greatest probability of academic success, whereas students with working-class origins will have disadvantages in the educational system because of the distance between their class culture and the 'legitimate' culture that dominates the school system (Andersen and Hansen, 2012).

A curriculum is built within a specific paradigm of regarding children and childhood and making sense of the world. Curricular approaches to ECE have been sorted into two broad categories:[2] the social pedagogic/

competence approach/model and the pre-primary/performance approach/model. The first category is found in Scandinavian countries, New Zealand (Te Whāriki) and Italy (Reggio Emilia). This category of curriculum sets broad orientations for children while viewing the acquisition of developmental skills as a secondary and unplanned result (Moore, 2008). The second category is found in France, the United Kingdom and the United States and is characterised by centralised development of the curriculum – often with detailed goals and outcomes that determine or influence curriculum decisions about what and how children learn (McLachlan et al, 2010). The goals and outcomes are often stated as learning standards or learning expectations and are related to school-readiness tasks and skills. McLachlan and colleagues (2010) note that the design of the latter curriculum category is underpinned by the scholarly academic ideology and is based on the notion that our culture has accumulated knowledge over the centuries that has been organised into academic disciplines within universities. The latter dimension is the dominant curricular discourse, which is given too much uncritical space and increasingly diminishes, impoverishes and undermines ECE's potential as a space where children's long-term life chances can be improved. However, it is not sufficient to look only to the long-term future of children – the quality of experiences that young children have are key with respect to the quality of their lives while they are children, and this in turn matters not only on an ethical-moral basis but specifically with respect to their chances of gaining the most from their educational encounters.

Moss and Bennett (2006) argue:

> Globally, there is a tendency to treat early childhood services as junior partners, preparing children for the demands of formal schooling; this threatens what the Swedes call 'schoolification', the school imposing its demands and practices on other services, making them school-like. (p 2)

Within contemporary policy frameworks, the ECE curriculum document has become the site through which content, coherence and control are articulated, as a means for aligning preschool and compulsory education policy, and ensuring that children achieve educational and school-readiness goals, which, in turn, contribute towards long-term economic and sociopolitical goals (Wood and Hedges, 2016, p 388).

The 'academic' nature of the curriculum filters down to early childhood education institutions and stands out as one of the major issues in ECE, while the emphasis in early childhood education has moved away from children's development and socialisation towards a matter of teaching specific academic skills. Dahlberg and Moss (2005) argue that, so far, the rationale for public investment in such programmes is the expectation of a demonstrable and calculable return, a quasi contract in which preschools receive funding in return for delivering certain outputs. The implicit assumption is that poverty and related social ills derive from individual failures – of children and/or parents – that interventions through early childhood education can rectify. Education is now regarded as an economic investment with a measurable outcome compared with other investments through cost-benefit analysis and children are experiencing an intensification of workload with a focus on marketable skills and an emphasis on technical competence and performativity as a guarantee of future prosperity.

Within this discourse, Tsatsaroni and colleagues (2003) point to the tendency to intensify the focus on academic knowledge in early childhood institutions. Hedges and Cullen (2005) argue that calls for early academic learning to give economic advantage and calls for an outcome-based model of learning and assessment risk adopting an overt approach to subjects. They refer to Marcon's (1999, 2002) research findings, which suggest that while an initial advantage may exist, there are no long-term gains for children from formal approaches. Instrumental views of the curriculum put an emphasis on its serving an extrinsic aim or external purposes such as producing citizens who will benefit society. This can be contrasted with the view that the curriculum should serve the intrinsic aim of providing a value in its own right, so that it is seen as self-fulfilling and providing experiences that are worthwhile (Soler and Miller, 2003). The curriculum should be seen as the incorporating normative frame under which the child will be enabled to reach her full potential and to be and to do what she has reason to value. Furthermore, it could serve as a tool to evaluate the level of implementation of the normative frame for each individual child within the ECE institution.

Reclaiming normative aims for ECE curricula through the capability approach

A capability-promoting policy is suggested here as an alternative vision for reclaiming the normative aims in ECE curricula. Such a curriculum has more things in common with the elements of the social pedagogic/competence approach/model referred above. A capability-promoting curriculum could serve as a critique to the instrumental and reductionist views of ECE curricula approaches, as the capability approach emphasises the value of basic human capabilities for themselves and not merely as a means to achieve better educational outcomes. Before elaborating on the potential of this curriculum, it is necessary to provide the context for the capability approach and to clarify the theoretical background that is considered adequate for such an endeavour.

The capability approach,[3] introduced by Amartya Sen and further developed by Martha Nussbaum, is a broad normative framework for the evaluation of individual wellbeing and social arrangements, the design of policies, and proposals about social change in society (Robeyns, 2003). The term capability represents the alternative combination of 'things' a person is able to do or be – the various 'functionings' a person can achieve. The term 'functionings' reflects the various beings and doings a person enjoys (what children are effectively able to do and to be). The difference between a functioning and a capability is similar to the difference between an achievement and the freedom to achieve something, or between an outcome and opportunity. Functionings are people's beings and doings whereas capabilities are the real or effective opportunities to achieve functionings. Sen and Nussbaum understand quality of life as sheding light on what beings are able to be and to do. Sen highlights 'public reasoning', a person's capacity to participate, communicate, read, and make informed choices and decisions (Sen, 1999). Nussbaum (2007) provides a philosophical underpinning for an account of core human entitlements that should be respected and implemented by governments of all nations, as a bare minimum of what respect for human dignity requires. Therefore she sets out a list of basic capabilities in order to develop a relatively definite standard of minimal justice (Richardson, 2015, p 163).

Saito (2003) highlights the potentially strong and mutually enhancing relationship between the capability approach and education – an interrelationship and interaction that could be crucial and groundbreaking. He calls for serious attention and research from educationists in order to realise the implications of the approach. Although efforts have been made to operationalise the capability approach within the field of education, to date, the context of early childhood education has not been a matter of thorough debate.

Nussbaum (2006, 2011) identifies 10 combined capabilities that, according to her, are central for human flourishing and a life of dignity, and need to be present for a fully human 'good life'. These are:

- life;
- bodily health;
- bodily integrity;
- senses, imagination, thought;
- emotions;
- practical reason;
- affiliation;
- other species;
- play;
- control over one's environment.

Diehm and Magyar-Haas (2010) praise the speciality of Nussbaum's accomplishment, the formulation of a vague, open, arbitrarily extendable, politically relevant list of functionings that is, on the one hand, non-detached, but, on the other hand, 'objective'. They argue that Nussbaum formulates a universalistic approach that is able to take both pluralism and cultural differences into account to the same degree (Diehm and Magyar-Haas, 2010, p 105).

Nussbaum (2011) argues that since its interception, the capabilities approach stresses the importance of education. For her, 'education ... forms people's existing capacities into developed internal capabilities of many kinds' (Nussbaum, 2011, p 152). Nussbaum (2006) perceives public education as a crucial element to the health of democracy and opposes the recent educational initiatives in many countries that focus narrowly on science and technology, neglecting the arts and humanities, and promoting the internalisation of information, rather than on the formation of the student's critical and imaginative capacities. Such a narrow focus is for Nussbaum a danger for democracy's future.

Nussbaum's list of basic human capabilities and her emphasis on offering a relative standard of minimal justice has great relevance for ECE settings, especially in fulfilling their role in combatting disadvantage right at the start. Most of Nussbaum's identified core basic capabilities are met in a great number of early childhood curricula in which they are endorsed either explicitly or implicitly. Many of them are deliberated in the Greek Cross-Thematic Curriculum Framework as well as in other curricula (for example, Te Whāriki, High Scope, Experimental Education, the Swedish curriculum or the Reggio Emilia approach). Indeed, ECE curricula highlight in particular the strong interaction between emotional, social and cognitive development in early childhood, which depends on environment and opportunity. Children can develop social/emotional competence through both planned and unplanned interactions with adults and peers. Moreover, a number of these basic human capabilities have been scrutinised by scholars such as Montessori, Piaget, Vygotsky, Freud and Fröbel within the context of educating and caring for young children. These scholars have produced eminent argumentations on their indisputable value that continue to influence and shape early childhood education to this day. The debate on these aspects of childhood is timely and yet timeless, revealing their interrelation as well as their instrumentality in child's development. Within early childhood education literature, the intrinsic and instrumental value of play, imagination, thought and socialisation–affiliation for children's development is emphasised. The child's free movement in space, and her mental, creative, emotional and imaginary expression and participation outside school, in current or future established social frameworks of work, constitute an axis for every current or future scheme pertaining to any preschool education strategy (Frangos, 1993).

An example of the wide use of basic capabilities in early childhood curricula can be found the Finnish national curriculum guidelines on early childhood education (2003), where such capabilities are prioritised and embodied in children's rights. The guidelines highlight, for example, children's right to 'warm personal relationships' and 'their own culture, language and beliefs', which could be linked to the capability of affiliation, as well as the right to 'secured growth, development and learning' and 'secure, and healthy environments that allow play and a wide range of activities', which may be linked to the capabilities of bodily health and bodily integrity. The following quote from the Finnish curriculum offers a sense of the common language used.

> A good combination of care, education and teaching can promote the child's positive self-image, expressive and interactive skills, and the development of thinking.... An activity that children find meaningful also gives an expression to their thoughts and feelings.... Children play for the sake of playing, and at best, play can give them deep satisfaction. Although children do not play in order to learn, they learn through play.... As playing is social by nature, peer groups have a significant effect on the way the playing situation develops.... At an early age, children also start to actively explore their object environment, which prepares them to a transition to imaginary play. Imaginary games mean detachment from here and now, and the onset of imagination and abstract thinking.... When they play,

they imitate and create new things. They pick up things that are meaningful for them from the sphere of both the real world and that of fantasy and fiction, translating them into a language of play.... Artistic activities and experiences introduce the child to an aesthetic world: the joy of learning, artistic drama, forms, sounds, colours, scents, sentiments and combinations of experiences based on the different senses. Art gives the child an opportunity to experience an imaginary world where everything is possible and true and in a make-believe way.

An additional example could be the well-known and highly respected Te Whāriki curriculum of New Zealand (1996) in which a similar discourse is evident and the interrelation between these aspects of childhood is highlighted:

Cognitive, social, cultural, physical, emotional, and spiritual dimensions of human development are integrally interwoven. The early childhood curriculum takes up a model of learning that weaves together intricate patterns of linked experience and meaning rather than emphasising the acquisition of discrete skills. The child's whole context, the physical surroundings, the emotional context, relationships with others, and the child's immediate needs at any moment will affect and modify how a particular experience contributes to the child's development. This integrated view of learning sees the child as a person who wants to learn, sees the task as a meaningful whole, and sees the whole as greater than the sum of its individual tasks or experiences.

In order to show the relevance of the basic human capabilities for ECE curricula, I focus on four key examples that support such a claim: play, senses–imagination–thought, affiliation and emotions. These capabilities comprise the cornerstone of ECE and are commonly found in early childhood curricula. Table 13.1 provides indicative quotes from ECE curricula where the role and the value of these capabilities is illustrated within this context.

Despite a tendency towards formalisation, unification and integration into the educational system as a whole, ECE still constitutes a space where more freedom is offered in comparison with other spheres of education. This does not by any means imply that within early childhood settings the power relations and the imposition of values and practices of the dominant discourse do not play a significant role. However, the structure, settings and actors involved provide the conditions for a unique way of interacting, learning and experiencing liberation that is not found in other educational settings, and facilitates the development of capability-promoting policy and the implementation of capability-promoting curricula. Such a policy would aim to redistribute social advantages and moderate the effects of disadvantage. Undoubtedly such an endeavour would require the use of Nussbaum's list as a basis for deliberation, not only among the professionals and the parents but also among children.[4] The essence of the approach should remain the same: to assure a standard of minimal justice that would set a threshold below which difference becomes a disadvantage within the early childhood educational setting. One of the specificities of the capability approach is that it 'leaves space for human diversity' (Alkire, 2003, p 15), a fact that should be a prerequisite in an educational setting. As 'a universal theory of the good' (Robeyns, 2003), the capability approach applies to all social justice issues, including education, and by being sensitive to local culture and context it permits transferability and applicability in diverse structures. The basic human capabilities that Nussbaum introduces are widely used within contemporary ECE curricula. One could argue that they share a common discourse on the value of those capabilities from a dual perspective: as ends in themselves that have as a secondary and unplanned result the acquisition of developmental skills (social pedagogic/competence approach/model); and as a means that serves to achieve predetermined academic goals and outcomes and facilitators for the accomplishment of expected learning standards among children (pre-primary/performance approach/model). However, the dominant case is that these capabilities play an instrumental role to serve academic knowledge acquisition within ECE curricula.

Taking as a given the shared discourse of the capability approach and the curricular approaches to ECE on the significance of the basic human capabilities in combination with the political urge to effectively address and interrupt the processes that start the journey of disadvantage for particular groups of children in the early years of their childhoods, it is important to reclaim normative aims in ECE curricula through the capability approach. A capability-promoting curriculum could be more easily developed within national contexts where the social pedagogic/competence approach/model prevails. The capability approach emphasises the value of the basic human capabilities for themselves and not merely as a means to achieve better educational outcomes. However, even in the case of the pre-primary/performance approach/model, and despite its instrumental and reductionist view of

Table 13.1: Children's capabilities in early childhood education curricula

	The capability of play	The capability of senses, imagination and thought	The capability of affiliation	The capability of emotions
Swedish curriculum Lpfö 98 (Skolverket, 2010)	Play is important for the child's development and learning. Conscious use of play to promote the development and learning of each individual child should always be present in preschool activities. Play and enjoyment in learning in all its various forms stimulate the imagination, insight, communication and the ability to think symbolically, as well as the ability to co-operate and solve problems. Through creative and gestalt play, the child is given opportunities to express and work through his or her experiences and feelings. (p 6)	Preschool should provide scope for the child's own plans, imagination and creativity in play, and learning, both indoors and outdoors. (p 7)		The preschool should take into account and develop children's ability to take responsibility and develop their social preparedness so that solidarity and tolerance are established at an early stage. (p 3)
Greek Cross Thematic Curriculum Framework (CTCF) (2003)	Play should be highlighted as the core of the entire program. (p 587) Play fills the greater part of the child's life at this age. It is the means by which the child gets to know itself, learns about people, and the world around it, understands its possibilities and limits. It contributes to the socialization of the child. Children through play learn to cooperate, to take responsibilities and roles, learn to follow and respect rules. (p 589)	Children in a safe and rich in stimuli environment explore with their senses, create ideas and construct knowledge. (p 586) They use initially their senses, make assumptions, and try to explore the world. (p 588) By using different materials to realize that senses help us understand the external environment; to name and describe the sensory organs and senses. (p 604) Children are encouraged to observe their surroundings, to use their senses to handle various materials to find specific features, to compare them, to study their properties and to classify them. (p 605)	CTCF (2003) focuses on the socialization of the children, the enrichment of their communication skills and the reinforcement of the interaction among children. (p 586)	CTCF (2003) suggest to the pedagogues the following on emotion: … provide opportunities to children to develop and express ideas and emotions in many ways, such as play, drama, writing, painting, among others. (p 587) With movement, voice, speech and materials chosen by the child, it expresses, alone or in cooperation with others, experiences, emotions and ideas. (p 589) Children should develop positive emotions about themselves [p 600]; develop feelings of love and brotherhood for all creatures of the earth. (p 601)

	The capability of play	The capability of senses, imagination and thought	The capability of affiliation	The capability of emotions
Norway's national curriculum (Ministry of Education and Research, Norway, 2006)	Playing is at the core of children's wellbeing and self-expression, and interaction with others whilst playing is important for a balanced development. (p 18) Kindergartens shall provide children with opportunities for play, self-expression and meaningful experiences and activities. (p 19) Play has intrinsic value and is an important part of child culture. (p 27)	They [children] must be actively encouraged to express their thoughts and opinions, and must receive acknowledgement for doing so. (p 15) Kindergartens must allow for the children's initiative, imagination and sense of wonderment. (p 18) **Kindergartens shall help to ensure that children use their imaginations and creative thought processes, and discover the joy of creating things.** (p 37) **Staff must start from children's curiosity, interests and backgrounds, and help them to experience with all of their senses, observe and wonder about phenomena in the natural and technological worlds.** (p 38)	The kindergartens shall be a challenging and safe place for community life and friendship. (p 29) Early experiences with peers are of great importance to children's ability to interact well, and this makes kindergartens important arenas for social development, learning, and the building of friendships. All children in kindergartens, regardless of age, gender, ethnic background and ability level must be given equal opportunities to participate in meaningful activities with their peer groups. (p 30)	Children's emotional expressions shall be taken seriously. (p 15)
Te Whāriki (Ministry of Education, 1996)		Children develop ... strategies for actively exploring and making sense of the world by using their bodies, including active exploration with all the senses, and the use of tools, materials, and equipment to extend skills [p 86]; ... the confidence to choose and experiment with materials, to play around with ideas, and to explore actively with all the senses. (p 88)		

education, it would be beneficial to use a curricular framework that aligns with the capability approach as an evaluative metric in order to unveil weaknesses and fallacies in the way cycles of disadvantage are addressed.

Conclusion

This chapter has explored the potential of a capability-promoting curriculum in early childhood education. It shows that the capability approach, and more specifically Martha Nussbaum's list of basic human capabilities, is highly interrelated with curricula frameworks within ECE. The central human capabilities, as the minimum entitlements a person should have, are deeply rooted in the normative principles that shape early childhood education. ECE institutions offer a chance for the establishment and support of the kind of habitus that supports longer-term means of fulfilling one's potential.

Contemporary ECE curricula share a discourse on the value of those capabilities from a dual perspective: as ends in themselves that have as a secondary and unplanned result the acquisition of developmental skills (social pedagogic/competence approach/model); and as a means that serves to achieve predetermined academic goals and outcomes and facilitators for the accomplishment of expected learning standards among children (pre-primary/performance approach/model). Each dimension reflects views of children and childhood espoused by the theorists or researchers who have developed it. The pre-primary/performance approach/model is the dominant curricular discourse and tends to be given too much uncritical space; its view of the child as a human becoming increasingly diminishes, impoverishes and undermines ECE's potential as a space where children's long-term life chances can be improved. However, it is not sufficient to look only to the long-term future of children. The quality of experiences that young children have are key to the quality of their lives while they are children, and this in turn matters not only on an ethical-moral basis but specifically with respect to their chances of gaining the most from their educational encounters. Children need to be seen as persons with a voice and as socially competent agents. Early childhood should not be perceived as a merely preparatory stage, a rehearsal for adulthood.

Democracy needs to be embedded in the curriculum, both as an object of learning and as an act of praxis (OECD, 2004). A capability-promoting curriculum, as suggested here and based on Nussbaum's theorising, could offer a relatively definite standard of minimal justice and reclaim a normative frame based on the central human capabilities as the minimum entitlements a person should have. Such a curriculum would align better with the perception of basic human capabilities mainly as ends in themselves within the ECE context, where the focus will be on each individual child's capability development, enabling her to choose a life of value. A capability-promoting curriculum could offer a meaningful understanding of what is worth seeking for its own sake without lacking academic content.

Nevertheless, assuring that the curriculum reflects the capability approach is not sufficient to ensure a successful capability-promoting policy within ECE. Obstacles and ambivalences will certainly occur when such a capability-promoting policy is put into practice. The most important challenge that needs to be addressed is the endorsement of the capability approach from practitioners in the field. Pedagogues and practitioners would also need to be encouraged to appreciate and embrace a capability-promoting curriculum. This would require initiating a plethora of engaging dialogical and debateable activities for the pedagogues, to enable them to 'walk the walk' of such a capability-promoting curriculum. Fullan (1989) argues that mastering practices and beliefs is the key to the success of policy implementation. If effective use of the capability-promoting curriculum is not achieved, especially with respect to the practices and beliefs of frontline implementers, outcomes will not be achieved. Frontline policy implementers are not usually involved in the process of curriculum formation and researchers often have little direct information about how pedagogues' personal pedagogy has evolved over the course of their career, so quite how the training and education of ECE staff operates is little known. Evidence suggests that the official curriculum may be only loosely connected to what teachers teach in the classroom (Cohen et al, cited in Lee Stevenson and Baker, 1991). Fleer and colleagues (2009) argue that we have little empirical evidence about the effectiveness of different curriculum models (p 192). According to Dahlberg and Moss (2005), although regulatory frameworks such as standards, curricula and guidelines provide external norms that may be reinforced through processes of inspection, practitioners also create their own internal norms, and these are indeed more important in determining their conduct.

Notes

[1] Well-known intervention studies with cost-benefit analyses such as the Chicago child–parent centres (Reynolds, 1997), the High Scope Perry Preschool Program (Schweinhart and Weikart, 1997) and the Carolina Abecedarian Project (Campbell et al, 2002) stress the long-term effects of preschool programmes on children's

cognitive and social development, especially for those living in poverty or at risk of it.

2   For more details on ECE curricular approaches and schoolification, see Bernstein, 1996; OECD, 2006; Bertrand, 2007; Moore, 2008; McLachlan et al, 2010; Potsi, 2014; Potsi et al, 2016.

3   Due to its interdisciplinary nature, the capability approach is the subject of a growing, voluminous literature, as it serves quite different epistemological goals and spans a wide range of traditional academic disciplines (see Andresen et al, 2006, 2008; Alkire, 2003, 2005, 2007; Clark, 2005, 2006; DiTommaso, 2006; Gasper, 2004; Kuklys and Robeyns, 2004; Osmani, 2000; Papadopoulos and Tsakloglou, 2005; Robeyns, 2000, 2003, 2005, 2006; Saito, 2003). This effort has led to the development of the approach in a variety of settings such as poverty or inequality assessment, quality of life measurement and so on. The capability approach has also received substantial attention by philosophers, ethicists, economists and other social scientists.

4   Although the capability approach offers a way of engaging with questions of educational equality, it should be a matter of concern that the absence of critical consideration on children's positioning within the approach as well as on intergenerational relationships may put the capability approach at risk of reproducing and reinforcing the material and knowledge-based power inequalities that are at the heart of the institutionalised educational system instead of combating the conditions of inequality. The controversy lies in the duality of the way in which children are perceived. Some researchers within the capability approach regard children as social actors who have values, make meaning and need opportunities in the here and now of their lives, whereas others regard them as humans to be, who need to be prepared for an adult life where opportunities will come to fruition. The importance of incorporating children's own views cannot be underestimated. Children have, over the past two decades, become visible to policymakers, politicians and academics concerned with promoting children's wellbeing in both the short and the long term.

References

Alkire, S. (2003) 'The capability approach as a development paradigm?' Material for the training session preceding the 3rd international conference on the capability approach, Pavia, pp 1–18, available at: www.researchgate.net/profile/Sabina_ Alkire/publication/228832403_The_Capability_Approach_as_a_ development_paradigm/links/004635231a3c01d715000000.pdf

Alkire, S. (2005) 'Why the capability approach?', *Journal of Human Development*, vol 6, no 1, pp 115-33, available at: www.tandfonline. com/doi/abs/10.1080/146498805200034275

Alkire, S. (2007) *Choosing dimensions: The capability approach and multidimensional poverty*, Working Paper No. 88, Chronic Poverty Research Centre, available at: http://dx.doi.org/10.2139/ ssrn.1646411

Andersen, P. and Hansen, M. (2012) 'Class and cultural capital: the case of class inequality in educational performance', *European Sociological Review*, vol 24, no 2, pp 243-56.

Andresen, S., Otto, H.-U. and Ziegler, H. (2006) 'Education and welfare: a pedagogical perspective on the capability approach', in *Freedom and social justice. Documentation of the 2006 International Conference of the Human Development and Capability Association*, pp 1–34, https://pub.uni-bielefeld.de/publication/1943033

Andresen, S., Otto, H.-U. and Ziegler, H. (2008) 'Bildung as human development: An educational view on the capabilities approach', in H.-U. Otto and H. Ziegler (eds) *Capabilities – Handlugsbefähigung und Verwirklichungschancen in der Erziehungswissenschaft*, Wiesbaden: Verlag für Sozialwissenschaften, pp 165-97.

Apple, M. (1982) 'Common curriculum and state control', *Discourse: Studies in the Cultural Politics of Education*, vol 2, no 2, pp 1-10.

Apple, M. (1988) 'Social crisis and curriculum accords', *Educational Theory*, vol 38, no 2, pp 191-201.

Bask, M. (2011) 'Cumulative disadvantage and connections between welfare problems', *Social Indicators Research*, vol 103, no 1, pp 443-64.

Bernstein, B. (1996) *Pedagogy, symbolic control and identity: Theory, research, critique*, London: Taylor and Francis.

Bertrand, J. (2007) 'Preschool programs: effective curriculum. Comments on Melhuish and Barnes, Kagan and Kauerz, Schweinhart and Leserman', in E. Tremblay, G. Barr and V. Peters (eds) *Encyclopedia on early childhood development*, Montreal: Centre of Excellence for Early Childhood Development, pp 1-7, available at www.child-encyclopedia.com/documents/BertrandANGxp.pdf.

Campbell, F., Ramey, C., Pungello, E., Sparling, J. and Miller-Johnson, S. (2002) 'Early childhood education: young adult outcomes from the Abecedarian project', *Applied Developmental Science*, vol 6, no 1, pp 42-57.

Clark, D. (2005) 'Sen's capability approach and the many spaces of human well-being', *The Journal of Development Studies*, vol 41, no 8, pp 1339-68.

Clark, D. (2006) 'The capability approach: Its development, critiques, and recent advances', Global Poverty Research Group GPRG-WPS-032, available at: www.gprg.org/pubs/workingpapers/pdfs/gprg-wps-032.pdf

Dahlberg, G. and Moss, P. (2005) *Ethics and politics in early childhood education. Contesting early childhood*, New York, NY: Routledge Falmer.

Diehm, I. and Magyar-Haas, V. (2010) 'Language education – for the "good life"?', in S. Andresen, I. Diehm, U. Sander and H. Ziegler (eds) *Children and the good life: New challenges for research on children*, Dordrecht: Springer, pp 103-14.

DiTommaso, M. (2006) *Measuring the well being of children using a capability approach: An application to Indian data*, Working papers ChilD n. 05/2006, Centre for household, income, labour and demographic economics.

Duncan, G.J., Magnuson, K., Kalil, A. and Ziol-Guest, K. (2012) 'The importance of early childhood poverty', *Social Indicators Research*, vol 108, no 1, pp 87-98.

Fleer, M., Anning, A. and Cullen, J. (2009) 'A framework for early childhood education', in A. Anning, J. Cullen and M. Fleer (eds) *Early childhood education: Society and culture*, Los Angeles, CA: Sage, pp 187-204.

Frangos, C. (1993) 'A Child Development Centre (CDC) based on the world of work and everyday life: a case of quality education provision for 2.5-5 year old children', *European Early Childhood Education Research Journal*, vol 1, no 1, pp 41-52.

Fullan, M. (1989) *Implementing educational change: What we know*, PHREE Background Paper No PHREE/89/18, Washington, CD: World Bank, available at www-wds.worldbank.org/external/default/ WDSContent Server/WDSP/IB/1989/07/01/000009265_396092 9042553/Rendered/PDF/multi_page.pdf.

Gasper, D. (2004) 'Human well-being: Concepts and conceptualizations', UNU – WIDER, Discussion Paper, 2004/06, pp 1–34, available at: www.wider.unu.edu/publication/human-well-being

Hedges, H. and Cullen, J. (2005) 'Subject knowledge in early childhood curriculum and pedagogy: beliefs and practices', *Contemporary Issues in Early Childhood*, vol 6, no 1, pp 66-79.

Kuklys, W. and Robeyns, I. (2004) 'Sen's capability approach to welfare economics', CWPE 0415 discussion paper, available at: https:// papers.econ.mpg.de/esi/discussionpapers/2004-03.pdf

Lee Stevenson, D. and Baker, D. (1991) 'State control of the curriculum and classroom instruction', *Sociology of Education*, vol 64, no 1, pp 1-10.

Lister, R. (2003) 'Investing in the citizen-workers of the future: transformations in citizenship and the state under New Labour', *Social Policy and Administration*, vol 37, no 5, pp 427-43.

Magnuson K.A., Meyers, M.K., Ruhm, C.J. and Waldvogel, J. (2004) 'Inequality in preschool education and school readiness', *American Educational Research Journal*, vol 41, no 1, pp 115-57.

Marcon, R. (1999) 'Differential impact of preschool models of development and early learning of inner-city children: a three-cohort study', *Developmental Psychology*, vol 35, no 2, pp 358-75.

Marcon, R. (2002) 'Moving up the grades: relationships between preschool model and later school success', *Early Childhood Research and Practice*, vol 4, no 1, available at www.ecrp.uiuc.edu/v4n1/marcon.html.

McLachlan, C., Fleer, M. and Edwards, S. (2010) *Early childhood curriculum. Planning, assessment and implementation*, Melbourne: Cambridge University Press.

Ministry of Education (1996) *Te Whāriki – He Whàriki Màtauranga mò ngà Mokopuna o Aotearoa – Early Childhood Curriculum*, Wellington, New Zealand: Learning Media.

Ministry of Education and Research, Norway (Kunnskapsdepartementet) (2006) *Framework plan for the content and tasks of kindergartens*, Oslo: Ministry of Education and Research.

Moore, T.G. (2008) *Towards an early years learning framework for Australia*, CCCH Working Paper 4, Parkville: Centre for Community Child Health.

Moss, P. and Bennett, J. (2006) 'Toward a new pedagogical meeting place? Bringing early childhood into the education system', Briefing Paper for Nuffield Educational Seminar, 26 September, available at http://89.28.209.149/fileLibrary/pdf/briefingpaper_Moss_Bennett.pdf.

Nussbaum, M. (2006) 'Education and democratic citizenship: capabilities and quality education', *Journal of Human Development*, vol 7, no 3, pp 385-95.

Nussbaum, M. (2007) *Frontiers of justice: Disability, nationality, species membership social contracts and three unsolved problems of justice*, Cambridge, MA: Harvard University Press.

Nussbaum, M. (2011) *Creating capabilities: The human development approach*, Cambridge, MA: Belknap Press of Harvard University Press.

OECD (Organisation for Economic Co-operation and Development) (2004) *Starting Strong: Curricula and pedagogies in early childhood education and care*, Paris: OECD.

OECD (2006) *Starting Strong II: Early childhood education and care*, Paris: OECD.

Osmani, S. (2000) 'Human rights to food, health, and education', *Journal of Human Development*, vol 1, no 2, pp 273-98.

Papadopoulos, F. and Tsakloglou, P. (2005) 'Social exclusion in the EU: A capability based approach', EI Working Paper, available at: www2.lse.ac.uk/europeanInstitute/LEQS/EIWP2005-01.pdf

Potsi, A. (2014) 'Greek pre-primary teachers' beliefs and practices: are they capabilities- or performance-based?', in H.-U. Otto and S. Schäfer (eds) *New approaches towards the 'good life' applications and transformations of the capability approach*, pp 89-106, Opladen: Barbara Budrich Publishers.

Potsi, A., D'Agostino, A., Giusti, C. and Porciani, L. (2016) 'Childhood and capability deprivation in Italy: a multidimensional and fuzzy set approach', *Quality and Quantity*, vol 50, no 6, pp 2571-90.

Reynolds, A. (1997) *The Chicago child–parent centers: A longitudinal study of extended early childhood intervention*, Institute for Research on Poverty Discussion Paper No 1126-97, available at www.irp.wisc.edu/publications/dps/pdfs/dp112697.pdf.

Richardson, H. (2015) 'Using final ends for the sake of better policy-making', *Journal of Human Development and Capabilities*, vol 16, no 2, pp 161-72, www.tandfonline.com/doi/abs/10.1080/19452829.2015.1036846.

Robeyns, I. (2000) 'An unworkable idea or a promising alternative? Sen's capability approach re-examined', Center for Economic Studies, Discussions Paper Series (DPS) 00.30, available at: https://core.ac.uk/download/pdf/6979068.pdf

Robeyns, I. (2003) 'The capability approach: an interdisciplinary introduction', Paper presented to the Training Course preceding the 3rd International Conference on the Capability Approach, Pavia, Italy, available at: www.academia.edu/621260/The_capability_approach_an_interdisciplinary_introduction

Robeyns, I. (2005) 'The capability approach: a theoretical survey', *Journal of Human Development*, vol 6, no 1, pp 93-114.

Robeyns, I. (2006) 'Three models of education: rights, capabilities and human capital', *Theory and Research in Education*, vol 4, no 1, pp 69-84.

Saito, M. (2003) 'Amartya Sen's capability approach to education: a critical exploration', *Journal of Philosophy of Education*, vol 37, no 1, pp 17-33.

Sardar, Z. (1986) 'Let the children be', *Afkar: Inquiry*, vol 3, no 8, pp 39–44 available at: http://ziauddinsardar.com/2011/02/children-and-tomorrow/

Schweinhart, L. and Weikart, D. (1997) 'The High/Scope preschool curriculum comparison study through age 23', *Early Childhood Research Quarterly*, vol 12, no 1, pp 117-43.

Sen, A. (1999) 'Breaking the poverty cycle – investing in early childhood', Keynote Speech at Inter-American Development Bank, Paris, 14 March 14, available at www.unicef.org/lac/spbarbados/Implementation/ECD/BreakingPovertyCycle_ECD_1999.pdf.

Skolverket (2010) Curriculum for the Preschool Lpfö 98, Revised 2010, available at: www.ibe.unesco.org/curricula/sweden/sw_ppfw_2010_eng.pdf

Soler, J. and Miller, L. (2003) 'The struggle for early childhood curricula: a comparison of the English Foundation Stage Curriculum, Te Whāriki and Reggio Emilia', *International Journal of Early Years Education*, vol 11, no 1, pp 57-68, DOI: 10.1080/0966976032000066091.

Tsatsaroni, A., Ravanis, K. and Falaga, A. (2003) 'Studying the recontextualisation of science in pre-school classrooms: drawing on Bernstein's insights into teaching and learning practices', *International Journal of Science and Mathematics Education*, vol 1, no 1, pp 385-417.

Unterhalter, E., Vaughan, R. and Walker, M. (2007) 'The capability approach and education', *Prospero*, November, available at www.nottingham.ac.uk/educationresearchprojects/documents/developmentdiscourses/rpg2008walkermclean9.pdf.

Wiborg, N.Ø. and Hansen, M.N. (2009) 'Change over time in the intergenerational transmission of social disadvantage', *European Sociological Review*, vol 25, no 3, pp 379-94.

Wood, E. and Hedges, H. (2016) 'Curriculum in the early childhood education: critical questions about content, coherence, and control', *The Curriculum Journal*, vol 27, no 3, pp 387-405.

Wright, C., Diener, M. and Kay, S.C. (2000) 'School readiness of low-income children at risk for school failure', *Sociology of Education*, vol 6, no 2, pp 99-117.

FOURTEEN

Education for all? Providing capabilities for young people with special needs

Christian Christrup Kjeldsen

Introduction

Policies that support human development among young people with special education needs (SEN) and other young people on the edge of the society are the main focus of this chapter. This will be addressed through the case of a promising policy from Denmark that entitles all young people to upper secondary education regardless of their special educational needs or disability. In order to set the scene for this policy, let me briefly describe the current situation and the historical development in this regard. According to Martha Nussbaum's central list of capabilities, the benchmark for measuring the freedom or capability for education can vary depending on the current economic state of the society in question. Ever since the Second World War, primary and lower-secondary education has developed into a formal freedom for all in European countries. This does not mean that everyone has the real freedom to take full advantage of basic schooling, but only that basic schooling has formally become a more or less universal entitlement within Europe. International assessments of literacy show that even in developed countries with highly supportive welfare systems offering compulsory free schooling for all, a good proportion of pupils still do not reach an acceptable level of reading proficiency. Those who lag behind become disadvantaged in their further life-course, and pupils with a low level of reading competence later on in life are found among the group being characterised as having only compulsory education (lower-secondary) as the highest education at the age of 27. This group can be contrasted with those who reach a high level of reading proficiency measured in PISA 2000. They more often have a tertiary education. Until the age of 27 they are lower on risk for receiving social benefits and they are less likely to drop out of different educational programmes (Rosdahl 2014).

Starting with the increasing focus on human capital in the mid-1960s pioneered by Gary Becker (Becker, 1993 [1964]) and the later introduction of mass education (mass universities) after the student revolts since the early 1970s, a larger proportion of the population in Europe is now educated to upper-secondary level or beyond. As a feature of this development in the educational landscape, the Danish parliament voted in favour of the so-called 'Specially Arranged Youth Education' (STU) Act, in 2007 (Ministry of Children and Education, 2007). This was related to some degree to the political ambition concerning the global economic competiveness of Denmark, and it was agreed that 95% of a youth cohort should finish youth education (upper-secondary level), either vocational or general (Danish Government, 2006). The main idea was to assist the Danish welfare state by increasing the proportion of young people with an upper-secondary education in the hope of a return on the investment required. In the Danish context, youth education is understood as a three-year, post-compulsory/upper-secondary period of education in the age range of 16 to 19 years. To achieve this high level of participation, several actions have been taken, of which the programme enacted by the STU legislation is just one example. This policy provides adolescents who cannot benefit from standard upper-secondary schooling with the legal right to receive individually arranged education for three years. After completing such a programme, the pupils concerned are included in the 95% goal mentioned earlier.

The main object of this chapter is therefore to consider this relatively new and innovative educational opportunity for young people with various disabilities in Denmark, which was initially provided by the STU Act (see also Kjeldsen, 2014). This Act was evaluated in 2012 and has been revised a number of times since, but with no major change to the overall aim of the programme as it is stated in the legislation. The latest revision of the Act was in 2015 (Ministry for Children, Education and Gender Equality, 2015), and was followed by a change relating to consolidation of the programme in 2016 (Ministry for Children, Education and Gender Equality, 2016). Policymaking is situated in societies and is thereby influenced by changing discourses when existing policies are revised. In order to empirically and analytically keep the effects of changes in public discourse (which is also the element of analysis) and interpretations of the Act distinct from the actual changes and adjustments of the Act, the empirical investigation will be limited to the period from 2007 to 2012, during which no adjustments in legislation were made.

From the start, the programme was seen as an individual *right* or entitlement, which, quite unusually, was and still is stated explicitly in the legislation as follows: 'Young mentally challenged and other young people with special needs have a legislative right to a youth education' (Ministry for Children, Education and Gender Equality, 2015, §2). In the Danish educational system, there is a distinction between vocational youth education and general youth education. General youth education qualifies young people for access to higher education, whereas vocational youth education is a preparation for transition into the labour market. Government policy is situated between these two main tracks, but the curriculum is strongly weighted in favour of general education, with a more practical focus aimed at eventual further training in the vocational track. General youth education is traditionally concerned with preparation for further education. But what about youth education for those who are mentally challenged and other young people with special needs who cannot pass through any of the other 'ordinary' channels of youth education? What are the aims for them?

This entitlement to upper-secondary education is supposed to give adolescents with special needs competences in three equally weighted areas. First, they should gain competences in various school subjects like reading, writing and mathematics, as well as more expressive subjects such as music and theatre (formal education). Second, their education must aid their personality development. And finally, their education must contribute to the acquisition of social skills. These three areas of development should foster the main aims of the programme, with pupils becoming adolescents who are capable of 'as independent and active participation in adult life as possible and if possible further education and employment' (Ministry for Children, Education and Gender Equality, 2015, §1). The main aims of the programme and the capabilities it is intended to develop are referred to in this chapter as the targeted capabilities for **e**mployment (E), personal **d**evelopment (D) in adulthood, **p**articipation in society and one's own life (P) and **f**urther education or vocational training (F).

In order to achieve these aims, when they are enrolled young people are given a written educational plan – a person-centred curriculum that describes the actual content of their individually planned programme. This is done after a clarification process. It is intended that the individual adolescent should have a significant influence on his or her STU curriculum for the three years. According to the Act, this curriculum should, at least in theory, be drawn up in collaboration with the young person and also with his or her parents or guardians. The educational plan provides an overview of the activities, including counselling sessions and internships, that the young person must be offered during his/her three years of upper-secondary education (Ministry of Children and Education, 2011; Ministry for Children, Education and Gender Equality, 2015, 2016). The aims of the programme may therefore be multidimensional and should be achieved through a specially arranged curriculum that takes into consideration each individual's level of competences, occupational interests and own wishes for a life they have reason to value. This individually shaped plan *may* aim at employment. However, this is not always the case, even though there may be good reasons for employment (not inevitably wage-labour), following Amartya Sen, having an impact on other aims such as the ability to engage socially, personal development and so on (Sen, 1997). In addition, further education or vocational training following on from upper-secondary youth education may be an aim of the individual's educational plan, although once again this is not necessarily the case. Sen gives a good reason for taking this goal into serious consideration when planning, because: 'Just as people "learn by doing",' they also "unlearn" by "not doing" – by being out of work and out of practice. Also, in addition to the depreciation of skill through non-practice, unemployment may generate a loss of cognitive abilities as a result of the unemployed person's loss of confidence and sense of control' (Sen, 1997, p 161). The consolidation Act for the programme states that pupils' potential for further education or labour-market entry should be taken into consideration. However, the overall aim of the policy is that the young people achieve 'as independent and active participation in adult life as possible" (Ministry of Children and Education, 2007, §1).

After only a few years, the programme was considered by the World Future Council in relation to an international study on the implementation of the United Nations Convention on the Rights of Persons with Disabilities (Heindorf and World Future Council, 2012). The programme was assessed to be promising in this regard. A content analysis of the many policy papers and the legislative text guided by the framework of the capability approach reveals that this policy encourages practice (arranged in the individual's educational plan) that could promote the capability development of all the 10 central capabilities on Martha Nussbaum's list for these young people with special needs (Kjeldsen and Jensen, 2010; Kjeldsen, 2014). The programme supports a didactic mixture of social work and educational intervention for mentally challenged young people and other young people with special needs. This opportunity to support the development of the central list of capabilities, and the right to education conferred on those young people who are not capable in the ordinary youth education system, means that this policy may be interpreted as an innovation in terms of social justice and the freedom of education for all (Kjeldsen, 2014), making it suitable as a case study in capability-promoting policies. Furthermore, one of the main characteristics of the policy is that the young people themselves should be given a say in the arrangement of their three years of youth education. This brings the policy well into line with the argument of Jean-Michel Bonvin, who holds that:

> In the capability-friendly model, the beneficiary is considered as an active citizen and invited to take part in the definition of ALMPs and the modalities of their implementation. Provided adequate means are granted to empower him/her and improve his/her capacity to act, this pattern engages him/her in a self-reflexive process ... on how to best develop his/her capabilities. The main difference with the marketised pattern lies in the possibility granted to the beneficiary to co-define and co-implement activation programmes. (Bonvin, 2011, p 152)

To sum up, if the policy documents are to be believed, this education programme promises to provide the legal right for individually based youth education for those who in the past would have left formal education after the completion of compulsory schooling. When only focusing on the legislative framework, it becomes apparent that the content of the individually planned curriculum can be shaped to become intrinsic to the individual's further development of the central capabilities that Martha Nussbaum advocates as essential elements of a truly human life (Nussbaum and Glover, 1995; Nussbaum, 2000; Nussbaum, 2006; Nussbaum, 2011). From now on, I will call this 'entitlement on policy paper'. The question is how this is reflected in the public discourse surrounding the programme and how this may change with changes in society. Josiane Vero argues that: 'One cannot take for granted that educational resources and rights provision (targeting early school leavers or aiming at increasing the access to tertiary education, etc) lead to increased capabilities' (Vero, 2012, p 11). I believe that one of the key factors affecting conversion is that of a changing public discourse regarding the interpretation of the opportunities provided by the programme – if the interpretation of the policy changes, so does the content it represents in practice and the freedoms it promises to offer.

Methodological approach to the discourse analysis and data

As already mentioned, the focus of this chapter is the discursive change related to the main capabilities targeted by the legislation. The analysis provides insights into how interpretations have altered over time in a changing society and how these interpretations relate to other discursive formations or changes in society. Changes in discourse are also a positional struggle between different key stakeholders who have different interests; in this case, for example, we have the intentions of the legislators on the one hand, and, on the other, the interpretation of the legislation by the local municipality that is responsible for implementing the programme. It turns out that municipal budgeting restraints influence decisions in this matter (Kjeldsen, 2014). Theoretically, the assumption is that public discourse is a combat zone for the positional struggle on discourse and this has in its widest sense social effects on the structure of society. The theoretical grounding for this form of analysis is found in the writing of Pierre Bourdieu and Norman Fairclough. Discourse analysis will not be used in that analysis for this chapter in the fashion of a Foucauldian critical discourse analysis with a simple focus on methodology. Instead, it departs from the argument that discourse analysis is 'a social theory of discourse' (Fairclough, 1992, p 62). This is furthermore 'based upon the assumption that language is an irreducible part of social life, dialectically interconnected with other elements of social life' (Fairclough, 2003, p 3) and thereby discourse becomes a dialectic matter that is formed by social life and forms social life. This is in contrast to the Bourdieuian epistemological stand of a 'constructivist structuralism or of structuralist constructivism' (Bourdieu, 1990b, p 122) approach. What is interesting are the structural and material circumstances that co-construct the discourse, in this case the economic downturn, but also the constructions of discourse that structure these structures. This is an objective analysis on empirical grounds along the lines of Bourdieu, who argues:

> Objective analysis obliges us to realize that the two approaches, structuralist and constructivist (by which I mean a kind of phenomenology of one's initial experience of the social world and the contribution which this experience makes towards one's own construction of that world),

are two complementary stages of the same procedure. If agents do indeed contribute to the construction of these structures, they do so at every stage within the limits of the structural constraints which affect their acts of construction. (Bourdieu, 1990a, p xiv)

However, it is important to bear in mind that 'the relationship between discourse and social structure should be seen dialectically if we are to avoid the pitfalls of overemphasizing on the one hand the social determination of discourse, and on the other hand the construction of the social discourse' (Fairclough, 1992, p 64). Discourse is seen as a social practice that co-constructs social life in relation to existing structures and the discourses have a 'constructive effect' on the societal structures of positions and the relation between knowledge, norms and belief systems (Fairclough, 1992, pp 62-4). One of the areas in which discourses about how to interpret the aims of the STU programme can be found is public media, such as newspapers and television. The public discourse surrounding this policy in newspapers also has socially constructive effects because 'People live in ways which are mediated by discourses which construct work, family, gender (femininity, masculinity), sexuality and so forth in particular ways, which emanate from experts attached to social systems and organizations, and which come to them through the mass media (print, radio, television, the internet)' (Fairclough, 2000, p 165). Public discourse therefore plays a significant role in the positional struggle, in that it relates to the relative power of dominant and dominated parties within the educational field (Bourdieu and Wacquant, 1992). This is understood as a field of power that is a 'relation of force that obtains between the social positions which guarantee their occupants a quantum of social force, or capital, such that they are able to enter into the struggles over monopoly of power' (Bourdieu and Wacquant, 1992, p 229). Municipalities, private and public social work institutions and parents and pupils also become forms of collective agents within this educational subfield and each collective 'belongs to a field inasmuch as it produces and suffers effects in it' (Bourdieu and Wacquant, 1992, p 232). It is these changes over time that are in focus, and therefore also this 'discourse analysis [is] focused upon variability, change, and struggle' (Fairclough, 1992, p 36).

Sample of newspaper articles for the content analysis of public discourses

In order to investigate the changes over time in the public discourse regarding the STU programme, it was necessary to obtain access to a searchable database of all written public media and then to perform content analysis on a subset of items that relates to the theme in question. This can be regarded as a form of unobtrusive research (Webb et al, 1966) as well as an observation method, whereas the analysis and the results are inferred only from existing text that is observable in the landscape of media (Krippendorff, 2010). Access to a searchable archive of all articles published in written media allows an analysis going back to the start of the programme in 2007 and over the years of financial downturn, in a period with no changes in the legislation relating to the programme. In Denmark, such a comprehensive search can be done through the news company Infomedia, which monitors approximately 600 Danish print media: 'Clippings are delivered digitally in full text.... Infomedia monitors approximately 150 key news programmes from Danish radio and television on a daily basis, producing short abstracts of each story.... Infomedia monitors approximately 2,500 Danish websites. In most of the sites, including the key Danish news sites, we make use of deep linking' (Infomedia A/S, 2013). Data is accessed through the State and University Library in Aarhus. The number of entries accumulated when building up a Boolean search query for articles with content related to this policy is enormous. One of the drawbacks of content analysis becomes apparent here because it is 'very time-consuming to complete large-scale studies' (Ishiyama and Breuning, 2010). Furthermore, after completing the content analysis, the data should be suitable for testing the hypothesis that there has been a shift from 2007 to 2012 in the way the capabilities targeted by the legislation in the STU programme are weighted in the public discourse by different positions in the educational subfield due to the field's struggles over doxa. The content analysis cannot rely solely on manifest content, but will have to interpret the texts for latent content as well, and therefore becomes more complex than simple word counts. The discursive struggle needs to be interpreted as Bourdieu argues: 'Accepting the radical separation which Saussure made between internal and external linguistics, between the science of language and the science of the social uses of language, one is condemned to looking within words for the power of words, that is, looking for it where it is not to be found' (Bourdieu, 2012 [1991], p 107). For this reason, all the articles chosen for analysis needed to be analysed qualitatively as well.

Therefore a sample strategy for reducing the total number was applied. The sample strategy known as systematic sampling (systematic random sampling) was used (Agresti and Finley, 2009, pp 21-2; Babbie, 2010, pp 211-14), and it is argued that this 'provides as good a representation of the population' (Agresti and Finley, 2009, p 22). In order to gain an estimate of the required sample size, statistical power analysis (Cohen, 1988) was conducted with an effect size for contingency tables of $w=0.2$ and $\alpha=0.05$. With these *a priori* choices, a sample size of at least 482 was needed in order to achieve a statistical power of 0.8. The total population of articles for the period 2007-12 was found to be 1,870; therefore, every third article was chosen and the random start became the second article. Six hundred and twenty-three articles were sampled for content analysis, which is well beyond the 482 needed.

Results: a struggle between life-first and work-first discourses

One of the main findings is the changing relationship between the aims of fostering employability and developing personal skills. The first stance can be placed within human capital thinking, where there is a lifelong obligation for personal development and skill formation for everyone in a Danish context. The policy only had employment or further education as a secondary aim. The overall aim was much more capability-appropriate in terms of central human capabilities, whereas on the level of legislation the policy was much more promising with regard to developing broad life skills and the different central capabilities that Nussbaum promotes. This is much more than simple employability in the ordinary labour market. On 'policy paper', the programme seems promising as a shift away from a one-eyed employability paradigm of education towards a capability paradigm of educational and social work interventions for those young people who have been excluded from the mainstream educational pathway. But there is a positional struggle in discourse between a work-first perspective directed towards the educational goals that should be set in the individual's plan and a life-first perspective where the target group develops as included citizens, becoming the executive editors of their own life, as Søren Kierkegaard advocated (Schou, 2009, p 505). The question is who and which aims dominate this production of the two discourses?

Changes and positional struggles in relation to the capabilities targeted in the legislation

In order to grasp the positional struggle surrounding capabilities, I now briefly describe the macro-political landscape at the birth of the policy. In 2007 when the Act was adopted, the spokesman for education affiliated to the Liberal Party of Denmark (Venstre) argued:

> We shall now consider the first reading of a great and thoroughly positive proposal.... The purpose of the bill is that young mentally challenged people and other young people with special needs should achieve personal, social and professional skills for independent and active participation in adult life, and that they are given the best possible opportunities for access to education or employment. (Nedergaard, 2007)

Five years later, when the Act was to be revised, the minister for education, Christine Antorini, argued that: 'It considers whether the youth education programme meets the established objectives, if the target group is correctly defined, if the funds are used appropriately in relation to ensuring that the target group get an education or employment' (Ministry of Children and Education, 2012). The secondary aims of education and employment are suddenly interpreted as the main aims, forgetting the aim of achieving 'their personal, social and subject competences for as much independent and active participation in adult life as possible' (Ministry of Children and Education, 2007, §1), as it was actually stated in the Act. This is a change in discursive interpretation and interest by the policymakers. There is a dialectic relationship between the discourse among policymakers and the public discourse surrounding the Act, which also changed over the years from 2007 to 2012. Another dialectic relationship is found between these discourses and the effects of the 2008 global financial crisis on the Danish economy. In 2007, when the policy was enacted, the municipalities responsible for conducting the programme were facing a quite different economic situation. Employment levels were high. Even people who had been excluded from the labour market for years could now find employment as a result of the labour shortage. This resulted in what Bourdieu calls an 'illusio'. In this case, the positions in the public discourse surrounding the policy are occupied either by providers or beneficiaries of the programme who are willingly or unwillingly drawn into the 'game' through their participation in the public debate and discourse formation. The illusio is that the agents involved are players in this social game without being aware that this is the case. Here it is worth noting Hill's argument in relation to the capability approach:

> One factor operating at all levels of society that has significant impact on social goals and their achievement is the exercise of social power. But this is a factor that has not received systematic consideration. Until the analytical frameworks being developed as extensions of the capability approach address the issue of social power, the analysis of well-being will be incomplete, and decisions made to enhance human capabilities will systematically fall short. (Hill, 2003, p 117)

By taking part in formulating the public discourse with their utterances in newspapers or other media, these actors indirectly show that it is a social game worth participating in. There is an interest at stake, and the interest in playing along increased steadily during the period considered here. Figure 14.1, which aggregates the sampled articles according to publication date, shows the dramatic increase in interest in the policy.

Figure 14.1: Frequency of articles published on the STU programme each academic year, 2007-12

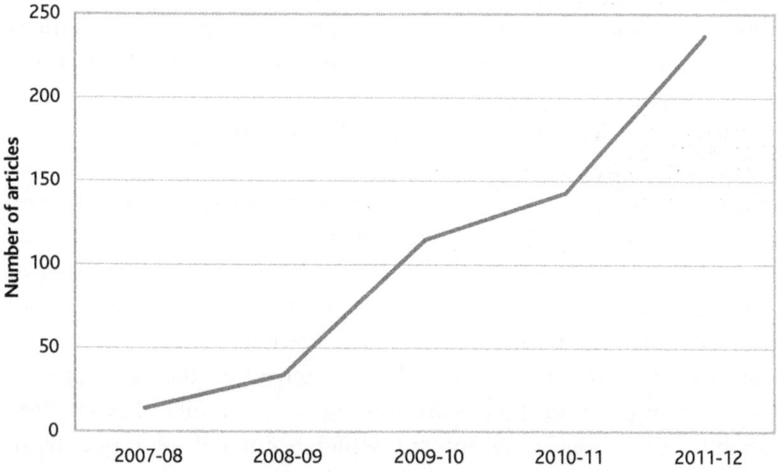

Note: Sampled articles per academic year excluding non-relevant sampled articles = 237.

Linear regression reveals that for the years investigated here there is a significant linear trend. One would expect a strong focus with the introduction of a new policy, with an initial rapid growth in interest followed by a levelling off shortly after, but in this case the focus increased every year over the five years researched. I would not argue for any causality, but it is remarkable that during the same period youth unemployment rates increased and the public discourse surrounding the aims of the policy shifted from a life-first to a work-first perspective.

The articles were then analysed using open coding and NVIVO software, and a categorisation sheet was completed for each article. One of the variables in the categorisation sheet was the policy aims and they were furthermore placed from 1 to 4 on the ordinal scale, with 1 representing the greatest emphasis on the given targeted capability:

- **e**mployment → E
- personal **d**evelopment → D
- **p**articipating in adult life in society and one's own life with 'as many competences for independent and active participation in adult life as possible' → P
- **f**urther education or vocational training → F

Furthermore, if any of the other central capabilities proposed by Nussbaum were latent in the article, they were gathered in a binary variable with 'yes' or 'no'. If the ordinal measure for each of the above categories is treated as interval scale data (with all the cautions this should lead to) and the timeframe investigated is divided into the academic years that these institutions follow, the mathematical mean () of the scores for each variable aggregated within each period differences is as shown in Figure 14.2.

The results show that the public discourse surrounding the main aims of the STU policy changed dramatically during the years of economic downturn. At the start of this period, the aim relating to employment was expressed less frequently and with less emphasis, but this then changes, with employment becoming the most important feature of the discourse by the end of the period. At the same time, all the other targeted capabilities diminished in importance. The targeted capability of personal development, which featured most frequently in the discourse when the policy was introduced, experienced the largest mean difference from period 1 to period 3. However, this says nothing about how the differences are distributed between the discourse producers. Let us therefore now examine the underlying structure through the explorative method of correspondence analysis, which will

Figure 14.2: Change in average ordinal representation of targeted capabilities over three periods

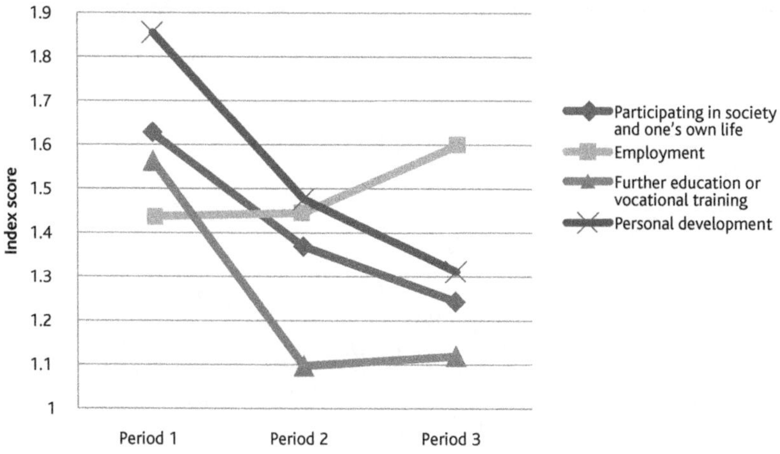

Source: Kjeldsen (2014).

reveal the positional differences in interests between the institutions conducting the programme, the municipalities, the parents and the pupils themselves. As already seen, in the first period the discourse on the goals was as one would expect if relating only to the legislation for this education, as the main purpose and goal of the STU programme is to foster citizens who are able to participate in society and their own lives and if possible to lead to further education or vocational training as well as employment.

The correspondence diagram reveals that the politician and municipality position places distinct in the other part of the map then parents, institutions and pupils. They are found in the area towards the east representing the least emphasis on the targeted capabilities as well as other central capabilities found through content analysis. P1, E1 and D1 are nearest to the politician and municipality position. This indicates that politicians and municipalities do not produce any public discourse in relation to the investigated targeted capabilities and they are not mentioned either explicitly or implicitly. In the northwest of the map enrolled pupils are positioned in the space where the capabilities targeted by the legislation are discursively emphasised most strongly. The capability for employment and further education or vocational training is found near the positioning for pupils and is therefore more explicitly named ('manifest') and given high importance ('interpretation', 'latent') in the articles.

Figure 14.3: Simple correspondence analysis, using Greenacre's proposal for an asymmetric map: 'who is in focus' crossed with the capabilities targeted in the legislation and other central capabilities present

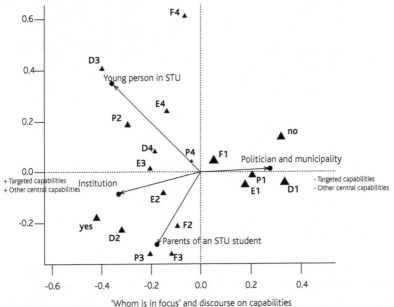

'Whom is in focus' and discourse on capabilities

Source: Kjeldsen (2014).

The STU programme emphasises the importance of enhancing capabilities. But when such intentions and formal entitlements are interpreted in practice, a much more blurred picture appears that is contextually bound to decision making and public discourse within each municipality. The social space and the physical space reflect each other (Bourdieu, 1996, 1999). On the macro level, there is a mismatch between the capabilities of pupils in terms of work and expectations and social structures. The pupils address all the capabilities targeted by the legislation in public discourse to a significantly higher degree than the other positions in the field, particularly with regard to employment. The pupils value work as an aim of their STU programme. But looking into the statistics for these pupils, the actuality of progression to further education or employment after completion of the programme remains unchanged (Kjeldsen, 2014).

Conclusion

As the analysis of the restricted bundle of main capabilities shows, the opportunities offered by the capability-promoting policy to young people with different special needs are compromised as different positions struggle over the doxa regarding the interpretation of the policy. This struggle is an indicator of which capabilities within the discourse are seen as valuable and how this perception changes over time to reflect the socioeconomic context. Over the course of the five years covered by the analysis, public discourse increases steadily and the interests of the main parties in the different aims of the programme fluctuate. Aggregating the changes for each position reveals that municipalities and other political representatives show an increasing interest in pupils within the programme having the capability of employment as the main target. They expect a return on investment as a result of these pupils being moved from social benefits into employment. From 2007 to 2012, the capabilities for employment and personal development attracted increasing focus within the public discourse regarding the cost of aims for further education or becoming active participants in society and one's own life. Different dominant positions are drivers for these changes. The dominant positions within the discourse regarding targeted capabilities are occupied by politicians and professionals working with the programme: they produce the public discourse surrounding the programme. The dominated positions in this struggle are occupied by the parents, who are mainly poorly educated, and the pupils themselves. They have no voice in the public discourse regarding which capabilities should be given prominence. The increasing interest in personal development was mainly influenced by the dominant position of the professionals. Within the articles analysed, discourses surrounding targeted capabilities are often presented in bundles. These discourses address one or more of the targeted capabilities at the same time. They become different combinations of capability sets constructed by the targeted capabilities. Not surprisingly, given the growth in representation of the capability for employment and personal development, these targeted capabilities are more often an ingredient of the bundle rather than the capability to engage in further education. Still, this is quite remarkable given that the capability to participate in society and one's own life is the overall aim of the programme. Over the same period, it can be found that the actuality of young people, and in particular young people with special needs, finding employment has declined in parallel with rising youth unemployment in general. Only very few of these targeted pupils do in fact go on to further education or employment, and those that do should probably be seen as exceptions (Kjeldsen, 2014). Figure 14.4 illustrates the effect of combining analytically the growing emphasis on employment as the aim for young people targeted by the STU policy with the changes in employment opportunities for this group.

Figure 14.4: Structural change as a capability mismatch

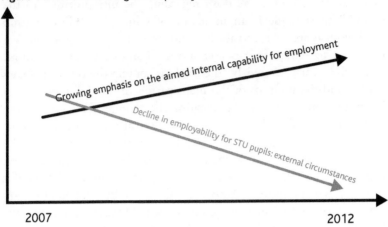

2007   2012

The analysis reveals that there is a growing gap between the actual possibilities for employment for this group and the emphasis on a work-first perspective in the policy aims. This is a form of capability mismatch between what Nussbaum calls external and internal capabilities. If this is related to the pupils' own discourse regarding the aims of the policy, another mismatch may be found between their expectations and the actual social structures in the labour market for these young people, as the pupils themselves address all the legislative aims, and in particular employment, to a high degree. On the one hand, the pupils are positions in the struggle on the discourse, and on the other hand, and to a greater extent, they are a factor in the public discourse regarding employment. The institutions are the other strong position in this regard. The young people value a life in which they can bring their competences into play in the labour market, but this is not a real option for them because the financial crisis has prevented from finding employment.

Similar to Bourdieu's critique of Marx's classes as 'classes on paper', when viewed in isolation, the intention of the policy – policy on paper – may be interpreted as promoting a capability approach, and yet a much more blurred picture arises when these intentions are interpreted in public discourse. As a social democratic welfare state, Denmark has been in transition from welfare to workfare since the early 19th century (Torfing, 1999). It is evident that the public discourse surrounding 'work first' and the latest changes resulting from active labour market policies have launched a second wave of modernisation of the welfare state for the most disadvantaged young people within society, with the current mantra being 'making work pay' (Diop-

Christensen, 2015). These young people, who, according to the STU policy are entitled to develop 'competences for the most independent and active participation in adult life possible' (Ministry of Children and Education, 2007, §1), are now facing a strong public discourse of 'work first'. This has affected programme take-up rates, and is being accelerated by a 'pay-fare' logic (Jensen and Kjeldsen, 2016) – that is, the young should only have access to such a programme if they can show a return on the investment in terms of being self-supportive and reducing social benefit expenditure. These findings reflect a tension between capability-promoting policies on paper and policies in context:

> So if what I have to say is disappointing, sometimes even depressing, it's not because I take any pleasure in discouraging people; on the contrary. It is because knowledge of realities inclines one to realism. (Bourdieu, 1993, p 60)

Even though a policy may seem on paper to adopt a capability-promoting approach, in practice it may become less so, owing to dynamic changes within society. Is there a way out, then? Truly capability-promoting policies need to have an evaluative dimension, involving empirical evaluation and follow-up of the actual results of the policy and the interpretations of key stakeholders. This is because:

> Justice cannot be indifferent to the lives that people can actually live. The importance of human lives, experiences and realizations cannot be supplanted by information about institutions that exists and the rules that operate ... the realized actuality goes well beyond the organizational picture, and includes the lives that people manage – or do not manage – to live. (Sen, 2009, p 18)

Furthermore, the success or failure of a capability-promoting policy rests on the ongoing support of the key producers of the attendant public discourse. A strong profession is therefore required to give voice to the needs of the disadvantaged young people in this case.

References

Agresti, A. and Finley, B. (2009) *Statistical methods for the social sciences* (4th edn), New Jersey: Pearson Prentice Hall.

Babbie, E. (2010) *The practice of social research* (12th edn), Belmont: Wadsworth Cengage Learning.

Becker, G. (1993 [1964]) *Human capital: A theoretical and empirical analysis, with special reference to education*, Chicago, IL and London: University of Chicago Press.

Bonvin, J.-M. (2011) 'Reframing the issue of responsibility in labour market activation policies', in *Transforming European employment policy: Labour market transitions and the promotion of capability*, Cheltenham: Edward Elgar Publishing, pp 138-56.

Bourdieu, P. (1990a) *Homo academicus*, Oxford: Blackwell.

Bourdieu, P. (1990b) *In other words*, Cambridge: Polity Press.

Bourdieu, P. (1993) *Sociology in question*, London: Sage Publications.

Bourdieu, P. (1996) *Rapport 10: Physical space, social space and habitus*, Oslo: University of Oslo.

Bourdieu, P. (1999) 'Site effects', in P. Bourdieu (ed) *The weight of the world: Social suffering in contemporary society*, Oxford: Blackwell, pp 123-29.

Bourdieu, P. (2012 [1991]) *Language and symbolic power*, Cambridge: Polity Press.

Bourdieu, P. and Wacquant, L.J. (1992) *An invitation to reflexive sociology*, Chicago, IL and London: University of Chicago Press.

Cohen, J. (1988) *Statistical power analysis for the behavioral sciences* (2nd edn), New York, NY: Lawrence Erlbaum Associates.

Danish Government (2006) *Fremgang, fornyelse og tryghed strategi for danmark i den globale* [Progress, renewal and security strategy for Denmark in the global], Albertslund: Schultz Information.

Diop-Christensen, A. (2015) 'Is "making work pay" effective for the "unemployable"? The impact of benefit sanctions on social assistance recipients in Denmark', *Journal of European Social Policy*, vol 25, no 2, pp 1-15.

Fairclough, N. (1992) *Discourse and social change*, Cambridge: Polity Press.

Fairclough, N. (2000) 'Discourse, social theory, and social research: the discourse of welfare reform', *Journal of Sociolinguistics*, vol 4, no 2, pp 163-95.

Fairclough, N. (2003) *Analysing discourse: Textual analysis for social research*, London: Routledge.

Heindorf, I. and World Future Council (2012) 'ZERO PROJECT: Innovative Policies to be presented in the Zero Project Report and discussed at the Zero Project Conference', Email correspondence. s.l.: s.n.

Hill, M. (2003) 'Development as empowerment', *Feminist Economics*, vol 9, no 2-3, pp 117-35.

Infomedia A/S (2013) 'A comprehensive source coverage', available at www.infomedia.dk/servicemenu/english/list-of-sources-for-media-monitoring.

Ishiyama, J. and Breuning, M. (eds) (2010) *21st-century political science: A reference handbook*, London: Sage Publications.

Jensen, N.R. and Kjeldsen, C.C. (2016) 'Capability-appropriate or capability-friendly policies: does it really matter? a perspective on the basic vocational education and training (EGU) in Denmark', *Sociologia del Lavoro*, vol 141, pp 55-71.

Kjeldsen, C.C. (2014) *Capabilities and special needs: An educational foundation*, Hamburg: Verlag Dr. Kovač.

Kjeldsen, C.C. and Jensen, H.I. (2010) *Capability approach: En tilgang til ligeværd og det 'gode liv'* [Capability approach: An approach to equality and the 'good life'], Aarhus: Ligeværd and Helhedstæning i UddannelsesGarantien.

Krippendorff, K. (2010) SAGE Reference online, available at www.sage-ereference.com/view/researchdesign/n73.xml (accessed 9 October 2011).

Ministry for Children, Education and Gender Equality (2015) *Bekendtgørelse af lov om ungdomsuddannelse for unge med særlige behov*, Act No. 783 of 15/06/2015, Copenhagen: Retsinformation.

Ministry for Children, Education and Gender Equality (2016) *Bekendtgørelse om ungdomsuddannelse for unge med særlige behov*, Act No. 739 of 03/06/2016, Copenhagen: Retsinformation.

Ministry of Children and Education (2007) *Lov om ungdomsuddannelse for unge med særlige behov*, Act No. 564 of 06/06/2007, Copenhagen: Retsinformation.

Ministry of Children and Education (2011) *Vejledning om ungdomsuddannelse for unge med særlige behov*, Legal Guidance No. 9569 of 16/11/2011, Copenhagen: Retsinformation, available at www.retsinformation.dk/Forms/R0710.aspx?id=139222.

Ministry of Children and Education (2012) 2011/1 SEL L 127, Copenhagen: Retsinformation.

Nedergaard, T. (2007) 'L 196 Forslag til lov om ungdomsuddannelse for unge med særlige behov: Forhandlinger', available at www.ft.dk/samling/20061/lovforslag/l196/beh1/1/forhandling.htm?startItem=#nav.

Nussbaum, M. (2000) *Women and human development: The capabilities approach*, New York, NY: Cambridge University Press.

Nussbaum, M. (2006) *Frontiers of justice: Disability nationality species membership*, London: The Belknap Press.

Nussbaum, M. (2011) *Creating capabilities: The human development approach*, London: The Belknap Press of Harvard University Press.

Nussbaum, M. and Glover, J. (1995) *Women, culture and development: A study of human capabilities*, Oxford: Clarendon Press.

Schou, S. (2009) *Dansk litteraturs historie: Bind 2*, [*The history of Danish literature: volume 2*]Copenhagen: Gyldendal.

Sen, A. (1997) 'Inequality, unemployment and contemporary Europe', *International Labour Review*, vol 136, no 2, pp 155-71.

Sen, A. (2009) *The Idea of Justice*, London: Penguin Books.

Torfing, J. (1999) 'Workfare with welfare: recent reforms of the Danish welfare state', *Journal of European Social Policy*, vol 9, no 1, pp 5-28.

Vero, J. (2012) 'From the Lisbon strategy to Europe 2020: the statistical landscape of the education and training objectives through the lens of the capability approach', *Social Work and Society*, vol 10, no 1, pp 1-16.

Webb, E.J., Campbell, D.T., Schwartz, R.D. and Sechrest, L. (1966) *Unobtrusive measures: Nonreactive research in the social sciences*, Chicago, IL: Rand McNally and Company

FIFTEEN

The instrumental values of education in the Southern Cone

Xavier Rambla

Introduction

Education is clearly an appropriate context for discussing the potential of capability-promoting policies. Certainly, in keeping with their explicit commitment to abstraction, Nussbaum (2000) and Sen (1999) do not necessarily make reference either to education or other policy fields. However, the United Nations Development Programme has included education in its Human Development Index since the early 1990s. Moreover, for the past decade, a growing literature has been discussing the underlying implications of the Education for All (EFA) goals for human capabilities. This chapter draws on the human capabilities approach in order to appraise to what extent an array of public policies may either contribute to (or dampen) the 'values of education'.

In 2015, the debate on education and development posited a good occasion for this discussion. Remarkably, the Millennium Development Goals and the EFA goals for 2000-15 were blamed for isolating education from other public policies (HLP, 2013; UNDP, 2013; EFA GMR, 2015). However, nowadays the Sustainable Development Goals (SDGs) not only foresee new educational targets but also entail an 'integrated approach' to the connections between these targets and the complementary goals regarding poverty, public health, the environment, inequality, cities, industrial policy and other areas (United Nations General Assembly, 2015, p 6; see § 17).

In this vein, the chapter discusses whether in recent decades a variety of public policies have affected the instrumental values of education in Latin American countries, with a particular focus on Argentina, Brazil and Chile. The first section outlines some theoretical arguments underpinning the relevance of the theme, the point being that the concept of instrumental values is very useful for identifying the crucial challenges. The next section comprises a general description of educational development in these countries, and the following section discusses the connections between education and social, employment, urban and language policies. The final section revisits these very general introductory comments to suggest more concrete indications of the current challenges to the global governance of education.

Public policies and the instrumental values of education

According to the human capabilities approach, freedoms are both constitutive of human development and instrumental to this aim. Freedoms are constitutive of development to the extent that they widen people's capabilities and functionings. The distinction between these two concepts is crucial. While capabilities define the potential of human beings to carry out the life they value, a functioning is the outcome of a given course of action. A well-known and graphic illustration compares voluntary and inexorable hunger. Starving for religious reasons is a functioning derived from a person's capability to engage in moral and spiritual issues. However, starving because food is not available damages a basic capability (Sen, 1999). Empirical research captures these courses of effective action, which normative theory evaluates as the self-actualisation of a given capability.

Scholars working on human capabilities normally argue that freedoms are instrumental for collective goods such as economic progress, public health and democratic deliberation and so on (Sen, 1999). This axiom means that people can generate these collective goods when they enact their capabilities. Simultaneously, any shortcoming of individuals' capabilities eventually disrupts the production of these collective goods.

The case of the human capabilities approach for gender equality is remarkably telling of the instrumental interaction between the dimensions of human development. They argue that people produce a better definition of health, employment and educational needs if the causes that lead many women to adapt their preferences to those corresponding to a subordinate social status are neutralised. If men lead social choice and women are secluded, the informational basis of social choice is obviously narrow. In contrast, if both men and women participate as equal subjects of human rights, the informational basis of choice automatically expands. Furthermore, research and policy evaluations also indicate that women excel in social practices that prove to be extremely favourable for human development. For instance, since they regularly pay micro-credits back, they can operate innovative financial schemes on a very small scale. Also, since they respond satisfactorily to the conditions attached to conditional cash transfers (CCTs), these social benefits are effectively delivered to children. Women's empowerment has also been instrumental to human development in this way. Therefore, women's rights are constitutive of human development and instrumental to it. On the one hand, as a constitutional component of development, there is no sound normative ground for conditioning this right to the instrumental contribution of women. On the other hand, the instrumental value of women's empowerment operates through sets of causal mechanisms that can be spelt out in empirical terms (Nussbaum, 2000).

Education is a positional good in so far as it renders some relative advantages. As a rule, in most societies higher education graduates are conferred with more prestige than those who do not achieve this level of education. Normally, they earn higher incomes than non-graduates. A crucial implication of the human capability approach for education has been the consideration of its intrinsic and instrumental values together with these positional advantages (Unterhalter and Brighouse, 2007). On the one hand, intrinsic values concern the impact of education on human capabilities such as emotional development, imagination and thought, practical reason and affiliation (living with others, self-respect) as well as political and material control over their environment (Nussbaum, 2000). On the other hand, education produces instrumental values by fostering the achievement of collective goods (McCowan, 2010, 2011; Tikly and Barrett, 2011).

Since the 1980s, the review of global development policies has resurrected the importance of the instrumental values of education. When Structural Adjustment Programmes were deployed at that time, the predominance of the World Bank in the educational sphere sparked an interest in the returns of education in terms of income and productivity. It was assumed that education was worthwhile because it helped individuals to earn more. Education allegedly produced a further aggregate effect to the extent that economies whose labour force had completed more years of schooling were expected to be more productive (Psacharopoulos and Patrinos, 2002). In contrast to this biased focus on productive outcomes, a long series of United Nations reports kept insisting on the multidimensional nature of development and the inevitable connections between these dimensions. International organisations searched for (and found) many positive externalities of increasing school enrolment and completion for health, family planning, trust, political participation and the education of future generations (EFA GMR, 2009, pp 29-37). In this view, poverty was conceived as a biographical process whereby specific people suffered from the multifarious effects of deprivation. It was convincingly shown that over time the causal accumulation of the eventual consequences shaped the life pathways of the most vulnerable population (UN Millennium Project, 2005; UNDP, 2005, 2013; UNSR, 2006).

Nowadays, the point is not only that education is instrumental for other dimensions of development, but also that these connections should be theorised and evaluated (EFA GMR, 2015). Thus, it is necessary to find out whether schools can overcome socioeconomic deprivation, or conversely, whether material destitution eventually annihilates the potential of education. It is also plausible to enquire whether children manage to learn if they feel insecure because of economic problems and urban violence. If not, these social problems may also be damaging education. Research on language diversity has also unveiled that all approaches to this issue are not effective and equitable in the same way. Therefore, the point is not only that these connections exist, but that poverty reduction, inclusive and safe cities, and the recognition of cultural diversity are necessary to enable all children to express their emotions, cultivate their imagination and thought, establish meaningful bonds with others, and learn to control their environment.

The capability approach offers a crucial insight to educational studies in so far as it highlights that the connection takes place in both ways. In this vein, education yields all the positive externalities that the human capital theory has acknowledged since the 1960s. In addition, the social conditions of education in terms of economic wellbeing, public health, security and so on also have to be guaranteed. School expansion is meaningless if these guarantees are absent (Unterhalter, 2005).

The instrumental values of education are not exclusively relevant for basic human capabilities. Similar bidirectional connections can be observed with the development of skills and creativity. Although these are not so necessary for human wellbeing, their potential contribution to the making of inclusive and sustainable economies should not be understated. If any society is to tackle such huge challenges as post-war recovery, climate change and the diversification of sources of energy, its population will need innovative, complex and sophisticated skills for sure. The same questions on the beneficial and detrimental interaction between education and other dimensions of human development should be asked in the field of technical and vocational education and training (EFA GMR, 2012; Tikly, 2013). Similarly, since innovation studies have identified national and regional systems whereby intra-firm processes are intertwined with an array of wider policies (Lundvall,

2007), the investigation of the two-way links between education and innovation is relevant too (CEPAL, 2015; OECD, 2015).

Bringing the instrumental values back in: education and poverty alleviation in Argentina, Brazil and Chile

The economics of development has widely documented the circles of poverty that spoil the lives of the worst-off, particularly in low-income countries and some regions located within middle-income countries. If households barely make a living, parents seldom have the time, money or emotional resources to support their children. When poverty affects many people, governments lack sufficient budget to build infrastructure, and the gross domestic product is too small for workers to be regularly employed on a formal basis. Vicious circles of poverty and insecurity often become inexorable mechanisms in these extreme circumstances (UN Millennium Project, 2005). As a consequence, the effective shortcomings that constrain a given dimension of development are likely to impinge on the other dimensions too.

Recent worldwide research on human development examined the configuration of a cluster of middle-income countries. Although the aforementioned perverse circular causality has been tackled to some extent, in these countries inequality continues to affect children (Vollmer et al, 2013). Unsurprisingly, when the sustained economic growth that raises an economy from low-income to middle-income ranking does not actually trickle down to the worst-off, the instrumental values of education are severely damaged. The study reports that the negative impact of economic poverty on education is reproduced in the most vulnerable sectors of middle-income countries. There, the spiral of weak governance, insecurity, illiteracy and early drop-out from schooling plagues urban slums and remote rural areas. Thus, the identification of a cluster of middle-income countries sheds light on the many linkages between education and other areas of public policy such as welfare, urban and language policies.

CCTs clearly illustrate the interactions that link the dimensions of development. The web of connections is specially telling in middle-income countries to the extent that relative prosperity and huge income gaps have fashioned a complex pattern. Since the 1990s, many governments have adopted a widely disseminated template of CCTs, whose design explicitly aims to break the perverse circle of poverty and widen the space for positive instrumental interaction between education and the other facets of human development. CCTs deliver social benefits to families provided they comply with clear-cut requirements such as school attendance and vaccination. Mothers are often officially granted the right to receive and manage these transfers. In both low- and middle-income countries, this small increase in family income has been enough to prevent child labour, since CCTs have diminished the number of working children. These schemes have also been effective in increasing school enrolment rates. Interestingly, CCTs highlight the instrumental value of women's empowerment for education in two ways. First, mothers have proved to be quite efficient in managing family income and taking care of their offspring's education and health. And second, although the average impact of these social benefits on academic performance appears to be very slight, a positive effect for girls has been observed in Brazil. This empirical observation sheds light on specific synergies between education and social policy in rural areas and marginal urban slums (Brauw et al, 2015).

Many commentators have blamed CCTs for authorities' tendency to overlook, and sometimes downplay, the contribution of pedagogic and management improvements that take place within schools. In fact, the education authorities have only played a minor role in designing and implementing CCTs (Reimers et al, 2006; Morais de Sa e Silva, 2015). However, this critique does not take into consideration that these social benefits have sometimes been aligned with pedagogic innovation targeting the poor, as happened in Argentina and Chile in about 2000. Nor have they noticed that ambitious plans for educational development have also complemented social benefits in other countries, as has happened in Brazil.

Crucial to my argument is the observation that these attempts to both strengthen welfare with educational measures and underpin educational expansion through welfare have highlighted the complexity of the instrumental values of education in middle-income countries. This conclusion of research and policy evaluation has been officially enshrined in the Ibero American Educational Goals. In accordance to the objectives of this international, educational, strategic plan, in 2010 the governments of the Latin American countries recognised the importance of the instrumental values of education by adopting broad notions of equity and inclusive education. By 2020 they are to:

> achieve educational equality and overcome discrimination
> in education by guaranteeing access and progression to
> all, providing extra support to ethnic minorities, African-
> Americans as well as children living in rural areas and
> urban slums, implementing quality intercultural bilingual

education, and fostering the educational inclusion of children with special education needs. (OEI, 2010, pp 148-9, 2nd General Goal)

Argentina, Brazil and Chile are clear illustrations of countries whose governments and civil societies have embraced such ambitions, and feel a strong need to address the undeniable, underlying predicaments. So far they have responded to special needs and social disadvantage, but their official policy is formally committed to creating a thoroughly inclusive educational system (Acedo and Opertti, 2012).

In Argentina, in the 1990s, the incumbent governments implemented a socio-educational programme specifically designed to tackle inequalities by deploying assertive action in the most vulnerable schools. Over time, a similar programme was implemented as a reaction to the financial crisis that ravaged the country in 2001. In a nutshell, the official approach put first the schools that catered for the most disadvantaged students. Many initiatives were deployed in order to strengthen student-centred pedagogies, define clearer guidelines for school management, facilitate in-service teacher training and open schools to parental and youth participation. These measures aimed to introduce reforms that were expected to eventually permeate the whole educational system. By starting with these schools, the programmes wanted to reach the neediest first, thus compensating for the negative effects of income inequality on education (Aguerrondo and Tedesco, 2005; Aguerrondo, 2007). After the 2001 financial catastrophe, cash transfers relating to unemployment and family support were also introduced. Initially, an array of different schemes targeting the unemployed and the worst-off families were piloted. But finally, an ambitious CCT scheme was launched so that most middle-class, working-class and poor families became eligible for a child benefit (Feldfeber and Saforcada, 2012).

Although most Argentinian commentators acknowledged the reduction of income poverty achieved by this massive scheme, many of them also pointed at the limits of these initiatives to reduce the huge inequality provoked by the financial crisis. On the one hand, policy evaluation detected positive impacts of socio-educational programmes on a variety of school-based processes, but the main report on socio-educational programmes could not find evidence of a significant impact on academic results (DINIECE, 2008). On the other hand, all these child benefit schemes were approved by means of presidential decrees that were not endorsed as fully-fledged Acts approved by the parliament. Thus, these pro-poor policies were not underpinned by a legal definition of rights including the right to education, but simply depended on the political will of the president (Campos, 2007).

Table 15.1 shows how the devastating effects of the crisis affected the school attendance rates of 13-to 19-year-olds. After increasing notoriously in the 1990s, between 2001 and 2006 the rate of school attendance remained stagnant. Even worse, the rate for the richest quintile actually declined. The data shows the correlation between the adoption of socio-educational plans and CCTs and the school attendance rate of the poorest quintile. Noticeably, when school reforms and welfare programmes were extended after 2003, the rate started to increase again, although progress stalled after a few years. Looking at the middle term of the two last decades and a half, the gap between the richest and the poorest youth seems to have declined, mainly because 10% of teenagers of affluent families have continued to drop out early for more than a decade.

Table 15.1: School attendance in Argentina: income quintiles 1 and 5 (% of 13- to 19-year-olds, urban areas)

	Q1 (poorest) %	Q5 %	Q5/Q1 Ratio
1990–01	61.6	79.2	1.29
1994–96	63.2	85	1.34
1999–01	74.9	91.5	1.22
2004–06	74.5	90.2	1.21
2009–11	78.4	89.1	1.14
2012–14	77.4	90.2	1.17

Source: CEPALSTAT (2015).

The well-known Brazilian CCT programme (*Bolsa Família*, or Family Social Benefit) was launched in 2003 together with a wider array of institutional initiatives aiming at educational development. Since the 1990s, a fiscal scheme has attempted to equalise school budgets throughout the country (*Fundo de Manutenção e Desenvolvimento da Educação Básica e de Valorização dos Profissionais da Educação* [Fund for Basic Education Maintenance, Development and Teachers Valorisation]). In compliance with a constitutional requirement, since the 1990s a series of strategic plans have been launched so as to align the goals of the educational policies conducted by all the municipalities, all the states and the federation (*Plano Nacional de Educação* [National Educational Plan]). Recently, a new programme has begun to deliver scholarships conditional on participation in vocational education and training (VET) (*Programa Nacional de Acesso ao Ensino Técnico e Emprego* [National VET and Employment Programme]).

Despite these wide-ranging endeavours and consistent expansive schooling trends, the persistent, extreme destitution of some people in urban slums and remote rural areas is still hindering the full achievement of universal primary enrolment in Brazil. In 2012, the school attendance rate of the population aged six to 14 years was 98.2%, that is, the country did not manage to achieve a round 100% (Federative Republic of Brazil, Ministry of Education, 2014, figure 3).

Although the poorest were largely excluded from secondary education in the 1990s (Table 15.2), the country has since caught up with its neighbours, so much so that currently the proportion of 13- to 19-year-olds attending school is very similar to that in Argentina. The Organisation for Economic Co-operation and Development's (OECD) Programme for International Student Assessment country report is quite conclusive:

> While Brazil performs below the OECD average, its mean performance in mathematics has improved since 2003 from 356 to 391 score points, making Brazil the country with the largest performance gains since 2003. Significant improvements are also found in reading and science. Improvements have been particularly strong among low performers in mathematics, reading and science. Between 2003 and 2012, Brazil also expanded enrolment in primary and secondary schools, with enrolment rates for 15-year-olds growing from 65% in 2003 to 78% in 2012. (OECD, 2013, p 1)

Table 15.2: School attendance in Brazil: income quintiles 1 and 5 (% of 13- to 19-year-olds, urban areas)

	Q1 (poorest) %	Q5 %	Q5/Q1 Ratio
1990-01	56	78.7	1.41
1994-96	61.3	86.6	1.41
1999-01	71.1	88.7	1.25
2004-06	73	88.1	1.21
2009-11	78.1	86.9	1.11
2012-14	75.8	85.1	1.12

Source: CEPALSTAT (2015).

Ever since a scheme of school vouchers was launched in Chile in the 1980s, a persistent trend of socioeconomic segregation has divided the school system here. However, since the inception of democratic rule in the early 1990s, Chilean administrations have attempted to reduce inequality through the use of innovative pedagogic and management techniques in the most vulnerable primary and secondary schools. Student-centred pedagogies, external expert consultancy, in-service teacher training and new management tools have been introduced in the country's most vulnerable schools. The authorities have also implemented a CCT scheme that in many cases depends on effective school attendance. In addition, for a long time Chilean democratic governments have attempted to compensate for the persisting equality gap by providing extra vouchers to the schools catering for the most vulnerable children as well as those with special education needs (Raczynski and Muñoz-Stuardo, 2007).

Generally speaking, the vouchers policy has dramatically exacerbated segregation and aggravated the divide in academic performance (Torche, 2005; Matear, 2007). However, a further programme that has extended full-day rather than a few hours' instruction to all the schools seems to have partially compensated for this gap (Bellei, 2009). So, the outcome is not as disappointing as in Argentina, in the sense that the gap in school attendance between the poorest and the richest quintiles somehow diminished between the 1990s and early 2000s. Furthermore, levels of inequality have remained stable for the past 10 years.

Table 15.3: School attendance in Chile: income quintiles 1 and 5 (% of 13- to 19-year-olds, urban areas)

	Q1 (poorest) %	Q5 %	Q5/Q1 Ratio
1990-01	74.7	86.1	1.15
1994-96	75.9	89.7	1.18
1999-01	76.4	88.6	1.16
2004-06	81.4	88.6	1.09
2009-11	81.8	89.6	1.10
2012-14	84.5	91.8	1.09

Source: CEPALSTAT (2015).

The recent history of Argentina, Brazil and Chile indicates that the instrumental values of education are remarkable in middle-income countries. Their importance concerns not only the economic conjuncture, as in Argentina, but also the connection between education and social policies. Some educational programmes have emulated means-tested welfare schemes in that they have targeted the most vulnerable schools in Argentina and Chile, but these initiatives have not been as successful as expected. Apparently, the extension of full-day schooling has had a stronger egalitarian impact in Chile. In Brazil, federal coordination has inspired reformers to align welfare with fiscal equalisation and development plans. The outcome appears to be relatively good.

In general, the measures affecting the whole education system have been more effective than measures of explicit positive discrimination. That is to say, according to the available evidence, full-day schooling and strategic multilevel planning have proved to be more egalitarian than educational and welfare initiatives targeting the poor. However, in spite of these pro-poor policies, a set of constraints is still dampening school expansion in so far as many young people leave school before they are 19 years old. This phenomenon amounts to 15-25% of young people coming from the poorest families. Around 10-15% of young people from the richest families drop out too.

Unveiling instrumental bottlenecks: the long shadow of inequality

The varied faces of development have both positive and negative consequences for their respective instrumental values. While prosperity, however temporary, and welfare expansion, however selective, appear to have had a positive impact on the educational development of Argentina, Brazil and Chile, a number of contradictions has also consolidated inequality – to the point where this disparity has stalled earlier expansive trends.

Nowadays, middle-income countries are notoriously divided by inequality (Vollmer et al, 2013). This societal feature clearly triggers influential causal mechanisms that eventually damage education (Ferreira, 2001). As a rule, inequality weakens the effect of targeted welfare schemes, compromises pedagogic innovation targeting the most vulnerable schools, and disrupts the coordination of skills supply and demand. Insecurity and cultural assimilation are also intermingled with inequality in very perverse ways for educational development. Some of these problems can be generalised to the whole of Latin America, but clearly most of them are pertinent in these three countries, even though democratic governments have been struggling with them for decades.

To start with, after substantial advancement, the previous pace of school expansion cannot be easily maintained because the most destitute children do not attend school and many youth leave the system too early. In so far as extreme income deprivation severely aggravates psychological stress, it puts considerable pressure on children's wellbeing, emotional maturation and academic learning. In addition, informal labour is widespread in Latin America, even in upper middle-income countries that have benefited from economic growth in recent decades. Argentina, Brazil and Chile posit paradigmatic illustrations. Informal labour entails a lower and more insecure wage. But it also exposes both parents and children to a very significant risk of economic catastrophe when breadwinners get sick, particularly if they suffer from any chronic disease. As a consequence of living in extremely miserable conditions, many students barely learn the basic academic competences when they attend school. Even worse, many of them do not even have a reasonable opportunity to do so because they drop out very early (López, 2012; Rambla et al, 2013).

Second, targeting the poor with pedagogic innovation a risky business. This strategy highlights the response of both students and their families in such a way that many of them are submitted to strict public scrutiny. If education authorities publicise the fact that they are piloting student-centred pedagogies, in-service teacher training methods and up-to-date management tools in the schools whose intake comprises those from the lowest socioeconomic status, and these schools do not catch up with other, average, schools, they are also inviting critics to blame the programme and the very beneficiaries for the alleged failure. Although officials try to make teachers aware of class, gender and ethnic stereotypes, they can seldom monitor all the subtle implications of these prejudices in everyday life. This problem may be aggravated if teachers discover that they are not overcoming social disadvantages despite using innovative, sophisticated and widely praised tools.

In fact, research shows that teachers generally stereotype vulnerable students, even in some schools that draw on the principle of positive discrimination. For many professionals, positive discrimination is the last resort for countering persistent disadvantage despite continued public intervention in favour of equity. But sometimes stereotyping retrieves deeply embedded prejudices. The point is that, despite continual official commitment to positive discrimination, a number of qualitative studies have found teachers denigrating students in schools that cater to more vulnerable students in Argentina, Brazil and Chile (Rambla and Verger, 2009; Bonal et al, 2010; Gluz and Rodríguez Moyano, 2013).

Third, educational outcomes also depend on the very difficult balance with labour policy. Certainly, in the middle term, higher rates of school attendance increase and improve the supply of skills in so far as secondary, tertiary and higher education graduates are normally better equipped for employment. However, it takes a long time to overcome the effects of low attendance, poor learning and early drop-out. At the same time, Latin American labour markets do not always respond to educational advancement. The educational level of the labour force is relatively low because it is the middle-aged population that feeds the labour force. Some decades ago, many of them were either out-of-school children, had hardly attended school, or left without completing the elementary stage. It is difficult for this cohort to engage in the economic activities that provide opportunities for newly graduated young people. This low-skills equilibrium certainly disrupts the balance between education and employment (Jacinto, 2010).

Fourth, Latin American cities are plagued with crime. Gangs control illegal trafficking and large neighbourhoods. If these gangs fight one another, or the police try to seize them, the streets and roads become battlefields. At the same time, weapons are available to large numbers of people. Robbing is also a common practice in these circumstances. In many cases, insecurity hinders human and educational development inasmuch as many young people suffer a premature death because of gang activities (Buvinic et al, 2005). But the damaging effect of crime is not restricted to these most fatal outcomes. Insecurity also spoils the educational potential of after-school programmes, and prevents students from using public spaces for leisure and learning. For the poorest, these effects reinforce the psychological stress derived from income deprivation (Bonal et al, 2010; Gallego, 2014).

Finally, albeit a small-scale phenomenon, language diversity has not yet been transformed into an educational asset in these three Southern Cone countries. A long tradition of educationalists has attempted to foster the bilingual capabilities of students who speak indigenous languages and have to learn either Spanish and Portuguese at school. A rich variety of methods that align bilingual with intercultural education has been proposed. Tupi-guarani and Amazonic peoples are normally taught on these grounds in Brazil. In Argentina and Chile, schools also use these pedagogies in some aymara and mapuche communities. Nevertheless, many prevailing approaches conceive these programmes as a transition phase before students learn the official language. Sometimes, teachers are not fluent in the indigenous language, and the curriculum is not fully respectful of cultural diversity. In many education systems in Latin America, particularly those in Argentina, Brazil and Chile, intercultural methods have been transformed into a merely compensatory strategy rather than a general approach designed to instil respect for diversity and concern with dialogue between cultures to the bulk of the student population. For this reason, language diversity is still correlated with severe academic under-performance is spite of a noticeable commitment to equitable and inclusive education (Candau and Russo, 2010; Unamuno, 2012).

Conclusion

Unterhalter and Brighouse (2007) were really insightful when claiming that the whole array of intrinsic, instrumental and positional values should be taken into account in order to conduct a sound evaluation of educational development. Despite the positional values having attracted the most attention thus far, their point reinforces the crucial relevance of the other two. This chapter has highlighted the importance of instrumental values.

This is not only an educational issue. If an 'integrated approach' to sustainable development is to be taken seriously, the connections between the dimensions of human development and the SDGs must be systematically conceptualised, discussed, researched, scrutinised and evaluated. This is an intellectual challenge, a research problem and an undeniable criterion for policy evaluation.

The current global agenda openly endorses a multidimensional understanding of human development. This tenet has inevitably led experts, policymakers and advocates to a logical corollary, namely that these dimensions may interact in both positive and negative directions. A strand of experts in Latin American education has convincingly argued that education cannot be isolated from citizenship (Gentili and Frigotto, 2000), social conditions (López and Tedesco, 2002), the rights of children, and inequalities (Mediavilla et al, 2013). This concern can be traced back to the late Paulo Freire (1991), who wrote on his experience as a policymaker in the field of education in the late 1980s. This is a rigorous, multifaceted scholarly position that directly posits new challenges to education, social sciences and philosophy.

The human capability approach invites engagement in a further discussion of the precise synergies that can be observed between education and social policy, as well as the obstacles raised by inequality. Concern with human flourishing is a sound basis for this necessary conversation. The conclusions may be relevant not just for Latin America but for the whole world. At least, the noticeable outcomes of cross-sectoral programmes such as generous social benefits, pedagogic innovation and multilevel strategic planning should not be forgotten easily. At the same time, the consequences of sharp social divides, stereotypes, disrupted labour markets, insecurity and language assimilation point at new frontiers of development studies. Noticeably, this academic speciality should pay more attention to the predicaments of middle-income countries in order to perceive these problems in a more coherent way.

In sum, Sen's (1999) and Nussbaum's (2000) interest in the instrumental connections that link one dimension of development with another have proved really helpful in making sense of the recent trends observed in Latin America. The common interest in empowering people to deploy their capabilities prevents generalised ideas of one-size-fits-all trade-offs, because the observation of these instrumental connections does not subordinate the moral relevance of education to any other dimension of development. Conversely, welfare, employment, security, language diversity and many other faces of development have their own value besides their empirical contribution to education.

The recent publication of the approved SDGs strongly reminds scholars and policymakers of this point (United Nations General Assembly, 2015). In Latin America, and elsewhere, the SDG 4 on quality education is connected to SDG 1 on poverty eradication, SDG 3 on good health and SDG 5 on gender parity. Between 2000 and 2015, the Millennium Development Goals already suggested these links, but they were not properly embedded. In addition, the wider thematic scope of the SDGs is certainly indicative of a wider set of connections, not least because education is also instrumental for SDG 8 on decent work and economic growth, SDG 10 on inequality reduction and SDG 11 on sustainable cities and communities. At the same time, any shortcoming in the achievement of these goals is likely to backfire on the very potential of educational development. Thus, capability-promoting education policies have to trigger these synergies and make the most of the benefits of an integral, multidimensional approach that takes into consideration the multifarious and interconnected nature of social phenomena.

References

Acedo, C. and Opertti, R. (2012) 'Educación inclusiva: de focalizar grupos y escuelas a lograr una educación de calidad como el corazón de una Educación para Todos' ['Inclusive education: from targeting groups and schools to achieving quality education as the core of Education for All'], in X. Rambla (ed) *La Educación para Todos en América Latina. Estudios sobre las desigualdades y la agenda política en educación* [*Education for All in Latin America. Studies on inequalities and the political agenda of education*], Buenos Aires: Miño y Dávila, OEI-UNESCO, pp 23-44.

Aguerrondo, I. (2007) 'Inclusión-exclusión' ['Inclusion-exclusion'], Paper presented at International Workshop on Inclusive Education (Latin America, Southern and Andean Region). Buenos Aires.

Aguerrondo, I. and Tedesco, J.C. (2005) 'Estrategias para mejorar la calidad y la equidad de la educación en Argentina' ['Strategies for improving the quality and the equity of education in Argentina'], in J.C. Tedesco (ed) *¿Cómo superar la fragmentación y la desigualdad del sistema educativo argentino?* [*How can we overcome the fragmentation and the inequality of the Argentinian education system?*], Buenos Aires: UNESCO-IIPE, pp 3584.

Bellei, C. (2009) 'Does lengthening the school day increase students' academic achievement? Results from a natural experiment in Chile', *Economics of Education Review*, vol 28, pp 629-40.

Bonal, X., Tarabini, A., Valiente, O. and Klickowkski, F. (2010) *Ser pobre en la escuela: hábitus de pobreza y condiciones de educabilidad* [*Being poor at school: The habitus of poverty and the conditions of educability*], Buenos Aires: Miño y Dávila editores.

Brauw, A.D., Gilligan, D., Hoddinott, J. and Roy, S. (2015) 'The impact of Bolsa Família on schooling', *World Development*, vol 70, pp 303-16.

Buvinic, M., Morrison, A. and Orlando, M.B. (2005) 'Violencia, crimen y desarrollo social en América Latina y el Caribe' ['Violence, crime and social development in Latin America and the Caribbean'], *Papeles de Población* [*Population Papers*], vol 11, pp 167-214.

Campos, L. (2007) *Programa Familias por la Inclusión Social. Entre el discurso de derechos y la práctica asistencial* [*Families for Social Inclusion Programme. Between the discourse of rights and the denigrative practice*], Buenos Aires: Centro de Estudios Legales y Sociales.

Candau, M. and Russo, K. (2010) 'Interculturalidade e educação na América Latina: uma construção plural, original e complexa' [Interculturality and education in Latin America: a plural, original and complex construction], *Revista Dialogo Educativo* [*Educational Dialogue Review*], vol 10, no 29, pp 151-69.

CEPAL (*Comisión Económica para América Latina y el Caribe* [Economic Commission for Latin America and the Caribbean]) (2015) *Fuentes del crecimiento económico y la productividad en América Latina y el Caribe 1990-2013* [*Sources of economic growth and productivity in Latin America and the Caribbean 1990-2013*], Santiago de Chile: CEPAL.

CEPALSTAT (2015) *Estadísticas de América Latina y el Caribe* [*Statistics of Latin America and the Caribbean*], Santiago de Chile: CEPAL.

DINIECE (*Dirección Nacional de Información y Evaluación de la Calidad Educativa* [National Office for Information and Evaluation of Educational Quality]) (2008) *Resultados. Evaluación del Programa Integral de Igualdad Educativa* [*Results. Evaluation of the Integral Programme for Educational Equality*], Buenos Aires: Gobierno de Argentina-Ministerio de Educación.

Federative Republic of Brazil, Ministry of Education (2014) *Report Education for All in Brazil 2000-2015*, Brasilia: Government of Brazil.

EFA GMR (EFA Global Monitoring Report) (2009) *Overcoming inequality: Why governance matters*, Paris: UNESCO.

EFA GMR (2012) *Youth and skills: Putting education to work*, Paris: UNESCO.

EFA GMR (2015) *Concept note for a 2016 report on "Education, sustainability and the post-2015 development agenda'*, EFA Global Monitoring Report, Paris: UNESCO.

Feldfeber, M. and Saforcada, F. (2012) 'Políticas educativas y derecho a la educación en Argentina: un análisis de las metas educativas en el nuevo escenario latinoamericano' [Educational policies and the right to education in Argentina: an analysis of educational goals in the new Latin American scenario], in X. Rambla (ed) *La Educación para Todos en América Latina. Estudios sobre las desigualdades y la agenda política en educación* [*Education for All in Latin America. Studies on inequalities and the political agenda of education*], Buenos Aires: Miño y Dávila, OEI-UNESCO, pp 169-200.

Ferreira, F.H.G. (2001) 'Education for the masses? The interaction between wealth, educational and political inequalities', *Economics of Transition*, vol 9, no 2, pp 533-52.

Freire, P. (1991) *A educação na cidade* [*Education in the city*], São Paulo: Cortez.

Gallego, L. (2014) 'Mecanismos causales de la educación y la pobreza. Aplicación a los casos de Medellín (Colombia) y Belo Horizonte (Brasil)' ['Causal mechanisms of education and poverty. Application to the cases of Medellin (Colombia) and Belo Horizonte (Brazil)'], Unpublished doctoral thesis, Cerdanyola del Vallès: Universitat Autònoma de Barcelona.

Gentili, P. and Frigotto, G. (2000) A *cidadania negada: politica de exclusao na educacao e no trabalho* [*Denied citizenship: The policy of exclusion in education and work*], Buenos Aires: CLACSO.

Gluz, N. and Rodríguez Moyano, I. (2013) 'Asignación Universal por Hijo, condiciones de vida y educación. Las política sociales y la inclusión escolar en la provincia de Buenos Aires' ['Universal Allowance per Child, life conditions and education. Social policies and inclusion in the province of Buenos Aires'] , *Archivos Analíticos de Políticas Educativas* [*Analytical Archives of Education Policies*], vol 21, no 2, pp 1-28.

HLP (High Level Panel of Eminent Persons on the Post-2015 Developmental Agenda) (2013) *A new global partnership: Eradicate poverty and transform economies through sustainable development*, New York, NY: United Nations.

Jacinto, C. (2010) *Recent trends in technical education in Latin America*, Buenos Aires: IIPE UNESCO.

López, N. (2012) 'Adolescentes en las aulas: la irrupción de la diferencia y el fin de la expansión educativa' ['Teenagers in the classroom: the irruption of difference and the end of educational expansion'], *Educaçao e Sociedade* [*Education and Society*], vol 33, no 120, pp 869-89.

López, N. and Tedesco, J.C. (2002) *Las condiciones de educabilidad de los niños y adolescentes en América Latina* [*The conditions of educability of children and teenagers in Latin America*], Buenos Aires: IIPE-UNESCO.

Lundvall, B.-A. (2007) 'National innovation systems: analytical concept and development tool', *Industry and Innovation*, vol 14, no 1, pp 95-119.

Matear, A. (2007) 'Equity in education in Chile: the tensions between policy and practice', *International Journal of Educational Development*, vol 27, no 1, pp 101-13.

McCowan, T. (2010) 'Reframing the universal right to education', *Comparative Education*, vol 46, no 4, pp 509-25.

McCowan, T. (2011) 'Human rights, capabilities and the normative basis of "Education for All"', *Theory and Research in Education*, vol 9, no 3, pp 283-98.

Mediavilla, M., Gallego, L. and Planells-Struse, S. (2013) 'Convergencia entre el enfoque de las capacidades y la educabilidad. Importancia de los factores de calidad en la educacion primaria en Brasil' ['Convergence between the capability approach and educability. The importance of quality factors in primary education in Brazil'], *Regional and Sectoral Economic Studies*, vol 13, no 3, pp 107-26.

Morais de Sa e Silva, M. (2015) 'Conditional cash transfers and improved education quality: a political search for the policy link', *International Journal of Educational Development*, 45, pp 169-81.

Nussbaum, M. (2000) *Women and human development*, Cambridge: Cambridge University Press.

OECD (Organisation for Economic Co-operation and Development) (2013) 'Brazil Country Note', in OECD Programme for International Student Assessment *Results from PISA 2012*, Paris: OECD.

OECD (2015) *OECD Employment Outlook 2015*, Paris: OECD.

OEI (*Organización de Estados Iberoamericanos* [Ibero American States Organisation]) (2010) *Metas Educativas 2021: la educación que queremos para la generación de los bicentenarios. Documento final* [*Educational Goals 2021: The education we want for the generation of the bicentenaries. Final document*], Madrid: OEI/CEPAL.

Psacharopoulos, G., G. and Patrinos, H.A. (2002) 'Returns to investment in education: a further update', *World Bank Policy Research Working Papers*, 2881, pp 1-29.

Raczynski, D. and Muñoz-Stuardo, G. (2007) 'Chilean educational reform: the intricate balance between a macro and micro policy', in. W.T. Pink and G.W. Noblit (eds) *International handbook of urban education*, Dondrecht: Springer, pp 641-63.

Rambla, X. and Verger, A. (2009) 'Pedagogising poverty alleviation: a discourse analysis of education and social policies in Argentina and Chile', *British Journal of Sociology of Education*, vol 30, no 4, pp 463-77.

Rambla, X., Pereira, R.S. and Espluga, J.L. (2013) 'La educación y las dimensiones del desarrollo humano en América Latina' [Education and the dimensions of human development'], *Papeles de Población* [*Population Papers*], vol 19, no 75, pp 1-25.

Reimers, F., Silva, C.S. and Trevino, E. (2006) 'Where is the "education" in conditional cash transfers in education?', *UNESIS Working Papers*, 4, pp 1-80.

Sen, A. (1999) *Development as freedom*, Oxford: Oxford University Press.

Tikly, L. (2013) *Revisiting global trends in TVET: Reflections on theory and practice*. Bonn: UNESCO-UNEVOC.

Tikly, L. and Barrett, A.M. (2011) 'Social justice, capabilities and the quality of education in low income countries', *International Journal of Educational Development*, vol 31, no 1, pp 3-14.

Torche, F. (2005) 'Privatization reform and equality of educational opportunity in Chile', *Sociology of Education*, vol 78, no 4, pp 316-43.

UN Millennium Project (2005) *Investing in development: A practical plan to achieve the Millennium Development Goals*, New York, NY: United Nations.

Unamuno, V. (2012) 'Gestión del multilingüismo y docencia indígena para una educación intercultural bilingüe en la Argentina' ['Managing multilingualism and indigenous teaching of an intercultural and bilingual education in Argentina'], *Praxis Educativa* [*Educational Praxis*], Special issue 2, pp 32-54.

UNDP (United Nations Development Programme) (2005) 'Inequality and human development', in UNDP (ed) *Human Development Report*, New York, NY: UNDP, pp 51-71.

UNDP (2013) *Humanity divided: Confronting inequality in developing countries*, New York, NY: UNDP.

United Nations General Assembly (2015) *Transforming our world: the 2030 Agenda for Sustainable Development*, Resolution adopted by the General Assembly on 25 September 2015, A/RES/70/1, New York, NY: United Nations.

UNSR (United Nations Department of Economic and Social Affairs) (2006) *The inequality predicament. Report on the World Social Summit 2005*, New York, NY: United Nations.

Unterhalter, E. (2005) 'Global inequality, capabilities, social justice: The Millennium Development Goal for gender equality in education', *International Journal of Educational Development*, vol 28, no 4, pp 111-22.

Unterhalter, E. and Brighouse, H. (2007) 'Distribution of what for social justice in education? The case of Education for All by 2015', in M. Walker and E. Unterhalter (eds) *Amartya Sen's capability approach and social justice in education*, Basingstoke: Palgrave Macmillan, pp 67-86.

Vollmer, S., Holzmann, H., Ketterer, F., Klasen, S. and Canning, D. (2013) 'The emergence of three human development clubs', *PLoS ONE*, vol 8, no 3, p e57624.

CONCLUSION

SIXTEEN

What is to be done about capability-promoting policies?

Hans-Uwe Otto, Melanie Walker and Holger Ziegler

While the capabilities approach is a convincing conception that attempts to theoretically reconcile allegedly competing demands associated with the fundamental principles of equality, recognition, welfare, liberty and human dignity, there is still surprisingly little research on capability-promoting policies in real-life contexts. The aspiration of this book has been to contribute to closing this gap. Some of the contributions have thus examined how a human development approach has been operationalised and these chapters assess the possibilities, obstacles and dilemmas of this approach when put into practice. In doing so, the contributions in this volume clearly demonstrate that the perspective of the capabilities approach makes a difference and opens up viable alternatives: the concept of capability-promoting policies is not only a political philosophical concept, but also a feasible and meaningful approach to analysing policy limitations – as some of the chapters do – and conceptualising real-world policies.

The chapters in this volume therefore have demonstrated how the capabilities approach provides a politically normative metric to critically assess given policies and public policy structures, as well as to analyse policy interventions driven by human development or human security concerns. By and large, they show that the realisation of capabilities or the feasibility of human flourishing are largely the result of existing social structures and institutions. Very often the effects of these structures are unnecessary and rather less secure than may appear – in the specific sense that significant changes in policy may alter these structures or at least largely moderate their effects. The point is that the policies of public institutions are often critical in ensuring or impeding people's chances to convert abstract and formal opportunities into genuine capabilities in the sense of 'real' and effective powers and freedoms.

Policies do obviously differ with respect to their contribution to human flourishing, and policies may contribute to restrict or to expand the opportunities individuals and groups have to realise lives they have reason to value. Drawing on empirical evidence and experiences in diverse contexts, a number of contributions show that some policies are more socially balanced, more inclusive and more successful in combating disadvantage and reducing – or at least in not (re)*producing* – social and human suffering than others. They thus point to comparatively more capability-friendly policies, and comparatively more rather than fewer equitable policies.

However, that some policies are comparatively more capability-promoting than others does not necessarily mean that they are *genuinely* capability-promoting, that is, oriented towards creating the conditions in which people can live flourishing lives.

The productivity of capitalism, in particular within Western liberal democracies, may not only have created affluence but also enhanced opportunities for human development. However, it tends to block the realisation of such opportunities for large segments of the population within these countries and for the vast majority of humans in the Global South, who are caught up in global economic developments that do not work well for people's flourishing in developing countries. Moreover, in Western democracies, some of the most significant domains of economic activity are excluded or obscured from democratic decision making. At the same time, these countries tend to allow a concentration of goods and privileges for a minority alongside growing pools of deprivation and social vulnerability, seriously limiting the conditions of effective 'real freedom' for the more disadvantaged classes of the population. The policies of a number of these countries might nevertheless be regarded as the relatively 'most capability-promoting', but they might often be rather far away from being genuinely capability-promoting. If really taken seriously, capability-promoting policies imply a redistribution of resources and powers alongside profound processes of democratisation and geopolitical arrangements that may hardly be accomplished without seriously challenging the real-world nature of capitalist institutions.

As it is a constitutive part of capability-promoting policies to conceptualise processes and activities aimed at bringing about social change in terms of what Sen (2009) denotes as the constructive dimension of deliberative democracy, it would be a performative self-contradiction to insist on a kind of comprehensive blueprint or authoritative road map of capability-friendly policies. Yet it is possible to explore some cardinal features of capability-promoting policies. Capability-promoting policies are socially empowering in a profound sense of this notion. The primary focus of capability-promoting policies is neither to strengthen 'economic power, based on the ownership and control of economic resources', nor to strengthen 'state power, based on the control of rule-making and rule-enforcing capacity over a given territory' (Wright 2006, p 106), but to strengthen democratic social power and to subordinate or at least to make accountable the former powers to this social power. This seems to be an essential aspect of the capabilities approach. The German title of Sen's seminal work on *Development as freedom* is translated as 'economy for humans'. While some have rightly argued that this is an inappropriate translation, it has at least one felicitous aspect, as indeed Sen does not propose centralised command-and-control planning as an alternative to libertarian fantasies about the 'free market', but insists that state institutions as well as the economy can and should be organised in ways that serve the needs, basic concerns and vital interests of ordinary people, nationally and globally.

This democratic aspect is central to a notion of capability-promoting policies that clearly acknowledges the significance of a radical redistribution of resources, yet does not reduce its focus to this issue alone. Rather, access to resources is conceptualised as one of several irreducibly necessary but not sufficient means to the end of human flourishing. From the perspective of capability-promoting policies, a progressive removal of unwanted obstacles is co-equal with concerns with material inequality. Central components of this emancipatory concern are the difference between 'functionings' in terms of people's access to those beings or doings that are fundamental to flourishing, on the one hand, and their 'capabilities' in terms of their effective freedom to choose or not to choose them on the other – a difference featuring prominently in conceptions of 'democratic equality' that are formulated in the space of capabilities (compare Anderson, 1999). Capability-promoting policies are committed to the aim of social and political justice, that is, they have a commitment to the aim that all people should have genuine and broadly equal access to the material and social means necessary to live flourishing lives. They also emphasise that people should, at the same time, be equally empowered to contribute to the collective control of the conditions and decisions that affect their common fate. This entails securing the chance for everybody to take an active part in shaping public policy, for which people have to be equipped with resources adequate to having a genuine capability to mount an effective defence of their (political) views and make them into a relevant part of the public political discourse.

In terms of its analytic fundament, the very notion of capability-promoting policies refers to an alliance between the capabilities approach and the tradition of critical social science. The capabilities approach may deliver a well-grounded evaluative metric for the elaboration and substantiation of a systematic diagnosis and critique of prevailing social, cultural and economic circumstances, and a sound conception of human flourishing in order to envision viable alternatives. Yet the approach is not an explanatory approach to power, domination and structural inequality. As Andrew Sayer (2011, p 238) puts it, the capabilities approach is most of all:

> a set of normative criteria that helps us assess the extent to which the various basic constituents of well-being are met within a certain population. It says nothing about the causes of their being met or not met. To identify these causes we need social science, albeit of a kind that is able to acknowledge and interpret well-being and ill-being as objective states of being, and not merely as norms or preferences.

The fact that the capabilities approach might be (and actually is) coupled with a broad range of different theories leads to the situation that it might be coupled with theories that are relatively silent, for instance on inequalities, or conditions and divisions of labour. This creates scope for opportunistic appropriations and interpretations when it comes to a political utilisation and domestication of perspectives and ideas associated with the capabilities approach.

An alliance with the tradition of critical social science may 'secure' the capabilities approach, with its analytic focus on real-world conditions and requirements for renegotiating social justice and creating more capabilities-promoting policies, and vice versa: a serious social scientific engagement with the capabilities approach does indeed have the potential to develop and refine the theoretical and ethical foundation of the emancipatory tasks of critical social science. Some years ago, Erik Ohlin Wright (2006, p 94) argued that emancipatory social science is *science* in so far as it is committed to the task of creating systematic scientific knowledge about how the real world works; it is *emancipatory* in so far as it is committed to the moral purpose of eliminating oppression and creating conditions for human flourishing; and it is *social and political* in so far as it stresses the fact that emancipation depends on the transformation of the social world, and is not just a version of identity politics that merely focuses on the inner self.

The evaluative metric sustained by the capabilities approach may provide a necessary foundation to understand the obstacles, chances and dilemmas of social and political transformation and inequalities in diverse country contexts and between countries. At the same time, an alliance of critical social science may forestall the capabilities approach from being used as a rhetorical appeal by hegemonic political and economic interests. This may allow the approach rather to deliver the analytical fundament for the capabilities approach to disclose its radical implications and to actually make a difference in terms of genuinely capability-promoting policies. To critical social science the normative principles embedded in the capabilities approach are congenial to the critique of policies, society and political economy. But this is precisely the radical point of envisioning capability-promoting policies. These include emancipatory and democratic strategies that transform unjust structures in order to enhance the agency of individual subjects in terms of human flourishing, that is, to enable them to realise their potentials as human beings and to develop their talents and capacities in order to conduct a non-alienated individual and social life that they have reason to value. That this is difficult and challenging is made clear by the chapters in the book; rigorous policy analysis through a capabilities lens is a good start to challenging current orthodoxies. That change may be possible, however, also emerges from chapters in the book to show that another kind of policy, another kind of way of organising human society is possible and worth pursuing.

References

Anderson, E. (1999) 'What is the point of equality?', *Ethics*, vol 109, no 2, pp 287-337.

Sayer, A. (2011) *Why things matter to people: Social science, values and ethical life*, Cambridge: Cambridge University Press.

Sen, A. (1999) *Development as freedom*, Oxford: Oxford University Press.

Wright, E.O. (2006) 'Compass points: towards a socialist alternative', *New Left Review*, vol 41 September-October, pp 93-124.

Index

Note: page numbers in italic type refer to Figures; those in bold type refer to Tables.

M

Magyar-Haas, V. 244
Mahendravada, Indira 12–13, 63–83
Mahmood, S. 49
Mahmud, S. 66
Mali, agency case study 12, 45–56, *50*, **53, 54, 55,** *55,* 58
Mandela, Nelson 161
Marcon, R. 242
market incorporation 92, **94,** 94–5, **95,** 103
    see also MITI (Market Incorporation Total Index)
Marshall, Thomas H. 224
Martin, K. E. 192
Martínez Franzoni, Juliana 93
Marx, Karl 274
Maternity Benefit Act 1961, India 68
May, J. 168
Mbao pension plan, Kenya 172, 173
McGhee, J. 184
McLachlan, C. 241
MDGs (Millennium Development Goals) 43–4, 87, 279, 293
Medical Termination of Pregnancy Act 1971 (India) 69
microfinance, India 66–7
'middle-income trap(s)' 18
migration 91
Milan *see* Giambellino, Milan case study
Millennium Development Goals (MDGs) 43–4, 87, 279, 293
Mind, society, and behavior (World Bank World Development Report 2015) 56
Mitchell, Ann 13–14, 111–29
MITI (Market Incorporation Total Index) 92, 94–5, **95,** 97–8, **98,** 103–4
Morales-Fernández, Emilio J. 13, 85–108
Moroni, S. 164
Morris, B. 204, 206, 207, 209
Morris, K. 193
Moss, P. 241, 242, 251
Movement of Third World Priests (*Movimiento de Sacerdotes del Tercer Mundo*) 122
Mugica, Carlos 122
multidimensional poverty, Mali case study 48, 49–50, *50*
    measurement of 51–2, **53**
    profiles 54–5, **55,** *55*

N

Naples *see* Scampia, Naples case study
NASSAA (national *stokvel* association) 173
National Commission for Women, India 70
National Development Plan, South Africa 167–8, 171, 175
National Endowment for the Arts, USA 132
National Mission for the Empowerment of Women, India 71
National Policy for the Empowerment of Women (Government of India, Ministry of Women and Child Development 2001) 70
National Policy for Women, India 71
Nedergaard, T. 268
neighbourhood effects 116
    and culture 133
    New York City cultural policy study 131, 140–2
neoliberalism 162, 163, 189–90
    and UK social policies 183, 185
neuroscience, and child development 186
New Labour government, UK 185
newspaper sources, Denmark's SEN education study 266–7
New York City:
    CAI (cultural asset index) 136, *136,* 140, 141
    cultural policy and social wellbeing study 14, 131, 135–42, *136, 137*
    political context 131–2
    social wellbeing clusters 137, *137*
'New York Consensus' 162
New Zealand, ECE (early childhood education) curriculum 241, 244, 246, **249**
NGOs (non-governmental organizations):
    and improved capabilities in India 66–8
    informal settlements in Buenos Aires 112
    Karnataka, India, women's empowerment case study 12–13, 64, 72–3, **74,** 75, **76,** 77, **78,** 79, **80,** 80–1
    see also CSOs (civil society organisations); third sector associations

313